CONSCIOUSNESS AND SELF-CONSCIOUSNESS

ADVANCES IN CONSCIOUSNESS RESEARCH

ADVANCES IN CONSCIOUSNESS RESEARCH provides a forum for scholars from different scientific disciplines and fields of knowledge who study consciousness in its multifaceted aspects. Thus the Series will include (but not be limited to) the various areas of cognitive science, including cognitive psychology, linguistics, brain science and philosophy. The orientation of the Series is toward developing new interdisciplinary and integrative approaches for the investigation, description and theory of consciousness, as well as the practical consequences of this research for the individual and society.

Volume 6

Rocco J. Gennaro

Consciousness and Self-Consciousness

CONSCIOUSNESS AND SELF-CONSCIOUSNESS

A DEFENSE OF THE HIGHER-ORDER THOUGHT THEORY OF CONSCIOUSNESS

ROCCO J. GENNARO
Indiana State University

JOHN BENJAMINS PUBLISHING COMPANY
AMSTERDAM/PHILADELPHIA

∞™ The paper used in this publication meets the minimum requirements of American National Standard for Information Sciences — Permanence of Paper for Printed Library Materials, ANSI Z39.48-1984.

Library of Congress Cataloging-in-Publication Data

Gennaro, Rocco J.
Consciousness and self-consciousness : a defense of the higher-order though theory of consciousness / Rocco J. Gennaro.
p. cm. -- (Advances in consciousness research, ISSN 1381-589X ; v. 6)
Includes bibliographical references and index.
1. Consciousness. 2. Self-consciousness. 3. Thought and thinking. 4. Phenomenological psychology, I. Title. II. Series.
B105.C477G46 1995
153--dc20 95-39111
ISBN 90 272 5126 6 (Eur.) / 1-55619-186-3 (US) (Pb; alk. paper) CIP

John Benjamins Publishing Co. • P.O.Box 75577 • 1070 AN Amsterdam • The Netherlands
John Benjamins North America • P.O.Box 27519 • Philadelphia PA 19118-0519 • USA

Acknowledgements

This work has of course benefited from the advice and criticism of many people. I owe the most to Robert Van Gulick for numerous comments on earlier drafts and for general guidance in the development of my work. It is difficult to articulate just how much I have learned from him. Jonathan Bennett's criticisms were helpful in the very early stages of this project. I have also learned in various ways from José Benardete, Thomas McKay and C.L. Hardin on relevant issues. Thanks are also due to Robert M. Francescotti and John O'Leary-Hawthorne for many helpful conversations and for general philosophical companionship going back to my graduate days at Syracuse University.

Parts of this book have been previously published. Some of chapter four (sections 4.5 and 4.9) originally appeared in my 1993 "Brute Experience and the Higher-Order Thought Theory of Consciousness," *Philosophical Papers* 22, 51-69. I thank the editor Michael Pendlebury for reprint permission. Chapter nine originally appeared in my 1992 "Consciousness, Self-Consciousness and Episodic Memory," *Philosophical Psychology* 5, 333-347. I thank Carfax Publishing Company and *Philosophical Psychology* for permission to reprint that material here. Part of chapter one and all of chapter five originally appeared in my 1994 "Does Mentality Entail Consciousness?," *Philosophia* 24. It is republished with permission of the editor Asa Kasher.

I also wish to thank my parents Vito and Marian Gennaro, my sisters Margaret and Maria, and the rest of my family for their support. Finally, I thank my wife, Deidra, for her love and encouragement throughout my work on this project. This book is dedicated to her.

Contents

CHAPTER 1

Introduction and Terminology

1.1 General Introduction

Contrary to what most philosophers believe, consciousness entails self-consciousness. The entailment is generally denied for two reasons: some primitive conscious creatures do not seem to be self-conscious, and self-consciousness is regarded as a sophisticated capacity that need not accompany all conscious states. However, neither of these reasons is persuasive given an adequate theory of consciousness. In the remainder of this chapter I primarily introduce some terminology, e.g. 'awareness' is distinguished from 'consciousness.' The existence of nonconscious mental states (particularly pains) is discussed, and I argue that there are nonconscious pains provided that the creature is capable of having conscious pains. There is also the crucial difference between 'consciousness' as it applies to mental states and 'consciousness' as it applies to organisms (or systems). We can call the former 'state consciousness' and the latter 'system consciousness.' The first six chapters are particularly concerned with conscious states.

In chapters two and three a theory of state consciousness is presented. Following the lead of David Rosenthal, I defend in detail the so-called "higher-order thought theory of consciousness" (hereafter 'HOT theory'). Specifically, I argue (in section 2.1) that the most plausible explanation for what makes a mental state conscious is that it is accompanied by a meta-psychological thought to the effect that one is in that state. Reductionist accounts do not yield the desired explanation since they cannot provide necessary conditions for conscious mentality. In section 2.2 I provide an account of self-consciousness and distinguish it from the more sophisticated capacity of 'introspection.' In doing so, I show that having conscious states requires at least some form of self-consciousness. I then discuss (in sections 2.3 and 2.4) David Rosenthal's HOT theory and show how mine differs from his, although there are many important similarities. I then present a taxonomy of conscious states and show how it differs from those offered by others, especially D.M. Armstrong (section 2.5).

The aim of chapter three is to show why the meta-psychological states which render mental states conscious must specifically be *thoughts.* For example, I argue that a meta-psychological *belief* would not be sufficient for rendering a mental state conscious (in section 3.2). More directly I argue (in a Kantian spirit) that having conscious states requires being able to apply concepts to them and, since it is most natural to construe concepts as constituents of thoughts, the meta-psychological states in question must be thoughts (3.3). In doing so, Kant's distinction between the sensibility and understanding is put to use. I further support my theory by examining Kant's claim that the "I think" must be able to accompany all of our representations" (3.4). An explicit discussion of the nature and role of concepts is needed in light of these considerations (3.5), and chapter three ends with a look at the relation between thought and language especially in light of the work of Donald Davidson (3.6). The issue of concept innateness is also briefly examined with special attention to Jerry Fodor's views.

In chapter four I further develop my theory of consciousness. Numerous objections are raised and responses are provided in an effort to bring out the details of the theory. For example, in section 4.5, I reply to the "content objection" which urges that such seemingly sophisticated thoughts cannot be had by many conscious organisms because some of the contained concepts are beyond their cognitive grasp. I also reply to Dennett's recent objection (4.7), and end with a discussion of the so-called "perceptual model" of the mind (4.10). Thus, this interdisciplinary work contains the most sustained attempt at developing and defending one of the few genuine theories of consciousness. Moreover, a valuable overall picture of the structure of the mind emerges with the help of various Kantian insights.

Chapter five is devoted entirely to the key related question of whether 'mentality requires consciousness,' and I argue that most interpretations of it are false. In doing so, the relationship between intentionality and consciousness is closely examined. I contend, for example, that having beliefs does *not* require having conscious mental states of any kind. This chapter is important because *if* mentality does entail consciousness, then, by my main thesis, it would also thereby entail self-consciousness.

In chapter six, I first distinguish two kinds of phenomenal states (6.1), and then show how having them entails self-consciousness (6.2 and 6.3). In section 6.4, I critically examine the idea that there are "unconscious sensations" while introducing the notion of "phenomenal information." The well-known blindsight phenomenon is also discussed, and I then critically assess the debate between Ned Block and Owen Flanagan on blindsight and related terminology (6.5). McGinn's reasons for believing that there is a "hidden structure" to consciousness are examined, and I show that some of what he says supports the HOT theory (6.6). Finally, explanations of other psychopathologies are offered and it is shown that they do not cause trouble for my theory (in 6.7).

Although I never entirely leave state consciousness, my attention is then somewhat shifted to system consciousness. Three arguments for the conclusion that 'being a conscious system entails being self-conscious' are explored. The fundamental strategy in each case is to argue first that being a conscious system involves having a specific mental capacity (e.g. having episodic memory), and then to show how having that capacity involves self-consciousness. Chapter seven contains the BEHAVIOR argument where I focus on whether self-consciousness is necessary for being able to modify one's own behavior. In chapter eight, the DE SE argument centers around the *prima facie* connection between *de se* attitudes and self-consciousness. In chapter nine the link between episodic memory and consciousness is exploited in the MEMORY argument. I show that episodic memory is necessary for being a conscious system, and sufficient for self-consciousness.

1.2 Some Terminological Matters

The term 'consciousness' derives from the Latin *con* ('with') and *scire* ('to know'). Consciousness and, therefore, self-consciousness has traditional ties to one's ability to know and perceive. One can have knowledge of the external world or of oneself and one's own mental states. Through self-consciousness one acquires knowledge about the latter.

What complicates the linguistic matter is that we can distinguish the following: (1) the abstract noun 'consciousness,' (2) the one-place predicate '...is conscious,' and (3) the two-place predicate '...is conscious of...'

My concern is primarily with (2) and (3). The one-place predicate '...is conscious' is sometimes applied to things or substances such as organisms or creatures. Human beings are conscious *creatures*. We say, for example, "Surely my dog is conscious." On the other hand, we also apply the predicate '...is conscious' to *states* of organisms. One's mental states are conscious. States of organisms, then, are often said to be conscious. Let us call this 'state consciousness'.

The two-place predicate '...is conscious of...' is also used in two importantly different ways. They mirror the ways in which one's knowledge or awareness can be directed, i.e. either at one's mental states or at some outer object. The locution "C is conscious of x" leaves open the value of 'x.' It might designate something outside of C (e.g. a tree, house, etc.), one of C's mental states, or even one of C's bodily states. The two-place predicate '...is conscious of...' reflects our tendency to treat consciousness as either a relation a subject bears to some external state of affairs or to his own mental states.

Thus far I have spoken of 'creatures' and 'organisms.' One might wonder whether any other sort of thing (e.g. a machine) could have conscious states. I will use the term 'system' to cover 'organisms' and 'machines' in order to remain neutral on this substantial question. It is, of course, notoriously difficult to define 'organism' and 'machine.' We might try to do so on the basis of the kind of matter that composes them, e.g. defining 'organisms' as those living things composed of organic or carbon-based materials. However, this would unjustly rule out the possibility of organisms composed of different kinds of matter. Thus, it seems wiser to appeal to certain functional properties. For example, organisms have a natural reproductive capacity which machines lack. They have various parts (e.g. organs) which function together to maintain their lives. Food is taken in and various nutrients are sent throughout the body, respiration is aided by their intake, and waste is excreted. Moreover, an organism's interaction with the environment involves a constant exchange of matter and will, over time, become composed of mostly different elementary particles. Machines are 'rigid' things, i.e. the particles of which they are composed remain relatively intact over time. These kinds of properties are perhaps what best serve to differentiate organisms from machines (if anything does). They are at least some of the ways we *in fact* distinguish them. I do not claim to provide a list of necessary conditions, but merely to indicate some common sense differences. The 'mode of organization' seems more important than the kind of matter of which it is composed. Let us simply understand machines as anything which is not an organism, but which could at least be a *prima facie* candidate for ascriptions of mentality. The point here is merely to introduce the neutral term 'system' without prejudging the possibility of machine consciousness.

Now mental states are standardly grouped into two overlapping classes. Intentional states, such as beliefs and desires, are those that are 'about' or 'represent' something. They have propositional content or are directed at an object. Phenomenal states (e.g. pains) are those that typically have a qualitative character or 'feel' associated with them. Some such states are not 'about' anything, e.g. there are no 'pains that p' or 'pains about x'.[1] Others have both qualitative and intentional properties (e.g. emotions and perceptions).

The notion of a 'conscious state' that I am aiming to capture is fundamentally Nagel's (1974) sense; namely, that there is 'something it is like to be in that state.' This is not to say that I share Nagel's conviction that consciousness presents an insurmountable obstacle to materialist theories of mind. I believe that his worries can be handled within a materialist framework. Although I will not often explicitly address this issue, I hope that this project can help to diffuse some of the mystery by providing a theory that is consistent with materialism.[2] I hold that every mental event is a physical event, but rarely rely on this view and so will not defend it here.[3]

1.3 Consciousness and Awareness

The terms 'conscious' and 'aware' are notoriously ambiguous. Any theory of consciousness should pay special attention to them. They are sometimes used interchangeably. We might ask: Aren't you conscious (aware) of your surroundings? We might say: Tom is aware (conscious) that the Jones' are coming for dinner tonight, or you should be more aware (conscious) of how you treat other people. However, it is clear that 'aware' and 'conscious' are not merely synonymous. For one thing, we can make sense of the locution "I must have been aware of it *in some sense*, but I was not conscious of it." It is not contradictory to speak of being 'nonconsciously aware' of something. Similarly, the expression 'consciously aware' is not redundant. Awareness does not necessarily carry connotations of consciousness. We can and do make room for nonconscious awareness. It is natural to ask: what senses does 'aware' have which allow us to speak coherently of 'nonconscious awareness'? There are at least two.

First, we can say of the day-dreaming long distance truck driver that he must have been aware *in some sense* of the twists and turns in the road. Otherwise, how could he have successfully completed his journey? The idea is that the long distance truck driver has certain internal states which direct his behavior. Those states play a critical role in the complex pattern of behavior required for him to navigate during his journey. These states might even be complex enough to warrant mental attributions, e.g. beliefs about the turns in the road, understanding of the best route to his destination, and so on. Dennett (1969: 118-9) comes close to capturing this sense of awareness in what he calls 'awareness$_2$':

> A is aware$_2$ that p at time t if and only if p is the content of an internal event in A at time t that is effective in directing current behavior.

One is aware$_2$ that p when one is able to organize and modify one's behavior on the basis of the content of p. But some qualification is needed. The internal state cannot just be any one if it is to be a kind of 'awareness.' It must be one that is responsive to the perceived environment, i.e. a state whose content depends upon some (perceptual) 'input' or 'channel.' Input from such channels lead to forming a state which, in turn, is effective in directing A's behavior at a given time. I will call this type of awareness 'behavioral awareness.' The long distance truck driver is 'behaviorally aware' of the turns in the road. Dennett has his reasons for recasting all talk of 'awareness *of*' into 'awareness *that*,' but my concern here is simply that one can have 'behavioral awareness' *of x* without being consciously aware of x. Behavioral awareness does not entail conscious awareness. I seriously doubt that flies or worms are consciously aware of their surroundings at all, but they can be behaviorally aware. It is also plausible to credit various complex robots with behavioral awareness whether or not we suppose that robots have conscious states.

Second, the notion of 'nonconscious awareness' gets support from the widespread acceptance of nonconscious mental states. In the post-Freudian era, we have grown accustomed to talk of nonconscious desires, motives, and beliefs. The plausibility of positing them arises, in part, from the quasi-behaviorist intuition that a third-person observer is often in a better position to determine one's state of mind. In fact, the idea that there are even nonconscious *phenomenal states* has been gaining noticable support in recent years (Nelkin 1986, 1989; Rosenthal 1986, 1991).

Nonconscious *thoughts* or 'thought processes' have also been widely accepted. We might remark "he must have thought that the paper was in the drawer or he wouldn't have looked for it there" without the least suggestion of conscious awareness. One can have nonconscious thoughts, for example, about objects in one's peripheral visual field. Thus a second reason for not treating 'aware' as synonymous with 'conscious' is that one can have nonconscious thoughts about things. I will refer to such nonconscious awareness as 'thought awareness.' It is distinct from 'behavioral awareness' because some creatures (e.g. worms and flies) might not be capable of thoughts at all while still being behaviorally aware. Behavioral awareness does not entail 'thought awareness.' Moreover, there is no principled reason to restrict such awareness to first-order nonconscious thoughts, i.e. nonconscious thoughts directed at the external world. Once we allow nonconscious thoughts at the first-order level, then the door is open for nonconscious second-order thoughts, i.e. nonconscious 'thought awareness' of one's own mental states.

1.4 Self-Intimation, Nonconscious Pains, and Infallibility

I accept the thesis that there are nonconscious mental states of various kinds. This is tantamount to rejecting one aspect of the so-called 'transparency thesis' which says that if one is in a mental state, then one is aware that one is in it, which is what Armstrong (1968) calls 'self-intimation.' The view that *all* of one's mental states are self-intimating is not very highly regarded today precisely because it rules out ignorance about our own mental states, i.e. the possibility of nonconscious mental states. But we do have nonconscious thoughts, emotions and desires.

What I have said thus far is not very controversial. However, I remarked earlier that it is reasonable to think that there are nonconscious *phenomenal* states. This is not as widely accepted, and so something ought to be said in its favor.

What is a phenomenal state? I define a phenomenal state as a mental state which has, or at least typically has, qualitative properties. Qualia are the properties of phenomenal states that determine their qualitative character, i.e. 'what it is like' to have them. When I say 'determine' I do not mean 'cause' merely in the sense that some underlying neural state might determine the qualitative character of a sensory experience. I simply mean that qualia are those properties that, from the first person point of view, give phenomenal states their qualitative character. Phenomenal states are typically accompanied by qualitative properties. When I speak of a 'qualitative state' or a 'sensory state' I have in mind a phenomenal state with a qualitative property. For example, being in pain typically has the property of 'painfulness' (e.g. searingness). The phenomenal state is 'being in pain' and the qualitative property is 'painfulness' or 'searingness.' I do not, as many philosophers do, use the terms 'phenomenal' and 'qualitative' interchangeably for reasons that will become clear.

My definition allows us to state clearly what a nonconscious phenomenal state would be: a phenomenal state without its qualitative property. This is why I say that phenomenal states *typically* have their qualitative properties. They need not have their qualitative properties. What reasons can be adduced in favor of such a view?

Earlier I proclaimed my adherence to a 'token identity' theory, i.e. every mental event is a physical event. I want to expand on that thesis. I do not merely hold that every mental event is a physical event. A defining feature of mental states is also the functional-behavioral role (FB role) of those states. That is, what (in part) makes mental states the states they are is their relation to what causes them (= input), to their typical behavioral effects (= outputs), and to other mental states. Most philosophers find it necessary to include the FB role in explaining what makes a token mental state the type of mental state it is. Some philosophers (e.g. Kripke 1971, 1972) hold that the sole defining feature of phenomenal states is the felt quality associated with them.[4] This is often used as a premise in so-called 'absent qualia arguments' against the plausibility of providing an adequate functional analysis of phenomenal states (see the debate between Shoemaker 1975, 1981b and Block 1980). On the other hand, one might also treat their FB role as a defining feature. My view takes the best of both. I hold that any *particular* phenomenal state need not have its typical felt quality, and so one can have particular nonconscious pains in virtue of having a mental state which plays the relevant FB role. I may truly have nonconscious pains attributed to me on the basis of certain characteristic behavior. For example, I can have many back and neck muscule twinges while I sleep, and which cause me to behave in ways that relieve them (e.g. changing my sleeping position). These are nonconscious pains. A football player might have a painful leg injury and limp off the field and then insist that he return to play. Throughout the game he favors that leg and often grimaces. He is, as we say, 'playing in pain.' He is in pain or has a pain *throughout* the game. At a post game interview, he might reveal that his leg only hurt between plays or when he sat on the sidelines for a period of time, and that he did not realize how much he was favoring it during the game. But it still seems perfectly reasonable to hold that he had a single continuous pain throughout the game of which he was sometimes aware. We often do not attend to our pains because, for example, we are focused intensely on something else. Mental states can sometimes intrude upon one's consciousness in such a way as to direct one's attention away from other states. There is little reason to deny that the pains existed during those sometimes very brief periods. From a materialist point of view, this amounts to the view that the relevant neural process (which is the pain) continues without the subject feeling the normally accompanying sensation. It is less plausible to construe our football player as having a long sequence of discontinuous, brief pains.

Some qualification is needed. I have said that one can truly be in pain on the basis of displaying certain typical behavior, i.e. having the right FB role of pain is sufficient for one's being in a *particular* pain. I do not hold that every individual phenomenal state must be conscious. However, a system could not be in a *kind* of phenomenal state K unless at least some of them are conscious (i.e. have qualitative properties). That is, a system cannot have phenomenal states which are *all* nonconscious. If we are to treat a system's behavior as indicating the presence of a nonconscious pain, then that system must also be capable of having conscious pains. Generally, if a system has nonconscious phenomenal states of kind K, it must have at least some conscious K states. It is reasonable to attribute nonconscious pains to a system only to the extent that that system is capable of having conscious pains. If a system behaved in the relevant way but was utterly incapable of having conscious pains, we ought not to treat it as having pains which are all nonconscious. We would rather say that it responds to stimuli in certain ways 'as if' it were in pain. Thus, whatever sense we can make of nonconscious phenomenal states is still somewhat parasitic on the conscious variety. To summarize: One can have a *particular* phenomenal state without its typical felt quality. However, what justifies us in treating it as a nonconscious *phenomenal state* is (a) that the behavior of the system exhibits the typical FB role associated with that type of state, *and* (b) the system is capable of conscious phenomenal states of that type.

Another qualification: It is reasonable to hold that the FB role associated with a nonconscious phenomenal state will differ to some extent from the FB role of the conscious phenomenal state of that type. For example, conscious pains might cause certain beliefs that nonconscious pains would not. They might even cause certain behavior that nonconscious pains typically do not, e.g. the 'avoidance behavior' might not be as readily manifested when one has a nonconscious pain. But their FB roles are close enough to warrant attributions of the same type of state. Their different FB roles fall within certain general parameters. Moreover, we can presume that a nonconscious phenomenal state and the corresponding conscious state would significantly share certain underlying neural events. This is further reason to treat them as the same type of phenomenal state.[5]

Even though we admit the existence of nonconscious pains, we should recognize the important fact that part of the function of pain is (typically) to intrude upon one's consciousness. It seems essential to the survival of a species (and its members) that pains normally be felt. If one were regularly unaware of one's pains, then one would be in the unfortunate position of regularly being unaware of damage caused to one's body. If such an individual could survive at all, he would require constant supervision. But, as I have urged above, if such an individual somehow *never* felt any pains then it is implausible to view it as having pains at all. Similarly, if a species somehow did not develop the ability to feel its pains, it would be difficult to see how it could survive. There are very good evolutionary reasons for why pains are typically felt which helps explain the natural tendency to treat them as essentially conscious. Nevertheless, the relationship between 'having pains' and 'being aware of pains' is a contingent one to the extent that an otherwise conscious system can have *particular* nonconscious pains.

Lastly, we ought to say something about the alleged 'infallibility' of our introspective states. Few philosophers today hold that if someone believes or thinks something about oneself *via* introspection, then one's belief must (logically) be true. The claim is that one cannot be mistaken about the content of one's own mental states. But we are notoriously bad at assessing the contents of our own minds. For example, we often mistake one emotion for another. One might falsely believe that one is angry, and really be jealous or envious. I do not deny that we are usually in the best position to know the contents of our minds. We are also probably better at knowing about certain kinds of our mental states over others. For example, we will not be as good at truly judging our emotions as we are at knowing whether we are in pain. My point here is only that we need not adopt an unnecessarily strong indubitability thesis which covers all types of mental states. (For more on the implausibility of the self-intimation and infallibility theses, see Armstrong 1968: 92-116; Armstrong and Malcolm 1984: 108-37; and Hill 1991: 126-30.)

CHAPTER 2

A Theory of State Consciousness

2.1 What is a Conscious Mental State?

What makes a mental state a conscious mental state? There are a variety of possible answers. I will discuss the options, discard the implausible alternatives, and briefly explain where my sympathy lies.

One possibilty is to take a reductivist approach, i.e. what best explains why some mental events are conscious is the presence of some brain property. This would be one way to 'naturalize the mental.' The idea would be to try to explain conscious mentality in nonmental, and specifically neurophysiological, terms. For example, there might be certain distinctive brain-wave patterns which one might *identify with* conscious mentality. While many materialists (including myself) have a certain natural sympathy with this type of approach, it is not one that I find reasonable to pursue in this work. One reason is simply that we do not know enough about the 'neurophysiology of consciousness' to even begin a successful reduction. We do not yet know what property of our brains can be successfully *correlated with* conscious states or even what property is *causally repsonsible for* us being conscious. We are presently in the dark as to how to complete the biconditional "S is a conscious mental state if and only if ..." in the language of neurophysiology or any other science. There also appears to be little help on the horizon.

Some philosophers have conjectured as to what that brain property might be. Lycan (1987) entertains the so-called "Volume Control hypothesis" which he ultimately credits to Dennett (1978: chapter eleven). The metaphorical suggestion is that some neural events are 'tuned up' higher than others and when a certain threshold is reached a state becomes conscious. We are to think of it on the analogy with the 'volume control' on a stereo or television. When tuned up high, the state becomes conscious. This is perhaps a 'higher-level' or functional (as opposed to 'neurophysiological') property with which one might try to explicate state consciousness.

Aside from the obvious metaphorical language and lack of serious evidence, there is a further reason to reject this type of answer. It is difficult to understand what *brain property* could fit the 'volume control' metaphor. One possibility is 'the firing of neurons.' The idea would be that neurons fire in different degrees and when one fires at a sufficiently high degree the state is conscious. The problem is that this is known empirically to be false. The firing of a neuron is an all or nothing matter. More specifically, neurons have a 'resting potential' of -70mV which is the normal voltage across the nerve cell membrane. If a neuron is excited *via* a neurotransmitter from a presynaptic neuron, then it causes a depolarization of the neuron. The depolarization causes brief changes in the neuron's permeability to potassium and sodium ions which, in turn, causes an electrical impulse (called an 'action potential') to occur at -50mV. The nerve cell fires at this point and not until that point. It does not fire 'to a lesser degree' at -60mV or -55mV. It also does not fire to any greater degree at -45mV and -40mV. (Just to complete the story, the firing will go on to cause the release of neurotransmitters into the synapse of the post-synaptic cells, and the cycle continues.) Of course, the volume control model need not adopt 'the firing of neurons' as the conscious rendering property, but what else it could be remains a mystery. Perhaps 'firing *rates*' is a *prima facie* possibility, but there is no empirical evidence to indicate that conscious states occur only when neurons fire at certain rates. Generally, we are presently ignorant about what brain property renders us conscious.

Furthermore, even if we did know what property was responsible for conscious states *in us*, that is not enough to satisfy the above biconditional. Most philosophers will acknowledge that consciousness could be had by organisms which are physically quite different from us (e.g. they might not even have neurons). But if a reductionist program is to provide *necessary* conditions for state consciousness, then merely finding out what *causes* us to be conscious or what it *is* for us to be conscious will not suffice. The reductionist program must fail if we allow the multiple realizability of conscious states, and we complete "S is a conscious mental state if and only if..." with terms referring to items that other conscious creatures might lack. The reductionist might opt to give up on providing any necessary conditions, but this would undermine much of the *philosophical* motivation and interest in this alternative.

More recently, Flanagan also goes too far in stressing the *actual* neural causes of consciousness. No doubt that the current trend toward the empirical study of consciousness is philosophically useful, but he leans too heavily on evidence (advanced by Crick and Koch 1990) which suggests that "subjective awareness is linked to oscillation patterns in the 40 hertz range in the relevant groups of neurons" (Flanagan 1992: 15). Such neural activity may be *sufficient* for consciousness, but doesn't seem *necessary* if we are to allow for multiple realizability. Flanagan (1992: 59-60, 215) even flirts with the idea that the 40-hertz oscillation pattern is necessary, but clearly he can only mean 'necessary *for humans*.' This would of course still be an important scientific discovery but leaves open the more philosophical question: "*Must any* creature have such neural activity in order to be conscious?"

There are, perhaps, other ways to 'naturalize the mental.' For example, one might try to do so in a way that many different levels of *functional* description are utilized. Dennett's (1978) cognitive theory of consciousness proceeds in this manner. I do not deny that such a project has some explanatory value, but it also has many shortcomings. First, it does not really explicate state consciousness if we desire an explanation of what makes a *particular* mental state conscious. It is too general. Second, it still does not provide necessary conditions for state consciousness. It is too specific in that it offers a cognitive model of consciousness *in us*. Such models are much too close to a *de facto* psychological explication of consciousness and cannot satisfy the more rigid philosophical constraint of providing necessary conditions. So it does not help complete the above biconditional. Third, it is not clear that mentalistic terms are avoided. For example, Dennett finds himself with a 'Control' subsystem with 'introspect' as one of its functions.

Thus, I think it best to explain conscious states in mentalistic terms. Since we cannot explain what makes a mental state conscious in physicalistic or in (non-mentalistic) functional language, then the only other option is to explain it in mentalistic language. Defining mentality and mental states in terms of other mental states is commonplace in contemporary philosophy of mind. For example, Shoemaker (1981a) describes 'weak functionalism' as a theory which allows concepts from the domain of the mental to appear in the definiens of a mental term. Weak functionalism reflects the general acceptance of defining mental states in mentalistic language, i.e. by reference to other mental states. For example, beliefs are often defined in terms of behavioral dispositions *and desires*. Shoemaker contrasts weak functionalism with 'strong functionalism' which does not permit reference to mental items in the explication of a mental term. My point thus far has been that strong functionalism with respect to state consciousness is not a plausible option. As far as I can see, however, a weak functionalist can leave open the possibility of a strong functionalist reduction. Indeed, many naturalistic accounts of the mental proceed in a two step manner. They first define some aspect of mentality in terms of another, and then define those states in naturalistic language. Thus, what follows is not *necessarily* opposed to the general project of naturalizing the mental.

We are left with two kinds of answers: what makes a mental state conscious is either something about the nature of that very state or something external to that state. That is, state consciousness is either an *intrinsic* (mental) feature of conscious states or an *extrinsic* property (i.e. what makes them conscious is some distinct state).

The extrinsicality view is implausible. Rosenthal (1986) is, as far as I know, the main philosopher of mind who takes it seriously, and I will show (in section 2.3) that his motivation is misguided. He fails to see how we can shed light on consciousness by treating it as an intrinsic feature of mental states. Consciousness surely seems to be an intrinsic feature of mental states from the first person point of view. When one is in a conscious state, it is natural to view its being conscious as an intrinsic property. Even Rosenthal (1986: 331) admits that this is so.

This leaves us with what I will call 'the intrinsicality view.' There is one version of it which ought to be dismissed as uninformative. It simply says 'what makes a mental state conscious is the presence of an ineffable quality which is part of it.' This is presumably what leads Nagel (1974: 435) to proclaim that "consciousness is what makes the mind-body problem really intractable." I will call this the 'narrow intrinsicality view' (hereafter NIV). It announces that the best or only answer to the problem of state consciousness is to be found in some nonrelational, simple, ineffable, and intrinsic feature of conscious states. The NIV stresses that we all know what makes a mental state conscious from the first person point of view. While this may be so, the problem is that it views conscious states (or the property of consciousness) as *simple*. In doing so, it resists any attempt at further analysis, and so cannot yield a theoretically satisfying *explanation* of consciousness. We should strive for an explanation that goes further. The NIV seems to offer little more than 'throwing up one's hands' or 'shrugging one's shoulders' at the problem of state consciousness.

The most plausible remaining option I will call the 'wide intrinsicality view' (hereafter WIV). I hold the WIV. Let 'CS' name the state that is rendered conscious. The WIV says that a mental state renders CS conscious, but not just any mental state will render it conscious. If the mental state is not importantly related to CS, then it is difficult to see how it could render CS conscious. It is most reasonable to think of the 'conscious rendering' mental state as directed at CS. That is, the conscious rendering state is about CS and so must be a meta-psychological state. My WIV does not treat the meta-psychological state as entirely distinct from CS (for reasons that will become clear throughout this chapter). Rather, it treats conscious mental states as complex states with both CS and the meta-psychological state as parts. Conscious states are individuated 'widely' so as to treat the meta-psychological state as intrinsic to the conscious mental state. It leaves room for further explication of conscious states. Treating them as complex will enable us to provide a theoretically satisfying explanation of state consciousness. On the NIV, no such explanation is forthcoming.

A key question is: What *kind* of mental state is the meta-psychological state? There are many kinds of mental states and it is reasonable to wonder which kind it is. Are the meta-psychological states 'beliefs,' 'desires,' 'thoughts,' 'hopes,' 'wishes,' etc.? Does it matter? It does matter. Not just any meta-psychological state can render a state conscious. Here I will simply announce my view that it must be a meta-psychological *thought* directed at a mental state. I agree with Rosenthal (1986: 335) that the most plausible account of conscious mental states will

> ...identify a mental state's being conscious with one's having a roughly contemporaneous thought that one is in that mental state.

The content of such thoughts are 'I am in mental state M.' It is a thought to the effect that one is in that mental state.

2.2 Self-Consciousness and Introspection

Self-consciousness consists is having meta-psychological thoughts. I take this to be a common sense view about self-consciousness. Thinking about one's own mental states is definitive of self-consciousness. It seems that having a thought about one of one's own mental states is necessary and sufficient for self-consciousness, although understanding what exactly is involved in having such 'thoughts' must be further developed throughout the next two chapters.

But I suggest that there is nothing in this account of self-consciousness which requires that the meta-psychological thought (hereafter MET) itself be conscious.[6] There are nonconscious thoughts and, so, there is no reason to deny the existence of nonconscious METs (cf. section 1.3). Just as one might have nonconscious thoughts directed at the world, one might have them directed at one's own mental states. We need not require that the METs which render mental states conscious are themselves conscious. Self-consciousness comes in varying degrees of 'self-awareness.' Sometimes it merely involves a *nonconscious thought awareness* of one's own mental states and, sometimes, it comes in the form of *conscious meta-psychological thoughts*. In the previous section I argued that what makes a mental state conscious is its being accompanied by a MET about that state. But such METs need not themselves be conscious. Indeed, we must insist on this point. Otherwise, the theory would be viciously circular. One should not define conscious states in terms of other conscious states. We cannot informatively explain what makes a mental states conscious by invoking the very notion that we are trying to explicate. Thus, there is good reason not to require that the conscious rendering METs are themselves conscious. The core notion of self-consciousness which includes nonconscious thought awareness allows that the MET may be nonconscious. So if I am right about what makes mental states conscious, then *having conscious states entails self-consciousness.*

Some might still wonder why self-*consciousness* need not be *consciousness of* something. I offer six reasons:

1. If a theory which allows for degrees of self-consciousness has some theoretical advantages which outweigh this more or less terminological issue, then it seems worth adopting. Of course, all of these advantages will not be clear for several chapters, but that is what I aim to show.
2. No one supposes that self-consciousness is literally "consciousness of a self" anyway, especially since Hume's observation that we are not aware of an unchanging or underlying self but only a succession of mental states. Thus the "ordinary meaning" of 'self-consciousness' is up for grabs in this regard since the term does not wear its meaning on its sleeve. It seems that we are somewhat free to stipulate a meaning (though not entirely arbitrarily of course).

3. One may suppose that we must at least be conscious of a mental state in order to be self-conscious at a given time. But even this is not clear given that we may rightly say that "someone is acting very self-conscious" when that person is not currently having any second-order conscious states.
4. As we saw in section 1.3, the terms 'conscious' and 'aware' are sometimes, but not always, used interchangeably. In the last chapter we stressed their differences, but, if we are to honor the authority of ordinary language, then we also must recognize their similarities. And if 'is conscious of' is sometimes used interchangeably with 'is aware of' and if awareness can be nonconscious in the ways earlier described, then it seems fair to allow for a nonconscious higher-order awareness to be called 'self-consciousness.' It may be that the adjectival use found in the one-place predicate "...is conscious" must carry with it connotations of consciousness in the Nagelian sense, but it is not clear that same goes for the "...is conscious of..." usage.
5. It is worth noting that Owen Flanagan also recognizes a "weaker" kind of self-consciousness and distinguishes it from a stronger version, so I am in good company. Although the context and his purpose are entirely different from mine, he does acknowledge, for example, that "all subjective experience is self-conscious in the weak sense that there is something it is like for the subject to have that experience. This involves a sense that the experience is the subject's experience, that it happens to her, occurs in her stream" (Flanagan 1992: 194). Unlike him, however, I will argue that such self-consciousness does involve an explicit (albeit nonconscious) thought and accompanies all conscious experience.
6. Other well respected philosophers put forth even weaker criteria for what counts as 'self-consciousness.' For example, Van Gulick (1988a) urges that it is simply the possession of meta-psychological *information*. While I will argue in chapter seven that his notion is too weak, I only want to point out here that my definition is clearly not the weakest one in the literature.

So one source of resistance to the idea that consciousness entails self-consciousness is due to mistakenly equating self-consciousness with introspection. But to introspect a mental state is to have a *conscious thought* about that state (cf. Rosenthal 1986: 338). When I introspect, my focus is 'inner' and my conscious attention is directed at my mental state. I will call this type of awareness 'introspective awareness.' On the other hand, self-consciousness need not involve having conscious METs. Self-consciousness is having

METs, conscious or not. Introspection requires having conscious METs. When we are in conscious states we are often not *consciously* thinking about our own states, but we are nonetheless thinking about or having 'thought awareness of' them. Having conscious states does not entail introspective awareness; my claim is only that it involves self-consciousness. Some more primitive creatures can have conscious states without being able to introspect at all. Introspection is a complex form of self-consciousness, which involves having *conscious* METs. One can be self-conscious without introspecting, but one cannot introspect without being self-conscious.

More needs to be said about introspection. A *MET* is conscious when *it* is accompanied by a further MET directed at it. Let 'CS' be a mental state that is rendered conscious by a MET, which can itself be made conscious by the presence of another MET, MET,' directed at it. In introspection, there is a conscious MET directed at CS, and so a MET' directed at MET. That is what it is to be introspectively aware of CS. Rosenthal (1986: 337-8) describes the situation as follows:

> Having a conscious mental state without introspectively focusing on it is having the second-order thought without the third-order thought...To introspect a mental state is to have a conscious thought about that state. So introspection is having a thought about some mental state one is in and, also, a yet higher-order thought that makes the first thought conscious.

We thus have conscious states, self-consciousness, and introspection. I also want to distinguish two types of introspection. Sometimes we *deliberate*, i.e. consciously think to ourselves in a deliberate manner in doing philosophy or in just creating a shopping list. We are also often engaged in deliberate activities directed at the external world, e.g. when our conscious attention is absorbed in constructing a book case. Even though all deliberate activity does not involve introspection, clearly some does involve sustained conscious thinking directed at one's inner states, which I will call 'deliberate introspection.' There is also a more modest type of introspection. One might consciously think about one's mental state without deliberating in any way, e.g. momentarily daydream or consciously think of a memory, or briefly consciously focus on a back pain or emotion. In these cases one is not engaged in deliberation or deliberate reasoning. Some animals seem able to introspect in this way though they cannot deliberate. Like deliberate introspection, such 'momentary focused introspection' involves having conscious thoughts about one's own mental states. I will often use the term 'introspection' to cover both types.

Introspection is a complex form of self-consciousness, and deliberate introspection is the more sophisticated kind of introspection. Rosenthal conflates these kinds of introspection when he says that "[i]ntrospection...involves *consciously and deliberately* paying attention to our contemporaneous mental states." (1986: 336, my emphasis) Perhaps he just ignores momentary focused introspection.

It is worth mentioning a threefold distinction made by Hill (1991: 117-22). *Inner vision* "occurs when one decides to attend to a sensation that is already in existence but that has not yet been subjected to scrutiny. The sensation itself is not altered...[r]ather there is a change in one's cognitive attitude toward the sensation" (1991: 118). Leaving aside for now the apparent implication that there are unconscious sensations, I simply want to note that inner vision sounds like what I have called 'momentary focused' introspection.

Secondly, *volume adjustment* is like inner vision, but "one adjusts the volume of a sensation by changing it in certain ways. One wants to bring the sensation into greater prominence [which changes] the intensity of the sensation..." (Hill 1991: 120). Hill is right to notice that we are sometimes able to alter the nature and intensity of a phenomenal state by focusing on it in various ways. For one thing, we can bring further thoughts (and so concepts) to bear on it, which, in turn, will affect the nature of the sensation itself. For example, we can further attend to the taste of a wine and considerably change the nature of the taste sensation. On the surface, this phenomenon seems to be another kind of momentary focused introspection since no particular extensive deliberative reasoning is involved. On the other hand, it does seem to involve a sustained ability to focus on a sensation which suggests a more sophisticated capacity. It may be that only creatures capable of deliberate introspection can perform volume adjustments on their sensations. This ability seems to straddle the line between momentary focused and deliberate introspection.

Third, *activation* involves bringing a kind of sensation "one has in mind" to consciousness. "Activation occurs if one succeeds in actualizing or activating a sensation of the right sort" (1991: 121). In this case, one actually brings a sensation into existence by intense thought about the type of sensation. Hill rightly recognizes that we are sometimes capable of such "creation" within us, e.g. by concentrating on a point on one's skin one can bring into consciousness a sensation of tingling or itching. Although Hill sometimes speaks as if even in these cases the sensation was "already there," he seems more often to mean that it was brought into existence. It seems to me that this ability is unique to us and those creatures capable of deliberate introspection since it often involves a rather sustained effort at conjuring up a sensation. It is not another *type* of introspection, but rather an ability which comes with deliberation that must be acknowledged. We not only can deliberate on preexisting mental states, but also can bring mental states into existence through this form of introspection.

2.3 Some Difficulties with Rosenthal's Methodology

David Rosenthal (1986, 1990) also offers a meta-psychological theory of state consciousness but, in developing it, he makes a number of questionable inferences involving such notions as 'essential,' 'intrinsic,' and 'analyzable.' He explicitly defines 'intrinsic' as follows:

> P is an intrinsic property of x if x's having P does *not* consist in x bearing some relation R to *something else* (1990: 21-22).

An 'extrinsic' property would just be one that is not intrinsic. He seems to understand essential properties in the standard way; namely, P is an essential property of x if x could not exist without P (or x has P in every possible world in which x exists). Rosenthal (1986: 341-3; 1990: 22) several times fallaciously infers from the fact that P is an extrinsic property of x to the conclusion that P is an inessential or contingent property of x. For example, he claims that since consciousness is a property which involves a relation between a mental state and some other state, "it would be natural to conclude that being conscious is a contingent property of mental states" (1990: 22). The inference is invalid as the following case shows. I might have a belief about the water in my pool. The property 'being about something composed of H_2O' is extrinsic to my belief because it involves a relation to a 'distinct existence.' My doppelganger on Twin Earth does not have the same belief because his belief is directed at XYZ and not water (see Kripke 1972, Putnam 1975, Burge 1986, Pettit and McDowell 1986). If one individuates belief states widely to incorporate this difference, then the type-identity of beliefs essentially involves reference to items in the external world. Thus some properties of beliefs can be both extrinsic and essential. This argument, admittedly, relies on the relatively controversial claim that my belief is essentially about H_2O. It might only show that x's being a belief that p depends upon certain relational facts which, in turn, may not be essential to x's existence. One might not think that 'being about H_2O' is essential to the belief's existence, i.e. an essential property of my belief.

My point can be more clearly and forcefully shown by considering the following extrinsic property of mine: being the son of Vito and Marian Gennaro. It is widely accepted that this is one of my essential properties, i.e. in any world in which I exist I have that property (see e.g. Kripke 1972). Here is a case where one of my extrinsic properties is uncontroversially essential to my identity. It is illegitimate to infer from extrinsicality to contingency and so it is still possible for consciousness to be both an extrinsic *and* essential property of mental states. Rosenthal is mistaken when he says that "[if] consciousness is essential to mental states, it is therefore a nonrelational [= intrinsic] property of those states" (1986: 341). It is also obvious that intrinsic properties need not be essential, my having dark hair is intrinsic but surely not essential. Thus, there is no clear logical connection between 'intrinsicality,' 'extrinsicality' and 'essentiality'.

Rosenthal's argument for the conclusion that there are nonconscious qualitative states is equally invalid because it also depends on this mistaken inference (1986: 347-9; 1990: 21-5). He argues for the independence of consciousness and sensory qualities on the grounds that consciousness is best understood as an extrinsic *and, therefore,* contingent property of qualitative states. If this inference is permitted, then qualitative states need not have their qualitative properties. Granted that 'what fixes the reference' of qualitative states *need not* pick out their essential natures,[7] but one cannot show the possibility of nonconscious qualitative states on the basis of an invalid inference from extrinsicality to contingency. He has given us no reason to deny the natural view that consciousness is an essential feature of *qualitative* states. Moreover, Rosenthal ignores the option that consciousness *per se* is essential to qualitative states but the particular form of consciousness associated with them is contingent. A pain with qualitative properties must be conscious, but the particular *way* that it feels to us is not essential to its being a pain. For example, alien pains might feel very different than ours. Of course, none of this is to say that consciousness is essential to *all* types of mental states, i.e. there are nonconscious mental states of various kinds.

The above difficulty springs from an even deeper fallacy in Rosenthal's thinking. He is concerned to provide a theoretically satisfying and informative theory of consciousness. He wants to be able to give some *explanation* of conscious mentality and so not merely to treat consciousness as a mysterious intrinsic property of mental states (in the way the NIV does). This is an admirable goal and one that I share. However, in supporting his position he ignores an alternative and so is guilty of setting up a false dilemma. Rosenthal (1986: 354; 1990: 23) urges that if we treat consciousness as an intrinsic property, then conscious states and the property of consciousness will be 'simple.' He then argues that since consciousness is 'simple,' it will be unanalyzable and so no informative explanation of it could then be provided. Rosenthal (1986: 330, 340-48; 1990: 22-4) often bypasses the 'simplicity' step and simply infers unanalyzability from intrinsicality. This is unjustified and leads him to abandon the idea that consciousness is an intrinsic property of mental states in the first place. Rosenthal wrongly thinks that the only informative account of consciousness is one that treats it as an extrinsic property. Let us concentrate on the following problematic inference:

> P is an intrinsic property of x.
> *Therefore*, P is unanalyzable (i.e. cannot be explained).

If consciousness is an intrinsic property of some mental states, it does *not* follow that it is unanalyzable. Nor does it follow that the state of which it is predicated is unanalyzable. We can understand consciousness as involving the property of 'accompanied by a MET' in much the same way as Rosenthal. But we might individuate conscious states 'widely,' i.e. in a way that treats consciousness as an intrinsic property of those states. On this account, the MET is part of the conscious state. I will call it the 'wide intrinsicality view,' or WIV. Conscious states are complex, and consciousness is an intrinsic property of conscious states. But, of course, an informative explanation of consciousness is not thereby ruled out. Thus, 'simplicity' does not follow from 'intrinsicality.' Indeed, much of Rosenthal's own analysis can be utilized within such a framework. Treating consciousness as an intrinsic property does not preclude an informative account of conscious states. Rosenthal fails to see this because he most often views the NIV as the *only* type of intrinsicality position. I agree that the NIV cannot offer a satisfying explanation of consciousness, but Rosenthal wrongly thinks that there are only two options: the NIV and his own 'extrinsicality' view. Since the NIV is unhelpful he sees his own position as the only plausible alternative. But there is another, and superior, alternative: the WIV. Rosenthal ignores it mainly because he is so concerned to discredit the radical Cartesian view that consciousness is essential to mentality. Since he often mistakenly equates 'essential' with 'intrinsic,' he takes his main opposition to hold that consciousness is an intrinsic property of mental states and then treats the NIV as the only type of intrinsicality view. After opting for his extrinsicality view, he then mistakenly infers contingency from extrinsicality.

2.4 The WIV and its Advantages over Rosenthal's Theory

The WIV holds that the MET is part of the conscious state which is rendered conscious. The MET is intrinsic to the conscious state, but this does not rule out an informative explanation of state consciousness. Conscious states are complex states. Consciousness is the intrinsic property of 'having a MET that one is in a mental state.' On Rosenthal's theory of conscious states (hereafter RTC) there are two distinct states, and so consciousness is an extrinsic property. In *introspection*, there is a first-order mental state which is rendered conscious by a *complex* MET. This MET is consciously directed at a (noncomplex) mental state. Introspection involves two states: a lower-order noncomplex mental state which is the object of a higher-order *conscious* and, so, complex state (see Figures 1 and 2).

The WIV retains the virtues of RTC and is, in many respects, similar to it. First, it is informative. Recall that Rosenthal's main concern in treating consciousness as an intrinsic property was that we would be left with simple, unanalyzable states. We have already seen how the WIV leaves room for an informative explanation of consciousness. It is difficult to see why we can only informatively explain state consciousness by appealing to entirely distinct states. Indeed, as Rosenthal (1986: 345, 1990: 22) admits, much of the evidence he adduces in favor of his theory can equally be used for the explanatory power of the WIV.

Secondly, the WIV still acknowledges the important role of *concepts* in one's ability to make various sensory discriminations. The concepts which figure into the METs are a vital element in this type of theory. The point here is simply that the WIV also explains how one has qualitatively differing conscious states on the basis of making fine-grained conceptual distinctions. As Rosenthal (1986: 350) notes, experiences such as wine tasting and listen-

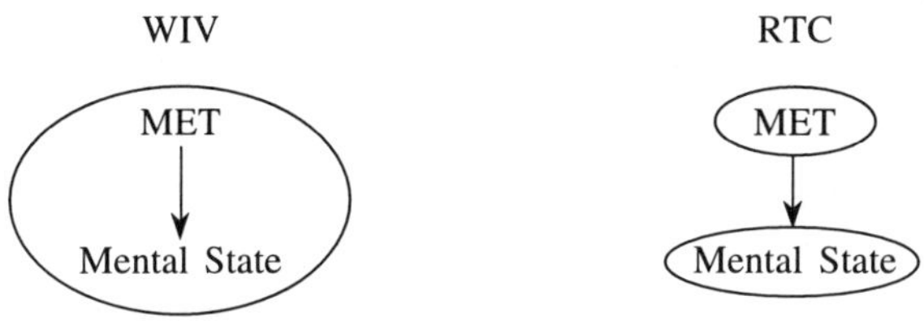

Figure 1. World-Directed Conscious Mental States

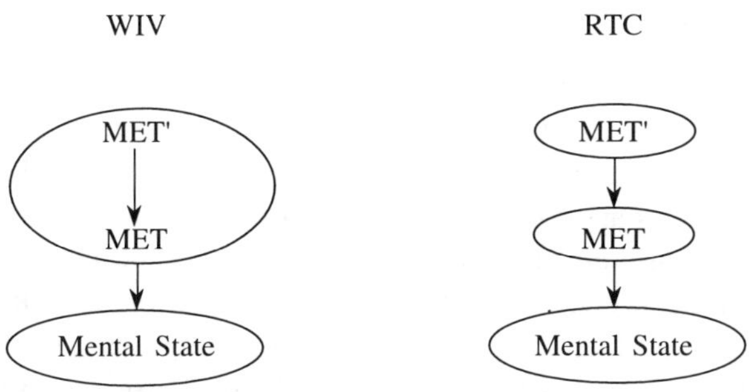

Figure 2. Introspective Conscious Mental States

ing to music provide vivid examples of this phenomenon. Both the WIV and the RTC explain how the possession of concepts can phenomenologically alter one's conscious states. This is related to the so-called 'theory ladenness of perception' whereby one's perceptual experiences are colored by background theory. There is also what we might call the 'concept ladenness' of conscious experience. The nature of conscious states are shaped by the concepts one possesses and the WIV can equally explain the relevance of concepts. Thus, Rosenthal (1986: 350) is mistaken when he says that "if consciousness is intrinsic to sensory states, the relevance of concepts remains mysterious." (See also Natsoulas 1992b: 390-1 for more on why both theories can accommodate the relevance of concepts.)

Interestingly, Rosenthal (1986: 343-6; 1990: 22) does briefly entertain the WIV at various points, but then dismisses it for misguided reasons. He at best shows that *if* one also holds a radical Cartesian concept of consciousness, then one cannot informatively explain consciousness. That is, he at best shows that:

> ...if consciousness is what makes a state a mental state, consciousness will not only be an intrinsic nonrelational property of all mental states; it will be unanalyzable as well. (1986: 341)

The Cartesian would be faced with regress and circularity problems because the MET invoked in the explanation would also have to be conscious. But, of course, one need not hold the radical Cartesian thesis that mental states are essentially conscious. There are nonconscious mental states and, in particular, nonconscious thoughts. The METs which render states conscious need not themselves be conscious. Rosenthal is so concerned to attack the Cartesian conception of consciousness that he does not give the WIV the attention it deserves. The false dilemma arises again.

At one point Rosenthal (1986: 345) does attempt an argument against the WIV. He rightly notes that if conscious states had 'parts' in this way, then either all of the parts are conscious, or only some. He correctly dismisses the former option for the same reason that the MET need not be conscious on his own view: fears of regress and circularity. But as for the alternative that the MET might be a nonconscious part of a conscious state, Rosenthal at best claims that there is no non-arbitrary way to distinguish the WIV from the RTC. But he is mistaken that the only reason to prefer the WIV is "the desire to sustain the Cartesian contention that all mental states are conscious states." (1986: 345) I do not hold (nor do I desire to hold) that all mental states are conscious.[8]

Thus far I have shown that Rosenthal's motivation for the extrinsicality view is miguided and that an informative explanation can still be provided. Moreover, he has offered us no further reason to treat consciousness as a contingent property of qualitative states. The WIV is a viable option and retains the virtues of the RTC. I now briefly turn to some further *advantages* the WIV has over the RTC, although the two theories are clearly very similar and I do not wish to understate my debt to Rosenthal's work. I have been primarily concerned with Rosenthal's *method* rather than his conclusion. Nevertheless, there are several reasons to *prefer* the WIV over the RTC.

1. The WIV ought to be favored on the grounds of simplicity. It requires the presence of one state for nonintrospective consciousness, and two states for introspective consciousness. The RTC requires two and three states respectively. One might naturally respond that this simplicity is gained only at the price of having states with complexity, which just reintroduces the levels in a different guise. Perhaps I am simply trading off simplicity in one place for it

elsewhere, but I am not convinced for the following reason:

There is a certain degree of artificiality on the RTC with respect to introspective consciousness. In giving his account, Rosenthal seems more concerned with what *must* be true as an extension from the nonintrospective case than with the details or elegance of his theory. He casually asserts that there must be third-order states if he is to avoid circularity problems. I disagree with Rosenthal on methodological and aesthetic grounds. Rosenthal captures the core of introspection in words when he says that "to introspect a mental state is to have a conscious thought about that state" (1986: 338). The WIV captures the core of introspection simply, accurately, and without unnecessary talk of third-order thoughts which render second-order thoughts conscious (See again Figure 2).

Many so-called 'adverbial theorists' are concerned with the ontology of mind, and contend that, whenever possible, one ought to avoid quantifying over mental objects.[9] This is best achieved by providing useful and accurate paraphrases which eliminate the need for the apparent quantification over mental objects reflected in the everyday use of mental terms. It is not clear that either the RTC or the WIV are *necessarily* opposed to the spirit behind the adverbial theory. But the WIV is in a *prima facie* better position to allay such worries because it makes reference to fewer states. It does so by individuating those states more widely, but this has always been a-common way of reducing the number of objects in one's ontology.

2. The WIV has the advantage of accommodating the intuitively appealing theses that consciousness is an intrinsic property of mental states. Once again, when we are in a conscious state, it certainly seems that consciousness is an intrinsic property of it. Consciousness surely seems to be an intrinsic feature of mental states from the first person point of view. It doesn't seem like 'being the cousin of...' or 'being to the left of...' It is clearly preferable to preserve this intuition if at all possible. Recall that Rosenthal agrees (1986: 331), but then steers away from an intrinsicality view for the misguided reasons explained in the last two sections.

3. The WIV also makes room for the historically influential thesis that conscious mental states are, in some sense, directed at themselves. There is an intuitive sense in which the consciousness of mental states is 'reflective' or 'self-referential.' Conscious mental states do not merely 'represent' the world, but also represent or understand themselves as doing so. Brentano

(1874/1973), for example, held that conscious mental states are secondarily directed at themselves. Part of his reasoning was that it is difficult to distinguish the 'mental act' of thinking or perceiving something from the mental act of thinking that one thinks or perceives something. Aware of the problems involved in having intentional states directed at nonexistent objects, Brentano stressed the very act of mental directedness. His view can be understood as a way to explain consciousness as an intrinsic property of some mental states.

Some care, however, is needed. Brentano's view literally says that a conscious mental state CMS is, in part, about CMS. This is not quite what the WIV says and is perhaps not even his considered position. Strictly speaking, on the WIV, a CMS is not directed at itself. There is rather an 'inner directedness' or 'inner relationality' in the CMS. The MET is also not directed back at the entire complex CMS, but rather at the psychological state it renders conscious. Conscious mental states are not about themselves, but there is a kind of indirect self-reference. The METs are directed at parts of states of which they are part. Hill (1991: 118) seems to echo the spirit behind this idea when he says of "basic awareness" that "[t]he object of awareness is included in the state of awareness." Rosenthal also recognizes the force of this intuition (1986: 344-5), and we should retain this element of self-referentiality in our theory insofar as it accords with common intuition and helps to explain the *structure* of state consciousness.

In a later paper, Rosenthal (1993a: 211-14) further discusses Brentano's theory, but rejects it mainly because he again fails to see what could motivate the belief that the MET is intrinsic to the conscious state. Of course, I have already argued that Rosenthal fails to show that we ought to accept the extrinsicality view and am now precisely offering additional reasons to prefer the WIV. But the point here is that Rosenthal thinks that the WIV "would be more tempting to hold if all mental states are conscious." (1993a: 213) I do not follow his reasons for this claim, but I have tried to show that it is not true. On the contrary, the WIV makes sense only if the MET *need not* be conscious. We can agree with Rosenthal against Brentano that there are unconscious mental states, but this is no reason to abandon his general view of the structure of conscious states. Rosenthal seems to think that only if the METs are distinct states, "can we explain why we are generally unaware of them" (1993a: 213). But this is surely wrong: we can equally be unaware of a nonconscious thought which is part of a conscious state. Rosenthal is again relying on the false dichotomy discussed in the previous section. He assumes the only other option involves the Cartesian view that all mental states are conscious. Admittedly, Brentano did mistakenly hold this view, but we need not hold it and so are free to retain the better aspects of his view.

David Woodruff Smith (1986) also defends Brentano's general idea, and has sparked Searle (1992: 141-3) to take issue with the idea that conscious states involve self-consciousness. In doing so, Searle casually sets aside this idea mainly because he does not adequately recognize that self-consciousness can come in degrees. He only seems to treat it as a very sophisticated form of introspection. For example, he imagines himself sitting in a restaurant eating a steak, and proclaims that "in the ordinary sense" he would not be self-conscious at all. But then he says that he might be conscious that the steak tastes good, that the wine he is washing down is too young, etc. But if self-consciousness is simply having meta-psychological thoughts, then Searle clearly is self-conscious. Moreover, in this case, he probably even has momentary focused *introspection* since he seems to be having a *conscious* MET about a taste sensation. Thus, for the reasons offered earlier in this chapter (and for many yet to come), Searle's challenge can be met. He fails to distinguish various forms of self-consciousness while not explaining what he means by self-consciousness in the "ordinary sense." Searle does seem to acknowledge the plausibility of the (weaker) claim that any (human) conscious state is itself *potentially* an object of consciousness, e.g. through a shift in attention. But he treats this as a "trivially true" version of the idea that consciousness entails self-consciousness. It doesn't strike me as a trivial claim even for all humans, and is clearly a very substantial claim if true of all conscious animals, i.e. all their conscious states are potentially objects of introspection. Indeed, even the HOT theory need not be committed to such a strong claim, since some conscious creatures may not be able to change each METs into a conscious MET. (For more on Brentano's view in the context of Rosenthal's theory, see Natsoulas 1989: 103-14; and Natsoulas 1992b: 376-9.)

4. One fact emerges from the concept-laden character of conscious experience; namely, that the nature of a conscious state is, in part, a function of the concepts which figure into the MET. Once again, the very *nature* of conscious states is colored by the concepts brought to bear on them. The sophisticated wine drinker has different qualitative states than the inexperienced wine drinker. The meta-psychological 'thought awareness' involved in having a MET actually changes the nature of the conscious state. The object of such awareness is not merely passively 'there' so that it remains unaltered by the

meta-awareness. The WIV can accommodate this fact because the MET is not a distinct state directed at another independent state. On the RTC, the state which is rendered conscious is viewed as an 'independent existent' and partly explains why Rosenthal thinks there are nonconscious qualitative states. But in treating the mental state and its MET as distinct, the fact that the MET contributes *essentially* to the very qualitative character of the conscious state is lost (on Rosenthal's own logic).

5. A related issue brings out a further advantage. I briefly noted one reason why Rosenthal should not conclude that there are nonconscious qualitative states (section 2.3). We have also seen how the WIV is able to explain the concept-laden character of sensory states. I would like to go further and offer another reason to deny the existence of nonconscious qualitative states. In doing so, we will see how the WIV is better equipped to explain why there could not be such states.

If having the ability to make certain conceptual distinctions is essential to *having* certain qualitative states and if those concepts figure into the METs which render states conscious, then it is very difficult to see how there could be nonconscious sensory states. Nonconscious qualitative states would be devoid of that conceptualization, but such conceptualization is essential to their identity *and* with the application of concepts comes the consciousness of those states. So a nonconscious qualitative state, *contra* Rosenthal, could not be the *very same state* as the conscious one because of the lack of conceptualization. Rosenthal agrees that it is the concepts (which figure into his HOTs) which render states conscious in the first place. My view says that the MET is, in part, what makes the conscious state the one it is. Claiming that there could be nonconscious states which are the same as concept-laden conscious states is absurd since the concepts are needed to render the states conscious in the first place. The problem is that Rosenthal wants it both ways. On the one hand, he recognizes that the identity and nature of qualitative states are bound up with one's possessed concepts. On the other hand, he wants to hold that *those very same qualitative states* can occur nonconsciously, and so without the conceptualization in question. It is wiser to stay with common sense and jettison the notion of nonconscious qualitative states. My theory explains why we should not suppose that there are, or even could be, such states.

2.5 A Taxomony of Conscious States

There are the following kinds of conscious states:

1. Conscious Phenomenal States.
   a. Conscious Bodily Sensations (e.g. pains).[10]
   b. Conscious World-Directed Perceptual States.
2. Conscious World-Directed Non-Perceptual Intentional States (e.g. desires and thoughts).
3. Self-Consciousness
   a. Non-Reflective Self-Consciousness, i.e. Nonconscious Meta-Psychological Thought Awareness.
   b. Momentary Focused Introspection.
   c. Deliberate Introspection.

Type (1a) states are more primitive than type (1b) because they are purely bodily states. Pains are not directed at anything, i.e. there are no 'pains that p' or 'pains about x.' Some phenomenal states do not have intentional properties. Type (1b) states, on the other hand, are states with both qualitiative and intentional properties. The difference in complexity can partly be seen by what renders them conscious. The MET which renders a type (1b) state conscious is a second-order *intentional* state; that is, an intentional state directed at another intentional state. The MET which renders a type (1a) state conscious is, of course, also meta-psychological but it is not a second-order intentional state in the sense that its object is also intentional. There is little need to elaborate on type (2) states here. Type (3) states have been explained in section 2.2. I believe that this taxonomy is superior to others that have been offered. For example, Armstrong (1980) distinguishes the following:

A1. Minimal consciousness.
A2. Perceptual consciousness.
A3. Introspective consciousness:
   a. Reflex consciousness.
   b. Introspection proper.

It is not clear that type-A1 states belong in any taxonomy of *conscious* states. Armstrong (1980: 55) often characterizes them as "minimal behavioral reactions to sensory stimuli," which sounds more like my 'behavioral awareness' (section 1.3). But one can be behaviorally aware without being consciously aware. It is also stretching our language to treat 'minimal' consciousness as a *sense* of consciousness. It is far from clear that there is, as a matter of linguistic usage, a use of 'conscious' which is what Armstrong calls 'minimal.' It was for this very reason that I originally distinguished between 'behavioral awareness' and 'conscious awareness'.

Armstrong's 'perceptual consciousness' (type A2) is much the same as my type-1b states. This at least includes "consciousness of what is currently going on in one's environment..." (1980: 58). It is also reasonable to include 'perceptions of one's own body' in this class. However, as far as I know, he does not explicitly note the more rudimentary type (1a) states. He also seems to ignore type (2) states, or at least does not properly distinguish them from the clearly perceptual type (1b) states.

Armstrong divides 'introspective consciousness' into "reflex" consciousness "which is normally always present while we are awake (but which is lost by the long-distance truck driver), and consciousness of a more explicit, self-conscious sort" (1980: 63). The former incorporates the idea that whenever we are in conscious states there is always some internal monitoring of those states. Introspective consciousness normally has only a "watching brief" with respect to our mental states. The more sophisticated 'introspection proper' involves "carefully scrutiniz[ing] our own current state of mind" (1980: 63). Armstrong draws the parallel with our awareness of the external environment. Sometimes there is a mere "reflex" seeing in contrast to a careful scrutinizing of the visual environment.

I suggest that Armstrong's 'reflex' consciousness is very much like my type (3a) states (i.e. non-reflective self-consciousness). Such states involve a meta-awareness of one's mental contents in the 'reflex' manner that Armstrong describes. They are not *themselves* conscious but, on my view, render their objects conscious. However, given my distinction between 'non-reflective self-consciousness' and 'introspection,' we should restrict 'introspection' to the more sophisticated mental states.

Perhaps Armstrong would agree that reflex consciousness is not really a type of introspection. This would explain his use of the term 'introspection *proper*' in characterizing his other type of introspection, but he still conflates 'deliberate' and 'momentary focused' introspection (i.e. my (3b) and (3c) states). It is not clear what 'carefully scrutinizing our states of mind' amounts to. He often seems to mean momentary focused introspection, but 'carefully scrutinizing' suggests deliberation. Armstrong's 'introspection proper' can thus at best be identified with either my 3b or 3c state (but not both), and so he has at least overlooked one type of introspective state. Nonetheless, Armstrong rightly explains that:

> It is a plausible hypothesis that [introspection proper] will normally involve not only introspective awareness of mental states and activities but also introspective awareness of that introspective awareness. (1980: 63)

My general theory echoes the spirit, if not the letter, of this sentiment. Introspection involves not only a MET directed at a mental state but also a further MET' directed at the MET. Introspective awareness does not merely involve being aware that one is in a mental state, but rather being aware that one is aware of being in it, i.e. being consciously aware that one is in that state.

It is also worth mentioning the work of psychologist Thomas Natsoulas who has perhaps led the charge to bring consciousness back into psychology after decades of deliberate neglect. He has distinguished six senses of consciousness (1978, 1983) based on the "consciousness" entry in the Oxford English Dictionary, and then goes on to examine many of them in depth (1985, 1991a, 1991b, 1992a). He distinguishes the following:

1. *Joint Knowledge*: Knowing or sharing the knowledge of anything.
2. *Internal Knowledge*: Knowledge as to which one has the testimony within oneself.
3. *Awareness*: The state or faculty of being mentally conscious or aware of anything.
4. *Direct Awareness*: The state or faculty of being conscious, as a condition or concomitant of all thought, feeling, and volition; the recognition by the thinking subject of its own acts and affections.
5. *Personal Unity*: The totality of the impressions, thoughts, and feelings, which make up a person's conscious being.
6. *The Normal Waking State*: The state of being conscious, regarded as the normal condition of healthy waking life.

Natsoulas' project differs from mine in that he is more concerned with etymology and definitions (e.g. in senses one and two), whereas my interest here has more to do with types of conscious states which can be had by an individual. Moreover, as was noted in chapter one, our concern is mostly with the adjectival sense of 'conscious' whereas many of Natsoulas' definitions apply to the abstract noun 'consciousness' (e.g. consciousness_5). In any case, several valuable points of comparison can still be made:

a. Natsoulas' consciousness$_4$ is obviously closest to my type (3a) state, i.e. non-reflective self-consciousness. In particular, Natsoulas makes it clear that the "direct awareness" in question is non-inferential which, as we shall see, will be central to our analysis of type (3a) states.
b. Consciousness$_3$ is the most general notion since it covers being conscious *of anything*. So we might say that it covers all of the states in our taxonomy whether they are directed at the world or toward a mental state. For example, it covers consciousness$_4$: "Every instance of consciousness$_4$ is an instance of consciousness$_3$, though not vice versa" (1992a: 213). We might say that every type (3a) state is an awareness of something, but not every awareness of something is a non-reflective awareness of a mental state.
c. Natsoulas' second sense seems more sophisticated than consciousness$_4$ since consciousness$_2$ seems to include *knowledge* acquired through deliberate reflection. This sounds more like introspection, e.g. a type (3c) state. As we have seen there are degrees of self-consciousness; some states are more sophisticated than others. Natsoulas acknowledges this point when he notes that consciousness$_2$ includes consciousness$_4$ and that the latter is less complex than the former (1991b: 353). We can put it by saying that introspection is an advanced form of self-consciousness, i.e. type (3a) states are less complex than (3b) and (3c) states.

Perhaps most relevant to my overall project is the more recent debate between Natsoulas (1993) and Rosenthal (1993b). My view is closest to what Natsoulas calls 'the self-intimational' account in contrast to Rosenthal's 'appendage theory' mainly because the former treats the MET as an intrinsic part of a conscious mental state whereas the latter does not. But I am not sure that we should follow Natsoulas in supposing that the 'mental-eye' perceptual model excludes adherence to the other two. If we define the mental-eye theory in such a way that makes the MET a distinct state, then of course it is inconsistent with the self-intimational model. But perhaps there is room for a fourth view which combines the mental-eye and self-intimational approaches. Indeed, I will argue in chapter four (4.10) that there are several good reasons to adopt a perceptual or 'inner sense' model. Moreover, we must keep in mind that when talking about *introspection* the higher-order (conscious) state is distinct from the lower-order state. The WIV should recognize the viability of the perceptual or 'mental-eye' view with regard to these types of states. Natsoulas (1989: 74-88) does not account for this when he addresses Armstrong's reasons for believing that a conscious state and the awareness of it must be 'distinct existences.' It seems to me that Armstrong was more concerned with *introspection* in which case the two states are distinct and a mental-eye view is at least more plausible.

CHAPTER 3

Why the Conscious Making State must be a Thought

3.1 Reducing the Alternatives

Given that the presence of meta-psychological *states* best explains conscious mentality, why must those states be *thoughts*? An indirect strategy might show that other propositional attitudes are not equipped to do the job. Although the term 'thought' is sometimes used in a generic sense that covers a variety of propositional attitudes, I restrict it to occurrent, momentary mental acts or events which are constituted by concepts.

Some propositional attitudes are not even *prima facie* candidates for the conscious rendering office even if they have the requisite content, i.e. '...that one is in a particular mental state.' For example, the meta-psychological state (hereafter MES) could not be hoping, desiring, expecting, wishing, doubting, or suspecting. Wishing or desiring to be in a mental state is never sufficient to render it conscious. One 'wishes' precisely because one is not in that state. The same goes for 'hoping' and 'expecting.' Doubting that I am in some mental state is also not sufficient for rendering a state conscious. These kinds of nonassertoric attitudes, by their very nature, show that one is even uncertain that their object is there. I can wonder whether some pain I have is 'piercing,' 'stabbing,' 'damaging' or 'passing.' We often wonder whether a conscious state has some property or not. But that is not what makes the state conscious. One can have conscious states in the absence of such attitudes. A state can be conscious *and then*, sometimes, we wonder whether or not it has some property. The MES must be, as Rosenthal recognizes, an assertoric state (1990: 40-1).

The most important remaining 'non-thought' candidate is belief. Beliefs present the most substantial challenge to the idea that the MES must be a thought. I suspect, however, that this is because the term 'belief' is often used interchangeably with 'thought.' As noted above, the term 'thought' is sometimes used in a generic sense covering most intentional attitudes, especially beliefs. When one is surprised at another's utterance in a philosophical debate, one might say: "I cannot believe that you think (believe) that." One might ask: "Why do you believe (think) that?" But there are important differences between thoughts and beliefs which need to be recognized in a mature theory of mind. The fact that two terms are often used interchangeably is not enough to show that they are synonymous (as we saw in the case of 'conscious' and 'aware'). We often speak of a nonconscious or sleeping person as having many beliefs, e.g. the sleeping physicist has many beliefs about the fundamental particles of the universe. But he need not be having the corresponding thoughts. Moreover, it is makes little sense to ask: What are you believing right now? On the other hand, it is perfectly proper to ask: What are you thinking now? The underlying reason for these differences is that beliefs are best understood as *dispositional* states whereas thoughts are *momentary* mental acts or events. This explains why we say that the sleeping physicist believes various things. *If* he were awake, he would be disposed to behave, linguistically and otherwise, in certain ways. One may *have* a belief that p at t, but that is not to say that there is an act of believ*ing* that p at t. Despite this difference between beliefs and thoughts, one cannot distinguish them on the basis of their objects. That is, for any value of 'p' or 'x' in 'S thinks that p or about x,' it might also be that 'S believes that p' or 'S believes something about x'.

3.2 Why Can't the Meta-State be a Meta-Psychological Belief?

The best available theories of belief treat believing that p as being disposed to behave, verbally or non-verbally, in certain ways under certain conditions (see Bennett 1976, Dennett 1987, and Stalnaker 1987). It is, of course, not quite that simple. If we see a person take his umbrella as he leaves his home, we might explain that behavior by attributing to him the belief that it will rain. But his behavior cannot be explained merely in terms of beliefs. Beliefs *and desires* must be attributed in tandem. If he does not *want* to keep dry, then he would not take his umbrella. Thus, even in simple cases, attributions of desires must accompany belief ascriptions in a satisfactory psychological explanation. An animal chases another because it wants to eat it, but that is not enough. It must also believe that it will get something to eat. Thus, in explaining the behavior of a system S, it is necessary to attribute both beliefs and desires to S. This is the so-called 'belief-desire-behavior' triangle. The emphasis here is on what best *explains* and so *usefully predicts* the behavior of systems (cf. Dennett 1987). One consequence of recognizing the 'triangle' is that desires are often just defined in terms of beliefs and vice versa. For example, 'S desires that p' is taken to mean that 'S is disposed to behave in ways that S believes will bring it about that p.' 'S believes that p' is understood as 'S is disposed to act in ways that would tend to satisfy S's desires in a world where p is true' (cf. Stalnaker 1987: 15; Bennett 1990). This kind of interdefinitional strategy is fundamentally the weak functionalist approach which allows reference to other mental items in defining mental terms. There are, of course, many schools of thought regarding the fundamental *nature* and *causal potency* of beliefs and desires, but my point here is only that our rough folk psychological concept of belief is a disposition to behave or act in certain ways under certain conditions. Part of the 'conditions' will be the accompanying desires.

I have been speaking of first-order beliefs, i.e. beliefs directed at the outer world, or a belief that a proposition is true. A similar, though more complicated, story ought to hold for meta-psychological beliefs (MEB). To have a belief about one's own mental state is presumably also to be disposed to act in certain ways under certain conditions, but the object of a MEB is different than the object of a first-order belief. I believe that I want to finish this manuscript by the end of July 1994. I have a MEB directed at a desire. What is it to have such a belief? It is at least that whenever I am in a situation conducive to fulfilling that desire, I behave in such a way as to do so. I am disposed to act in ways which would satisfy my desire, i.e. to bring it about that I will finish by the end of July 1994. It will presumably also involve my being disposed to answer questions about the finished product.[11] Similarly, I might believe that I am angry and so have a MEB about an emotion. I would, for example, be disposed to answer "Yes" to the question "Are you upset right now?" as long as I desire to speak truthfully. One can have a MEB about a mental state while the object of the MEB is conscious, but it is not the MEB that makes it conscious. There is at best a contingent connection between the presence of a conscious state and any MEB that might be directed at it. Let us see exactly why MEBs cannot render states conscious:

1. I have said that a key difference between beliefs and thoughts is that the former are best understood dispositionally and the latter as momentary mental events. One reason to treat systems as having a large number of MEBs is their dispositional nature. It makes sense for us to speak of each other as having many MEBs at time t because that is to say something about how we would behave in certain situtations. Presumably I have hundreds of MEBs *now*, but if they are what render mental states conscious then I would be overwhelmed by a flood of conscious states. Since I am not so overwhelmed, a MEB cannot be what renders a state conscious. METs, on the other hand, come in sequences of momentary episodes and a system cannot have very many at any instant. I can have a few different conscious states at the same time (e.g. a pain in the toe and a visual experience), but the number falls far short of my present number of MEBs. Moreover, my MEB that I want to finish this book by the end of July 1994 clearly does not render that desire conscious. I have that MEB all the time. It is a dispositional and enduring state of mine. *Sometimes* that desire is conscious, but it is not made so by any MEB directed at it.

2. Georges Rey (1988) provides us with another way to show why MEBs are ill equipped to render mental states conscious. Rey is skeptical as to the existence of consciousness (or, at least, its explanatory usefulness). I do not agree with Rey's conclusions, but am more concerned with his method. His strategy is to show how various aspects of mentality can be built into a system without any inclination to treat it as conscious. If all of the important features of mind can be incorporated, then Rey wonders what role consciousness has left to play. Van Gulick (1989: 212) rightly notes that the argument

> ...is a variant of what are sometimes called "absent qualia arguments," arguments that attempt to show that one or another functionally specified condition for possessing mentality can be satisfied by systems which lack any [conscious] states.

Rey takes his argument to show that there is no room for 'consciousness' to play in his functionalist (i.e. computationalist) theory of mind. But the conclusion drawn provides us with a classic example of the principle that "one philosopher's *modus ponens* is another's *modus tollens*." That is, we might instead take the moral to be that his theory of mind is inadequate because it leaves out the conscious aspect of mentality. Since consciousness does not find a place in the story, the computational theory on which it rests must be incomplete.

But let us return to Rey's method. He imagines a first-order intentional system which "has beliefs and preferences merely by virtue of obeying rational regularities" (1988: 13). Rey then argues, *via* his computational theory, that such a system can be easily programmed to be a second-order intentional system by allowing the program to access itself at various junctures. This would render it capable of having beliefs and preferences about beliefs and preferences. It would have MEBs. The program that performs this further function is the 'Recursive Believer System,' and Rey is right that we have no reason to treat the system as thereby conscious. A system can be endowed with a Recursive Believer System without even being conscious at all.

One can object to Rey's method in at least two ways. First, we might wonder whether the states in question even deserve to be called 'mental' as opposed to merely 'as-if' intentional states (cf. Searle 1984, 1989). Second, Rey might be oversimplifying what is involved in having second-order intentional states. These are important lines of objection in their own right and bring out issues of independent interest. An adequate repsonse to the first objection would require a full discussion of the minimal necessary conditions for mental representational states, which is well beyond the scope of this work.[12] An adequate response to the second objection would take us even further into how various theories of mind handle second-order states (cf. again Van Gulick 1980, 1982). It is, for example, not obvious that the presence of second-order beliefs can be justifiably attributed purely on the basis of non-verbal behavioral evidence. But my point here is simply that *if* Rey's kind of story is at all plausible, then MEBs cannot render mental states conscious. The addition of a Recursive Believer System provides us with no further reason to treat a system as having conscious mental states. More specifically, the addition of the MEBs do not render their objects conscious.

I take the above arguments as sufficient to show that MEBs *qua* dispositions cannot be the conscious rendering states. But a natural response is that I have neglected the possibility of an occurrent/dispositional division within the class of beliefs. Perhaps *occurrent* beliefs can render their objects conscious.

Beliefs are best understood as dispositional states of systems, but there is still room for the notion of an 'occurrent belief.' I have the belief, B, that the best way to walk to the University is to make a right on University Avenue. I have B at all times which is just to reinforce its dispositional nature. Most of the time B does not play any role in the production or explanation of my behavior, e.g. while I am eating dinner at home. However, when I am walking to campus and make a right onto University Avenue, B is involved in the explanation of my behavior at that time. Beliefs function as part of the explanation for a system's behavior at a particular time. So although beliefs are dispositional in character, they can also be occurrent in the sense that they explain a system's behavior at a given time. It is one and the same belief that becomes 'occurrent,' i.e. beliefs are 'activated' or 'manifested' at various times. When a belief is manifested at time t it is occurrent at t. The analogy that suggests itself is: B *qua* dispositional state is to B *qua* occurrent state as the 'fragility' of a glass is to its 'breaking'.

Nothing about 'occurrent' beliefs shows that they can render their objects conscious. They are not *additional* kinds of beliefs that we have. My occurrent belief that I want to turn right on University Avenue does not render its object conscious. I may not even be thinking about University Avenue at all. The object of a belief need not be conscious in order for the belief to play an active role in one's present behavior. Similarly with MEBs. I can have an occurrent MEB without its object being conscious. My MEB that I want to finish this manuscript by the end of July 1994 is often occurrent, e.g. most of the time that I am working. But, of course, that desire is not always conscious at those times. Moreover, I can presumably have many occurrent MEBs at one time, e.g. a belief that I want a drink of water, a belief that I want to finish this chapter, a belief that I like one of my arguments, a belief that I want to call my wife at work, and so on. But, as was argued earlier, if they are what renderend states conscious, then I would be overwhelmed with a flood of conscious states. But I am not, and so MEBs cannot be what render states conscious. I can presumably *manifest* many different MEBs at a given time without their objects becoming conscious, although I admit it is very difficult to *know* whether another is having a MEB purely on the basis of non-verbal behavioral evidence.

There may be other ways to understand occurrent beliefs, e.g. one might treat them more like real causally efficacious representational states (cf. Lewis 1966 and Armstrong 1968). I do not think that this is inconsistent with my view. It makes a further claim about the nature and causal power of such beliefs; namely, that when one has an occurrent belief one is in some inner state that causally produces the behavior *and* it is best to interpret that state as representing the belief. But this does not help show that MEBs can render their objects conscious. I can still have the occurrent belief that I want to finish this book without the desire becoming conscious. A causally efficacious mental state might produce the relevant behavior without its object becoming conscious. I suggest that when one is at all inclined to treat MEBs as conscious rendering states, one is not really differentiating them from my 'METs'.

Recall that I initially contrasted beliefs and thoughts by noting that the former are enduring dispositional states while the latter are momentary datable mental events. It would be a mistake to treat my acknowledgement of occurrent beliefs as a retreat from that fundamental contrast. When a belief is occurrent it is not some *additional* belief of the system which is a momentary and datable mental event. What is momentary and datable is the *behavioral manifestation* of the belief, not the belief itself. The crucial point is that in neither case does the belief render its object conscious.

It is also wise to allow for what I will call 'episodic beliefs' which are not equivalent to 'occurrent beliefs.' The former are those which are consciously thought about by the believer. A belief B is episodic at t for S when S is entertaining or introspecting B. Humans have the sophisticated capacity to consciously think about their own beliefs. When the psychiatrist's patient is made conscious of one of his beliefs at time t, then it is episodic at t. Episodic beliefs are conscious, and all conscious beliefs are episodic. I purposely define episodic beliefs as requiring *conscious* thoughts about them because I think that this is the only way for beliefs to be conscious. Beliefs are different than other mental states: there is 'nothing it is like to be in them.' Thus, I find no place in my theory for a conscious belief with *only a nonconscious MET directed at it.* It is difficult to understand what such a state could be, whereas the division between other conscious states and introspecting them is clear. It would again be a mistake to treat this as a difficulty for my account. I hold that that METs render mental states conscious, and this is still so for episodic beliefs. What makes them conscious, and so episodic, is that they are being thought about by the subject. One can have an episodic MEB, but what renders its object conscious is not its being a MEB but rather that it is accompanied by a (conscious) MET.

There are other good theoretical reasons for distinguishing METs from MEBs. It seems possible for a system to have METs without MEBs and vice versa. A system might have relatively complex long term dispositions to behave in certain ways without being able to have momentary meta-psychological thoughts (e.g. Rey's imagined system). Indeed, if Rey is right, then a system might have MEBs without being conscious at all. If so and the present theory is right, then this entails that a system could have MEBs without having any METs. Conversely, some creatures might be capable of some rudimentary conscious states without having MEBs at all. A frog might have a conscious pain or visual experience which, if I am correct, involves having a MET that it is in that state. But we might also be hesitant to treat frogs as having beliefs at all, not to mention MEBs. The best reasons seem to be either that their behavior is not complex enough to demand anything more than relatively simple mechanistic explanations (Dennett 1987), or such creatures do not have a significant degree of inferential integration or 'promiscuity' amongst its putative beliefs (Stich 1978).[13]

The capacity to have METs is typically accompanied by an ability to have MEBs *in us*. I might form a belief that I am in pain on the basis of having a thought that I am in pain. But I see little reason to treat the connection as a necessary one. It seems possible for a system to have long-term dispositions to behave in certain ways in the absence of momentary thinkings, and vice versa.

3.3 The More Direct Approach: Sensibility and Understanding

Thus far I have argued negatively. No meta-psychological state other than a thought could serve as our conscious rendering state. We might try to argue in a more positive manner.

What is thinking? What is a thought? These are some of the most difficult questions in philosophy of mind. But more needs to be said about them given their key place in the theory. Thinking involves some internal representations of the world or item thought about. That is, creatures represent reality in thought *via some* medium of representation, although we need not suppose that it *must* be linguistic in nature, i.e. that there must be a language of thought (cf. Fodor 1975).[14] What, then, is the 'medium of thought?' A natural answer is that thoughts are constituted by concepts which "consist in [possessing] some kind of non-linguistic internal representation..." (McGinn 1982: 71). Thinking is the exercise of concepts. This is so for both first-order thoughts and for METs, and we have already (in sections 2.3 and 2.4) alluded to the importance of the role of concepts in the HOT theory.

Thoughts would seem to have a logical structure analogous to the structure of sentences: concepts are to thoughts as words or terms are to sentences. Intuitively, we understand concepts as the building blocks of thought just as sentences are built up out of terms. More accurately, we should say that the possession and application of certain concepts are to thoughts as terms are to sentences, because the concepts themselves are probably best understood as abstract objects whereas their exercise and possession are embodied in concrete mental abilities or items. In any event, this general sentiment is found in Samet (1986: 588-9):

> It is very natural to think of concepts...as the counterparts of *terms*. Terms...express concepts, a concept gives the meaning of a term, it fixes the extension of a term...concepts are term-sized."

This type of analogy is taken to the extreme by Fodor (1975, 1981) who understands concepts just to *be* terms in the language of thought, i.e. as mental representations that combine to form propositions. But Fodor is thus committed to the highly controversial view that virtually all concepts are innate.

This general analogy is also vividly recognized by Bennett (1974: 23-6) in the context of interpreting Kant's theory of judgment. He raises the potential problem that it also seems very natural to regard judgments or thoughts as more basic than concepts in the way that one might treat sentence-meaning as more basic than word-meaning. We understand concepts not in isolation but relative to the thoughts into which they figure. This seems to run counter to the notion that concepts are the building blocks of thoughts because thoughts are viewed as more primitive. This point is also recognized by Samet (1986: 589) when he rightly notes that concepts are themselves often understood as sets of propositions, which makes it seem that propositions are more primitive than the concepts which are analyzed in terms of them. The issue is of a piece with the traditional debate between the 'holists' and the 'atomists.' However, one can acknowledge a kind of primitiveness of the whole (thoughts) over the parts (concepts) while retaining the natural picture of concepts as prior to thoughts. It may not be possible to *explain* a concept (or its possession) without appealing to the set of possible thoughts containing it. Analogously, it is difficult to explain the meaning of a word or term without reference to sentences which contain that word. There is an *explanatory* priority of the whole over the parts, but this need not run counter to treating concept-possession as prior to a capacity to have thoughts (cf. Geach 1957: 104-5).

It is also natural to understand concepts as playing 'a Kantian role,' i.e. they make experience possible. I wish to exploit this idea in defending my theory of consciousness throughout this and the next chapter. The Kantian role of concepts is eloquently described by Samet (1986: 589) as follows:

> ...[concepts] make our experience of a world possible...experience is the effect of our applying concepts (or: of concepts being applied) to an inherently unparsed stimulus array — to the busy, bustling, blooming confusion of sensation. Because we have concepts, our experience is organized, coherent, and regular. If we didn't have them, we wouldn't experience anything at all...they are *preexperiential*; they are logically prior to experience.

Some version of this idea can be found in any commentary on Kant, and I think it is fair to say that all philosophers are sympathetic to it in varying degrees. Strawson (1966: 20), for example, echoes this sentiment when he says that:

> [if] any item is even to enter our conscious experience we must be able to classify it in some way, to recognize it as possessing some general characteristics.

This consideration helps support my contention that the conscious rendering states must be thoughts: since concepts play a Kantian role and they figure into thinking, the conscious rendering state must be a thought. One way to explain how states become conscious is to exploit the Kantian idea that concept application makes experience possible. Many philosophers will, of course, think of concepts as constituents of representational and intentional states in general. They do not limit concepts to thoughts as I understand them. I agree that they can figure into other intentional states, but I have already shown that they cannot be the conscious rendering states. However, it is not clear even that MEBs really *apply* their concepts to their objects. Beliefs are not inner momentary mental episodes which involve the exercise of concepts; they are (at best) inner states which are *interpreted as* having content on the basis of the system's behavior.[15]

Let us pursue this more direct strategy by looking at Kant's (1781/1965) own reasons for why concepts are required for experience. Kant explained that there are two stems of human knowledge:

> *sensibility* and *understanding*...through the former, objects are given to us; through the latter, they are thought (A15=B29). Objects are *given* to us by means of sensibility, and it alone yields *intuitions*; they are *thought* through the understanding, and from the understanding arise *concepts* (A19=B33).

We are presented with the 'raw data of experience' through sensibility. The understanding works on that data intellectually by classifying, judging, recognizing, and comparing it to other data. It is the faculty which brings the 'raw data' under intellectual control *via* the application of concepts. To 'have an intuition' is 'to be in a sensory or conscious state.' To have an intuition of x is to be consciously aware of x *via* a sensory modality when 'x' is an object of outer sense.

Kant stresses the fundamental duality of the 'understanding' (or the cognitive) and the 'sensory.' He draws the sharpest of lines between them, and shows how only such a division can explain how experience is possible, i.e. through the cooperation of the sensibility and the understanding. Conscious experience is possible only when intuitions are brought under concepts. This was Kant's great insight, and resulted in his famous dictum: Thoughts without content are empty, intuitions without concepts are blind (A51=B75). Kant rightly saw that many earlier philosophers unwisely viewed the sensory on a continuum with the intellectual. They mistakenly treated a difference in kind as one of degree. He wrote that "Leibniz *intellectualized* appearances, just as Locke...*sensualized* all concepts of the understanding (A271=B327; cf. A44=B61)." Spinoza, Hume, Berkeley, and Descartes made similar errors as is evidenced by their notoriously ambiguous use of the term 'idea.' They found themselves having to make sense of such obscurities as 'faded impressions' (Hume) and 'confused perceptions' (Leibniz). For Kant, the division between the sensory and the intellectual is absolute.[16]

Kant also stresses the passive nature of sensibility and the *activity* of the understanding. The active/passive dichotomy aligns with the understanding/sensible. This is an equally important way to explicate the fundamental duality between the sensory and thought. The understanding's role is to synthesize the raw data of experience (see e.g. A77=B103). The understanding, *via* the exercise of concepts, 'grasps' the items which it synthesizes. Kant's term for concept is *Begriff* which has as one of its cognates *begreifen* (= to grasp). The understanding, then, acts upon the disperate array of raw data and produces an intelligible stream of conscious experience. The key idea for us is that there are internal states which are made conscious when synthesized by the concepts of the understanding.

The ways in which these considerations support the present theory should be obvious. First, the conscious rendering states must be thoughts because they are constituted by concepts which play a Kantian role and no other intentional state will do. Second, we can now better see how conscious states are composed by a lower-order state and a MET directed at it. A conscious mental state is produced through the cooperation of the understanding operating on the otherwise passive contents of one's mind. Mental states are rendered conscious through the work of meta-psychological intellectual operation. Third, the so-called 'concept-ladenness' of experience is a natural consequence of the above story. Simply having conscious states *presupposes* the application of concepts.

Hundert (1989: chapter seven) provides a provocative discussion of the sensibility and understanding. First, he shows how the Kantian model is realized in the brain with the help of neurophysiological evidence. For example, he urges that 'lower' parts of the brain work together with the more sophisticated 'thinking' or 'higher-order' areas to produce a unity of consciousness (see Hundert 1989: 195-201, 210-15 for some of the neurophysiological details).

Second, and even more important, Hundert brings back the 'faculty psychology' of Kant in more contemporary language. He notes that the faculty approach has been recently revived under the heading of the "modularity of mind," i.e. the idea that experience is best explained by the presence of distinct and discrete modules operating in relative ignorance of what goes on in others (Fodor 1983; cf. Gazzaniga 1988). He then does us the great service of drawing several crucial similarities between the Fodorian and Kantian models. Of course, Fodor comes at the issue from artificial intelligence and cognitive science, but the comparisons are striking and instructive.

Taking center stage is Fodor's distinction between "input systems" and "central systems." The former takes in external stimuli and converts it, *via* the "input analyzer," into usable information which is then 'synthesized' by higher-order central systems. Although Hundert rightly urges that the input system is more active than Kant's passive sensibility (given the work of the input *analyzer*), he also rightly draws the general analogy: input systems are to sensibility as central systems are to the understanding (see especially his 1989: 190-5, 201-10). Input systems have two key properties: (1) they are specific to one modality, i.e. can only process one type of information, such as 'visual;' and (2) they are 'informationally encapsulated,' i.e. analyze input in ignorance of what is going on in the other input and the central systems. The latter feature helps explain phenomena such as the well-known Müller-Lyer arrows that *look* unequal even when we know that it is an optical illusion.

So, for example, in the case of vision, certain neurons in area 17 are selectively sensitive to the specific visual properties of shape, movement, size, and depth. Such processing continues to the point where it is synthesized into experience by the understanding. As Hundert (1989: 213) puts it:

> We seem to have a system in which certain properties of our visual fields are organized and analysed by identifiable neuroanatomical structures, and then *these properties* are synthesized by the central processing systems of Understanding into human visual experience.

It is once again worth stressing that the boundary between the sensibility and understanding is blurry for at least two reasons. First, the sensibility (or any input system) is somewhat more 'active' than Kant had theorized. Second, input systems are no longer informationally encapsulated at higher levels of input analysis:

> it must be an open question precisely where we want to say the input analysis of Sensibility has stopped and the central processing of Understanding started. (1989: 206)

Fodor does stress that 'modularity' is a matter of degree. Kant, of course, also saw the need for cooperation and interaction between the sensibility and understanding despite urging their fundamental duality in nature.

One question, however, is where along the 'upward' information flow does a *mental state* emerge. Clearly, many of the input system states do not deserve to be called 'mental' at all, and are merely some kind of primitive informational states. This is a large issue in itself, but I suggest that the key distinction lies in when a state in the input system is able to interact with those in the central system. In other words, the more informationally encapsulated, the less likely to be a mental state. This coincides nicely with the widely held idea that mental states must be able to intract with others in an "inferentially promiscuous" way (cf. Stich 1978). In any case, we must allow for the distinction between genuine mentality and mere information possession *within* sensibility, since the understanding operates on sensibility and involves having a thought about a mental state.

3.4 Another Kantian Theme: The "I Think"

I have shown that Kant's theory of mind and my theory of consciousness are of the same spirit. One might wonder how far the similarities can be taken.

For instance, it might be objected that Kant was not obviously concerned with *meta-psychological thoughts* in his program. I suggest that Kant did indeed hold that METs render states conscious. Consider the following well-known passage:

> It must be possible for the 'I think' to accompany all my representations; for otherwise something would be represented in me which could not be thought at all, and that is equivalent to saying that the representation would be impossible, or at least nothing to me. (B131-2)

Kant is closely relating mentality and self-consciousness. Presumably, the 'I think' is not just any thought, but a thought directed at one's 'representations.' The above quotation is embedded in the complexity of the Transcendental Deduction. My aim is not to delve deeply into that part of the *Critique*, but it is relatively clear that Kant utilizes the implicit premise that consciousness entails self-consciousness. My aim here is to unravel various interpretations of this quote and show its close relation to the WIV. Consider the following portion of Kant's claim:

> (S) It must be possible for the 'I think' to accompany all my representations.

S can be understood in many ways depending upon how one interprets 'I think' and 'representation.' The term 'representation' can be taken as either 'mental state' or as 'conscious mental state.' It is not always clear which Kant had in mind and so commentators do not always properly distinguish them. The 'I think' also admits of two possible interpretations: I *nonconsciously* think and I *consciously* think. Once again, it is not always clear what is meant. Thus, just as 'representation' is ambiguous between mental state and conscious mental state so 'I think' is ambiguous between I nonconsciously think and I consciously think. Consider, then, the following interpretation of S:

> (S1) All of my mental states must be able to be accompanied by a thought about them.

Kant thinks that S1 is true. He is using himself as an example of a self-conscious creature as is evidenced by his use of the first-person pronoun. He might just be claiming that all of *his* mental states might become an object of *his* thought. Kant can in principle think about any of his mental states, and presumably so can any cognitively similar creature. S1 does seem true. Any of *our* nonconscious mental states might become the object of a MET. On the WIV, this is to claim that any of our mental states could become conscious if accompanied by the appropriate MET. Is there any reason to think that some of our mental states could not become conscious? One reason hinges on just how far one extends mental ascriptions, e.g. to some states involved in early perceptual processing. If such states are understood as genuinely mental, then they do not seem to be the kinds of states that even *could* become conscious. But this is rather controversial as many will want to treat such crude states as mere rudimentary 'informational' states. Perhaps Kant's claim is the following:

> (S2) Any of an organism's mental states must be able to be accompanied by thoughts about them.

S2 extends S1 to all organisms, i.e. it says that any creature with mental states must be able to have thoughts about them. One might deny S2 for the same reasons as S1. S2 is even less convincing than S1 because some lower animals would seem to have various nonconscious intentional mental states, but it is not obvious that they are capable of METs directed at them. If dogs and cats have beliefs, it is not clear that they are capable of thoughts about *them*. So S2 seems much too strong. In S1 and S2 'representation' is understood as 'mental states' and the 'I think' need not be a conscious one. So let us explore an option which treats the 'I think' as I consciously think:

> (S3) Having a mental state involves the ability to consciously think about (i.e. introspect) it.

S3 is clearly false on the WIV. An organism can be in mental states without introspecting them. A creature can even be in *conscious* mental states without *being able* to introspect them at all. Various lower animals have mental states of different kinds but clearly do not have a sophisticated introspective capacity. It is unreasonable to withhold ascriptions of mentality solely on the grounds that a system lacks *introspective* ability. Let us contrast S3 with:

> (S4) Having a *conscious* mental state involves being able to consciously think about (i.e. introspect) that state.

In S3 and S4 the 'I think' is read as 'I consciously think.' In S3 the 'representation' is not conscious, but in S4 it is. They are both false on the WIV even though Kant seems not to think so, but the reason for this is that he does not properly distinguish between 'self-consciousness' and 'introspection.' He equates the two and so holds that every representation (conscious or not) must occur in a self-conscious being which for Kant just means that every representation can be introspected. Bennett characterizes this point as follows:

> Kant says that every representation must occur not just in some mind but specifically in the mind of a *self-conscious or self-aware* being. Sometimes he concedes that a representation might exist unaccompanied by *self-consciousness*, but insists that such a representation would be nothing to its owner. (1966: 104, my emphasis)

Bennett makes only one claim on Kant's behalf; namely, that every mental state must occur in a self-conscious being (where 'self-conscious' covers both 'non-reflective self-consciousness' and 'introspection'). But if we identify self-consciousness with introspection, then we are only left with the problematic S3 and S4 interpretations. The fact that Kant had 'introspection' in mind would help explain his resistance to the idea that lower animals have conscious mental states that are 'anything to' the animal. They might have representations in some sense but they would be 'nothing to' them. But surely dogs have conscious states, e.g. conscious perceptions and pains. This does not entail that they are capable of introspecting those states. However, it is difficult to see why that fact justifies the claim that they are 'nothing to' the dog. A representation might exist unaccompanied by *introspection*, but it can still be something "it is like" to its owner because it is accompanied by a (nonconscious) MET. It is *also* true that a representation can exist without self-consciousness, but this is just to say that there are nonconscious mental states. These representations would be 'nothing to' its owner because there would be nothing it is like to be in those states. Thus Bennett follows Kant's conflation of self-consciousness and introspection. In doing so, he fails to recognize an interpretation of S, and thus is unable to see how distinguishing them can shed light on the claim that representations unaccompanied by self-consciousness would be 'nothing to' its owner. Distinguishing non-reflective self-consciousness from introspection leaves the following interpretation open to us:

> (S5) Having conscious mental states requires being able to have (nonconscious) thoughts about them.

S5 is very close to the present theory of consciousness. The 'I think' is read as 'I nonconsciously think' and 'representation' is understood as 'conscious mental state.' It is perhaps more reasonable to understand 'representation' in this way since Kant often uses it to cover 'sensory states,' which suggests conscious experiences. S5 avoids the troublesome S3 and S4 interpretations since it does not claim that introspection is required for conscious mentality. S5 also avoids the problematic S1 and S2 interpretations because it does not treat self-consciousness as a necessary condition for mentality *per se*. Kant could, and should, have held S5. It does not suffer from the problems with the other interpretations and retains many virtues of his theory of mind. The application of concepts to one's representations need not be conscious in order for them to become conscious.

The above conflation by Bennett is partly what leads him and others to abandon this "self-consciousness" reading of B131-132, and opt for the so-called "ownership" or "self-ascription" reading which has Kant claiming that "whenever there is a cognitive state, there must also be a thinker." However, when we are careful about making the above distinctions we see that the self-consciousness reading is not only a viable alternative, but even preferable to having Kant as claiming that an "owner" ("I") must accompany any mental state. Patricia Kitcher (1990a) is also led astray in the same way: rejecting the self-consciousness reading and then searching for the most unproblematic way of saving the ownership reading (cf. Kitcher 1990b: 92ff). My aim here is not to critique the latter reading *per se* (though there are significant problems of textual support), but rather to defend the self-consciousness reading especially since even Kitcher acknowledges Kant's clear equation of "apperception" with "self-consciousness" and her admission that Kant's vocabulary is "much better suited to a thesis about self-consciousness" (1990a: 275).

First, Kitcher relies too heavily on Bennett's claim that this reading is "obviously false" since a conscious being need not be self-conscious. Of course, most of this work is designed to show that consciousness does indeed entail self-consciousness. But more to the present point, she follows Bennett in saying that "creatures could enjoy cognitive states that inform them about their environments and never *think* of themselves" (1990a: 274, my emphasis). Once again, it is not clear which of the above interpretations they have in mind, e.g. whether or not the "thinking" must itself be conscious. If it is either S3 or S4, then we can agree on its falsity, but still insist on the truth of S5.

Second, Kitcher believes that the self-consciousness reading is repudiated in the text when Kant says that "all my cognitive states (*even if I am not directly conscious of them as such*) must conform to the condition under which they alone *can* stand together in one universal self-consciousness" (B132). But by "not *directly* conscious," Kant presumably means to be stressing the special complex form of self-consciousness which is *introspec-*

tion. So here Kant might simply be rightly asserting that one can have a cognitive state without introspecting it.

Third, Kitcher cites passages where Kant indicates agreement with the familiar Humean thesis that we are not conscious of a single unchanging or underlying self (e.g. A107, B134; cf. The Paralogisms). But I fail to see why accepting such a dubious thesis is central to the self-consciousness reading. No one believes that "self-consciousness" literally must mean "consciousness of an unchanging self," which is all the more reason to define it simply as having meta-psychological thoughts. Indeed, this construal explains why there is no consciousness of any unchanging self: we are, as Hume rightly observed, only aware of successive states of consciousness when we turn our attention inward. This is all that self-consciousness can be expected to reveal.

In any case, by now it will have been noticed that S5 is not quite my view since our claim is that what makes a mental state conscious is that it *is* accompanied by a MET. My theory requires *actual* self-consciousness to accompany any conscious state whereas S5 only mentions *potential* self-consciousness, i.e. it only says that in order for a state to be conscious one must *be able to* think about it. This is reflected in Kant's wording: *it must be possible for* the 'I think' to accompany all my representations. For this reason Rosenthal (1993a: 207-8) dismisses the idea that Kant's position is the same as ours. While I agree with him that *we* must require the actual presence of the 'I think,' I believe it is nonetheless still reasonable to interpret Kant as also holding this position. I base this on the idea that what makes mental states conscious is the *actual* application of concepts to them (as I urged in the last section). If it is reasonable to construe Kant's 'I think' as performing the concept application role, then it must actually accompany one's conscious states. In discussing the 'imagination' and the 'threefold synthesis' presupposed in conscious experience, Kant explains that one's present conscious states must *actually* be apprehended *via* concepts.[17] As Kitcher (1990b: 119) notes, "[t]he unity of apperception (and cognition) can only be generated by actual synthesis." If a present state is to 'be anything to its owner,' then there must be actual recognition in a concept. One must rationally and so conceptually grasp one's present states if experience is to be possible. Of course, all commentators would agree that the synthesis and so the concept application *itself* need not be conscious. This is as it should be: when one has a first-order conscious state, the higher-order thought is not itself conscious.

But even if one remains unconvinced that Kant held the stronger 'actual' interpretation of S5, it is clear that *we* should and so not opt for the weaker 'dispositional' account. Mental states will not be made conscious by the mere dispositional presence of METs, i.e. being disposed to have a thought about a mental state will not make it conscious. As Rosenthal notes, the MET must be occurrent and consciousness is clearly "a non-dispositional, occurrent property of mental states (1993a: 208; cf. Rosenthal 1990: 41-2)." Conscious states must be accompanied by actual self-consciousness. Dispositions to self-consciousness or 'potential' self-consciousness will not do the job.

The above line of argument can be used as a reply on behalf of Pippin (1987) who has argued that ealier verisons of Kitcher's analysis leaves out a fundamental part of Kant's view; namely, the reflexivity of conscious experience. Kitcher (1990b: 105-6) objects to Pippin's interpretation that "all human experience is ineliminably reflexive...because, according to Kant, whenever I am conscious of anything, I also "apperceive" that it is I who am thusly conscious." (1987: 459). I have tried to show that the self-consciousness reading of B131-2 is very plausible and that it must be actual self-consciousness. If I am right, then Pippin has a reply to Kitcher who again too quickly dismisses these interpretations. Moreover, Pippin's notion of reflexivity of conscious states fits in well with the HOT theory and should also remind the reader of the Brentano-like view presented in chapter two.

3.5 Concepts

The more direct approach I have utilized in the previous sections relies heavily on the notion of a 'concept.' For example, I have urged that one's inner states must be conceptualized in some way in order for them to be rendered conscious. The meta-psychological thought awareness which renders states conscious has been partly explicated in terms of the application of concepts.

What *is* a concept? On one standard account, concepts are understood as abstract objects and, in particular, universals. Two creatures can possess, share, or grasp, the very same concept. This is not so for various mental entities. Concepts are universals which fix the extension of a term. They should not be identified with 'properties' since different concepts can pick out the same property. This can be seen from many cases of theoretical identities, e.g. 'being a lightning flash' and 'luminous electrical discharge,' or even 'being in pain P' and 'neural firing N.' I will simply adopt this view of concepts especially since I fail to see how our apparent quantification over them can be eliminated or paraphrased away.

"What is a concept?" must be distinguished from "What is it to *possess* a concept?" which is far more central to my concerns. However, it is also notoriously more difficult to answer. First, it is not likely that there is a single uniform answer to the question. The answer or any analysis just seems to depend on the concept. Second, there are presumably many different *types* of concepts although there is far from universal agreement on where and how to draw the lines. Philosophers have long tried to distinguish simple from complex concepts, and observational from theoretical concepts. Furthermore, some concepts are of objects and others are of properties. The concept 'chair' importantly differs from 'brown' or 'triangular.' This is all the more reason to wonder how there could be a single uniform answer to the question.

Third, the most valiant historical attempts to explain concept possession are beset with well-known difficulties. The empiricist attempt to understand concepts in terms of *mental images* encounters serious problems with complex and theoretical concepts. More recent attempts to explicate concept possession *via linguistic competence* in using certain terms seems equally doomed to failure. Many lower animals can possess concepts in the absence of a language. Quasi-behaviorist analyses of concept possession are also unsatisfactory. Being able to *discriminate* objects that are F from objects that are non-F might be necessary for having the concept F, but it is hardly sufficient. A behavioral analysis need not be restricted to mere discrimination, e.g. it can include how one uses certain items and otherwise behaves in their presence. But, again, it is far from obvious that such an analysis can produce necessary and sufficient conditions (cf. Wittgenstein 1958). Moreover, merely being able to *identify* or *recognize* Fs cannot be necessary for having the concept F (cf. Geach 1957, Chipman 1972). We should at least indicate what concept possession is *not*, even if we do not know exactly what it is.

I am inclined to conclude from this that the search for necessary and sufficient conditions is misguided, or at least that it is unlikely to yield the desired results. At best we might hope for a hybrid theory whereby different kinds of concepts are understood in different ways. For example, possessing certain simple concepts (e.g. red) might be best understood in terms of a capacity for having mental images, whereas the possession of theoretical concepts (e.g. electron) is better understood in terms of linguistic competence. I do not have, and nor could I provide here, a detailed theory of concept possession. If there is anything that is a primitive capacity of minds, perhaps concept possession is the leading candidate. This is perhaps an unsatisfying and somewhat deflationary answer, especially since the notion of a 'concept' plays a fairly prominent role in my quasi-Kantian defense of the theory.[18] We all have a reasonably good, if somewhat limited, sense of what it is to possess a concept. To possess the concept F involves some degree of *understanding* Fs or things that are Fs, i.e. being able to *grasp* F-ness. Terms such as 'grasping' and 'understanding' are, of course, also somewhat unhelpful. But recent attempts at explicating concept possession in more familiar terms are similarly unsatisfying (although perhaps not entirely worthless or unimportant).[19] One might accuse me of adhering to certain standard Fregean, Searlean and Nagelian intuitions — so be it. But I know of no satisfactory *analysis* of what it is to possess a concept.

What is clear is that to have a concept of F is to have some kind of *capacity* with respect to Fs (Geach 1957: 11-18; McGinn 1984: 167-9). How best to understood that capacity is open, although some possibilities are clearly inadequate and the search for necessary and sufficient conditions seems doomed to failure. A promising general answer is that concept possession is best explained in terms of the very *judgments* or *thoughts* into which they can figure. This is the option alluded to earlier (in section 3.3) when I noted that judgments have an explanatory primitiveness over concepts. In the absence of any reductivist account, perhaps the only plausible remaining explanation is in terms of judgments or thoughts (see Armstrong 1973: chapter four). We explain what it is to have the concept F *via* an analysis of the judgments into which F can figure. To have the concept 'man' is to be able to make judgments or have thoughts about men. This view does fit well with my theory of consciousness which makes use of meta-psychological thoughts or judgments which render states conscious. These thoughts (into which the exercise of concepts figure) have the unique capacity to render mental states conscious.

Would an examination of Kant's theory of concept-application help here? I am inclined not to think so despite the obvious independent interest. Such a task would require a careful study of the Schematism chapter in the *Critique* which is beyond the scope of this work. We might here simply note the following standard description of Kant's view:

> In opposition to the image-based accounts of his predecessors, he argued that we [apply concepts to objects] through the use of *schemata* — not images but *rules for constructing* images. These rules indicate the sequence of operations that the perceptual system goes through in producing images of instances of the concept. (Kitcher 1990b: 209)

I am not convinced that a detailed examination of Kant will yield fruitful results because it is not clear that a helpful *analysis* of concept-possession can be extracted from it.[20] Perhaps this is why, in the end, Kant confesses that

> This schematism of our understanding...is an art concealed in the depths of the human soul, whose real modes of activity nature is hardly ever likely to allow us to discover, and to have open to our gaze. (A141=B180)

For our purposes, however, two relevant points are worth making:

1. The difficulties with finding necessary and sufficient conditions has, in part, sparked many to propose that the mental representation of a concept is best understood in terms of a so-called 'prototype,' i.e. a typical *example*, with certain typical characteristic features, of the type of object. So rather than run through a list of necessary and sufficient conditions when we perceive some object, we instead compare the item to the prototype and judge its similarity.
2. If Kitcher is right (1990b: 205ff), Kant actually helps to explain why the search for necessary and sufficient conditions is doomed to failure: we must be prepared to revise our concepts in light of new experience.

> Since empirical concepts derive their epistemological warrant by being malleable by experience and since experience is open-ended, they cannot be defined...A definition model implies rigidity in the face of new experience, but the basic theoretical assumption about concepts is that they are molded by experience. And, as Kant observes, in experience, ever new characteristics of concepts may be discovered. (1990b: 211, 212-3)

3.6 Language, Thought and Innateness

It seems clear that language depends upon thought in some important way, but some have argued that they are mutually dependent. Does thought depend on language? If so, how? Naturally, the answer will partly turn on what we mean by 'language' and 'thought.' Once again, I understand 'thoughts' to be momentary, episodic, occurrent states of mind which involve the exercise of concepts.[21] Thus, we must further explore the nature of concepts, and, as we will see, the issue of innateness is relevant as well.

'Language' is very ambiguous and difficult to define. For one thing, there seems to be the broad division between a 'public' and 'private' language. The former might divide into verbal language and some other kind of overt (but) non-verbal communication. Private language might just mean some inner medium of representation with concepts as constituents, or perhaps even more explicit syntactic structures embodying a "language of thought" such that there are literally "mental sentences" in our heads composed of mostly innate concepts which are "triggered" upon experience (Fodor 1975, 1981). Aside from the obvious independent interest, the importance of this for us is twofold:

a. If thought requires (public) language, then many non-linguistic creatures would seem incapable of thought (contrary to my view and common sense), and
b. If thoughts require some inner "language of thought," then we must be clear about how concepts constitute them and which (if any) concepts are innate within the context of our Kantian model.

One view I wish to set aside is Wittgenstein's so-called "private language argument" which urges that one cannot have a private language at all (see his 1958: paragraphs 243ff). The basic idea is that one cannot have 'private' meanings because language requires following rules which, in turn, requires membership in a linguistic community. As Kripke (1982: 110) puts it: "The falsity of the private model need not mean that a *physically isolated* individual cannot be said to follow rules; rather that an individual, *considered in isolation* (whether or not he is physically isolated), cannot be said to do so." At the least, there could not be an individual with a language which no one else could understand. Perhaps having a language entails that it not be "private" in Wittgenstein's sense, but I am more concerned with whether having thoughts requires language in the first place. Moreover, it is not clear that the impossiblity of a private language automatically rules out having all and any private *thoughts*.

So let us distinguish several questions and treat them in turn. My aim will mainly be to sketch critically the possible alternatives and offer some reason for where my sympathies lie.

(1) Does thought require a public language in the sense of a verbal language?

Donald Davidson (1984, 1985) is probably the best known supporter of an affirmative answer to this question. This is not the place for a thorough examination of Davidson's arguments, but a summary and critique seems appropriate. He uses two related arguments: one emphasizes the commonly held 'holistic' approach such that in order to have a mental state one must have many others; and the other stresses the connection between having beliefs and having beliefs about beliefs.

First Argument:

(1) Intentional ascriptions require semantic opacity, i.e. substitution of co-referring expressions does not guarantee the same truth-value of the containing statement.
(2) Fixing intentional semantic opacity requires a dense network of other intentional states (or 'holism').
(3) Any creature with the requisite network of intentional states will exhibit complex patterns of behavior.
(4) The complexity of behavior must include linguistic behavior.

Therefore,

(5) Intentional attitudes (i.e. all 'thoughts') require the capacity for linguistic behavior.

Of course, there are clearly many individual thoughts that probably do require a verbal language, e.g. the thought that 202+345=547, or the thought that Pluto is the ninth planet. But this does not really help answer question (1) since the issue is whether *all* thought requires verbal language.

Most of us are prepared to go along with Davidson up through premise (3), although there is some question about what kinds of other intentional states must be had by any thinker. We all can agree with some version of premise (2), but Davidson notoriously holds a very extreme version of it. He espouses an all-or-nothing holism whereby a dog cannot believe that a cat is in the tree without also having many *general* beliefs about trees, e.g. that they are growing things, that they have leaves, etc. (1985: 475). But it is unlcear that every thinker must be capable of these and other rather sophisticated thoughts in order to have beliefs about cats and trees, and so it seems wiser to opt for a more modest holism (Heil 1992: 191, 220ff). Perhaps we can accept that the dog must at least have some general beliefs (e.g. that they have branches, that squirrels climb them, etc.), but surely they needn't be all of the ones that Davidson mentions. Any thinker must be capable of many intentional states, but the entire group can be simpler than Davidson believes. If not, we should begin to wonder whether a four year old child can believe that a cat is in the tree.

In any case, premise (4) is the link that causes most of the dissention. First, it is tempting to accuse Davidson of confusing the *evidence* we may have for another's thinking with the thinking itself. That is, perhaps the best and most decisive evidence that Spot has thoughts would be linguistic evidence, but without it we still cannot conclude that Spot does not *have* thoughts (cf. Heil 1992: 195-6, 211ff). I agree with Heil that we should give Davidson the benefit of the doubt here, and that it is unlikely that someone of his prominence would make such a mistake.

Second, and more important, the key question becomes: Why should we suppose that only verbal linguistic behavior could be complex enough to manifest intentionality? Several points: (a) 'Language,' and particularly the ability to communicate, can certainly come in many different forms; only one of which is verbal human-like speech. (b) As Heil notes, Davidson must surely be wrong if he means to say that "utterances, considered just as instances of behavior, possess a built-in complexity and organization absent from nonlinguistic stretches of behavior" (1992: 212). (c) There is a large body of work aimed at showing that non-linguistic behavior can serve as very good evidence for the presence of beliefs and desires (Bennett 1976), not to mention that such attributions are often extremely useful explanations and help to predict behavior (Dennett 1987). (d) Heil (1992: 223) also points to Martin's (1987) work on so-called "proto-language" which is nonlinguistic activity with structured sophisticated patterns that parallel language. So perhaps language requires some kind of proto-language, but not verbal (human-like) language. (e) Dretske (1993b) has argued that although thought may require objects distinct from the thinker, it does not require that any of them be other people or speakers. Thus, thought may be "extrinsic" in some sense, but not social in a way that requires a public language. His main reason for resisting the socialization of thought has to do with the important explanatory role and causal efficacy of thought. We seem to be able to imagine scenarios whereby an isolated creature's behavior is best explained and caused by its having thoughts.

Second Argument:

(1) Having intentionality in general requires having beliefs.
(2) Having beliefs requires having the concept of belief, i.e. a belief about a belief.
(3) Having the concept of belief requires being a member of a speech community, i.e. requires having a public language.

Therefore,

(4) Having intentional states requires having a public language, i.e. human-like speech.

There are several ways that Davidson attempts to fill out this argument and defend premises (2) and (3). Concerning premise (2), he explains that having genuine beliefs involves appreciating and acting on them in such a way that the agent distinguishes between the representation and what is represented, between the subjective and objective, and between opinion and truth. In particular, a believer must understand the possibility of error and be able to distinguish truth from falsehood, which is often manifested is the phenomenon of surprise.

I do not wish to challenge premise (2) at this point because I am sympathetic with the general idea that having mental states entails having higher-order states, especially if this means that having *conscious* intentional states entails having a meta-psychological thought about it. I am also very symapthetic with premise (2) because many of his supporting reasons have a significant Kantian flavor.

My main worry about premise (2) stems from the apparent implication that having beliefs entails consciousness (and even self-consciousness). This is a large issue which I will address at length in chapter five under the title "Does Mentality Require Consciousness?" One problem has to do with the terms 'belief,' 'thought,' and 'self-consciousness.' If beliefs are, as I have urged, merely dispositions to behave in certain ways, then it is not at all clear why an utterly nonconscious system could not have beliefs. Perhaps having first-order beliefs entails having second-order beliefs for some of the reasons Davidson offers, but again we might wonder why consciousness must enter the picture at all. Indeed, if Rey's Recursive Believer System is possible, then (as we saw in section 3.2) a system could have meta-psychological beliefs without being conscious at all (not to mention self-conscious). Davidson may be willing to allow for a sub-class of intentional states which does not entail consciousness, but his examples and use of terminology often seem to rule that out. In any case, we can still accept the general implications that having first-order intentionality entails having second-order intentionality and that having *conscious* first-order mental states entails having second-order thoughts.

The real problem, however, lies with premise (3), i.e. the move from meta-psychological beliefs, or what Davidson would call 'self-consciousness,' to being a member of a speech community. The idea is that having the abilities mentioned earlier (e.g. distinguishing truth from falsehood) entails there being a shared intersubjective domain which ultimately involves one's being able to interpret and understand another's speech.

Several objections come to mind: First, many of the replies to the first argument also apply here, e.g. it is a mistake to think that only verbal (human-like) speech can be complex enough for such an interpretive understanding of others. Second, it seems possible for even a single thinker to count as a 'speech community' in the sense that she could think of herself as a speaker *over time* and thus to 'triangulate' in arriving at the concept of an intersubjective world. If so, then thinking does not require there to be any *other* members of a speech community, which takes the force out of Davidson's implication that thought requires more than one thinker (see Heil 1992: 214-20). Third, to anticipate our next question, we need to ask: why the kind of language required by Davidson must be verbal or human-like rather than some other kind of (public) communication? Thus, Heil summarizes:

> What is required for thought is a sophisticated array of capacities, including interpretive capacities. Perhaps [they] could be had only by a creature who possessed the concepts of representation, of an objective world, and of alternative possibilities of representation....we can perfectly well agree with all this, and much more, yet stop just this side of Davidson's claim that [they] are impossible in the absence of language. (1992: 224-5)

When even such a sympathetic commentator stops short of endorsing premise (4) perhaps we also should do so, although we should not forget how far we can still agree with Davidson. We must, however, conclude that the answer to (1) is *no*.

(2) Does thought require some form of overt communicative ability which constitutes a 'language'?

Given the answer to question (1), we should at least acknowledge an affirmative answer to (2). Cases of paralysis aside where the 'ability' in question cannot be manifested due to physical injury, it seems that we should grant that thought entails some ability to communicate. Of course, exactly when such communicative ability is legitimately construed as a 'language' is a difficult and controversial matter. It is arguable that a complex enough set of (non-verbal) behavioral communicative patterns can constitute a language, and, if so, then thought does require language in this sense. Dretske (1993b: 185) seems right when he says that communication is "the heart and soul of language." But of course this is not to say that speech or a verbal human-like language is necessary for thought. Moreover, there are various forms of animal communication; some of which involve nothing like verbal speech at all whereas others do involve speech-like vocalizations (e.g. whales). We might then distinguish between these two kinds of non-human communication. Moreover, there is an enormous body of growing evidence suggesting that "increasing understanding of the versatility of animal communication makes the distinction between animal communication and human language a less crucial criterion of human uniqueness" (Griffin 1992: 22; see also chapters eight through eleven).

But we must be careful about the line of reasoning here. Griffin and others are often concerned with what behavior and apparent communication can tell us about an animal's inner life, e.g. whether or not it is conscious and capable of thoughts. Here the argument goes *from* the communicative behavior *to* thought, i.e. that such behavior is very good evidence for thinking. This is a very large, but distinct, issue. Controversies will arise when, for example, we look at the complex communicative behavior patterns of honeybees (Bennett 1964; Griffin 1992: chapter nine). No doubt such behavior often provides good evidence for thinking, but *our* question is different since it asks whether overt communicative ability is *necessary* for thought. The issue here runs *from* inner thinking *to* complex communicative behavior, and the idea that thought requires overt communicative behavior seems much less controversial. Perhaps we cannot be conclusively sure about inferring from behavior to thought, but it seems right to infer from thinking to at least some ability to (non-verbally) communicate those thoughts. Thus the answer to (2) is yes.

Of course, exactly when some set of complex behavioral patterns is properly called a 'language' is a complex matter in its own right. Principles including rationality, semantically structured behavior, and great flexibility are crucial and so might rule out bees as 'having a language' (Bennett 1964). I am not sure if Bennett is right, but if he is, then we can of course still answer yes to question (2) but then suppose that bees therefore do not think. If he is wrong, then we also need not treat that, by itself, as conclusive evidence for honeybee thinking. My point here is only that it is difficult to imagine an organism which *does* think, but yet could have no ability to manifest any communicative behavior. Some primitive forms of "communication" may not deserve to be called a 'language,' but that should not cause us to answer negatively to question (2).

Let us turn our attention, then, to the so-called 'private' language side of the issue and recall the rather modest claim that thought involves an inner medium of representation with concepts as constituents (3.3). Recall also the Kantian model of sensibility and understanding and the idea that experience itself presupposes concepts, i.e. concepts make experience possible. One issue that needs attention has to do with innateness and the acquisition of concepts.

The ultimate problem is this: If conscious experience requires concepts, then they must already be present within the subject. So it seems that unless many of our concepts are innate, conscious experience would not even be possible. But it seems that we do acquire many of our concepts.

This issue is importantly related to the 'thought and language' question mainly due to the work of Jerry Fodor who, we might say, argues that thought requires language in the sense that there is a *language* of thought. Moreover, Fodor controversially believes that most of our concepts are innate, which, if true, suggests a way out of the above problem but at a very high price. This also suggests an affinity with Kant's idea that sensory experience presupposes having concepts. Thus, keeping in mind that we are primarily concerned with sensory or perceptual concepts, several points must be made before we address the above problem more directly.

Although Fodor is committed to the idea that most of our concepts are innate, it is not clear that we must adopt such an extreme position. This is not the place for a throrough summary and critique of Fodor's arguments, but some remarks are in order. We should first note that whether or not thought requires (a private) language in Fodor's sense largely depends upon the idea that most of our concepts are innate since those very concepts constitute the language in question. In other words, if we answer no to question (4) below, then we have good reason to answer no to question (3).

(3) Does thought require a private language in Fodor's sense of an explicit language of thought?
(4) Must *we* suppose that most of our concepts are innate (even though Fodor does)?

Following Kaye (1993), it seems that Fodor's main reason for holding 'concept nativism' stems from the core idea that any acquired predicate must be coextensive with some already known (simple or complex) predicates. Moreover, any examination of a concept learning paradigm in psychology reveals that there is no such thing as acquiring an entirely new concept because the "new" concept must definitionally reduce to already known concepts in order to explain the inevitable process of background hypothesis formation.

In any case, there are numerous standard replies to Fodor's arguments which I will only briefly touch on here. For example: (a) We seem to be explicitly taught certain concepts, e.g. artifactual and scientific; (b) We seem to be able to create or invent new concepts in a way that contradicts Fodor's hypothesis; (c) Fodor seems to assume that "for a concept to be acquired, the learner must be able to formulate *explicitly* a hypothesis that uses that concept" and there is little reason to grant this to Fodor (Kaye 1993: 194).

However, I wish to focus on two related issues. First, Fodor attempts to acknowledge the obvious sensitivity of our stock of concepts to experience by explaining that concepts are not learnt, but are *triggered*. But this distinction between triggering by experience and learning from experience is notoriously difficult to make. Fodor urges, for example, that the former is a 'brute causal' process whereas the latter is a 'rational causal' process. However, it seems that mere contact with appropriate instances is insufficient for concept triggering, and that at least *some* concept acquisition is mediated by a 'rational' process, e.g. sensitive to other cognitive states of the thinker. Furthermore, we might sometimes wonder why Fodor's view does not simply collapse into a widely acknowledged but very uninformative 'trivial nativism' which merely says that there are innate *capacities* to acquire concepts (see Sterelny 1989 for an excellent discussion of this point).

Second, many authors have objected in one way or another to the apparent Fodorian inference from 'unlearned' to 'innate.' Consider the following representative quote:

> Fodor seems to move straight from the idea that primitive concepts are unlearnt to the idea that they are innate. But this inference surely isn't sound....Fodor has at most shown that *certain kinds* of learning don't

> constitute the acquisition of primitive concepts. It doesn't follow that the concepts are innate; they may be acquired by a different kind of learning process, or acquired but unlearnt. Perhaps not all *acquisition* is learning. (Sterelny 1989: 126; see also Samet 1986: 580ff)

Interestingly, Bennett (1966: 95-9) anticipates this objection in his analysis of Kant's Categories as compared to the Lockean and Leibnizian opposing positions on innateness. We might disagree with Bennett about the innate status of Kantian Categories and perhaps a few other concepts, but much of what he says applies to Fodor's methodology:

> Within the genus concept-acquisition there is the species concept-learning...Nothing is logically prerequisite to a concept's having been acquired except its being not possessed and then later possessed; but...[learning] involves the active, rational co-operation of the learner...Are concepts like those of totality and negation therefore innate? If 'innate' meant 'possessed but not learned,' the answer would be affirmative; but since it means 'possessed but not acquired,' there is no reason to say that those concepts are innate. Some philosophers have overlooked the possibility of acquisition other than by learning, and have thereby tilled the ground in which the dispute over innate concepts flourishes. (Bennett 1966: 97-8)

Fodor clearly did not learn this historical lesson.

Thus, we need not accept the idea that thought requires a (private) language partly because we need not suppose that most of our concepts are innate. In other words, we can answer no to questions (3) and (4). However, we are still left with our initial problem given our earlier Kantian defense. So let us now recall that problem:

> If conscious experience requires concepts, then they must already be present within the subject. So it seems that unless many of our concepts are innate, conscious experience would not even be possible. But it seems that we do acquire many of our concepts.

We can perhaps reduce it to the following question:

(5) How can we acquire (perceptual) concepts through experience if they are presupposed in experience?

It would be silly for me to pretend that I have a satisfactory answer to this question. However, we can make the following three points:

a. To be clear about the above discussion: We can agree with Fodor and

Bennett that learning is a 'rational-causal' process, but we must disagree with Fodor that all concept acquisition must be learned and that virtually all concepts must therefore be innate. Second, we can agree that *some* primitive concepts are innate, e.g. Kant's Categories and even some basic perceptual concepts like 'square.' But we should not accept that all or even most concepts are innate especially in Fodor's sense involving a language of thought.

b. We can take the lead from Samet (1986: 582) who sketches an alternative account:

> Roughly put...if we go out into the world with our sensory channels open we 'catch' (sensory) concepts. This, in fact, is very close to the traditional empiricist conception of the matter....All we can say about concept acquisition is that there are input-output regularities of a certain sort, and we might develop a neurophysiological theory to explain these regularities. What the empiricist should deny is that there is any *mental* process that eventuates in sensory concepts; we don't 'think them up' or 'figure them out.' They are simply recorded in us as a result of our interactions with the world.

Of course, this account is unsatisfying in many ways but it is perhaps the best available at this point. Naturally, we would like to know more about just *how* we 'catch' sensory concepts in terms of a neurophysiological theory. It seems we must have some faith that child psychologists and neurophysiologists (along with philosophers of mind) will be able to fill out the theory in more detail through empirical investigation. But the important point is that this alternative is nonetheless preferable to both the idea that 'rational' processes are involved in acquiring sensory concepts and that sensory concepts are already innately within the subject. We should note, however, that Fodor's notion of a 'brute-causal' process is useful but only because acquiring sensory concepts is brute-causal, not because mere 'triggering' of already present concepts is.

c. So returning directly to question (5) we can sketch the following solution:

We begin experiencing objects *as* certain things very early, i.e. *as* having certain properties. This is due to us having a select few innate concepts. As we acquire more and more sensory concepts in a brute-causal way, we are more and more able to experience objects as having the corresponding properties. We are able to build up a stock of sensory concepts very quickly and we clearly do not 'think them up' or 'figure them out.' We nonetheless can experience an object with property F without first having the concept F, but *at that time* we would not be experiencing the object *as having F*. Similarly, we can experience an object x without first having the concept x, but *at that time* we would not be experiencing that object *as an x*. For example, a two-week old can experience a table without having the concept 'table,' but at that time she does not experience the object as a table (but perhaps only as a rectangular colored object). The same might go for 'dogs,' 'television,' 'grass,' etc. Over time and through repeated exposure to the object, she will acquire the concept 'table' and then will have experiences of tables in the sense that *does* presuppose the concept 'table.' So we need to start with some concepts in order to, so to speak, 'get experience started.' We can also still have experiences *of* objects and properties for which we lack the relevant concepts, but such experiences will not presuppose having those concepts.

Thus: we go from (1) Experiences of an object with F; to (2) Acquiring the concept F over time in a brute-causal way; to (3) Having experiences of objects *as having F*.

Similarly, we go from (1) Experiences of an object x; to (2) Acquiring the concept x over time in a brute-causal way; to (3) Having experiences of objects *as x*.

So we can acquire a sensory concept C through experiences because C is not presupposed in *those* experiences, though other already possessed concepts will be. That is, at the time we are acquiring a sensory concept (an 'x' or property 'F') through experience we are not experiencing the objects in question *as* an x or *as* having F.

Naturally, the transition from (1) to (3) is still somewhat mysterious, but no more so than any alternative account. Moreover, as we all know, providing a philosophically adequate analysis of the experiences themselves is difficult enough. But it seems to me that if we do not view explaining what happens *in* (1) and (3) as insurmountable obstacles, then we also need not be skeptical about the prospects for explaining what happens *between* (1) and (3).

Chapter 4

Objections and Replies

Various objections might be raised at this point. In this chapter I will consider some of them and provide responses. In doing so, the details of my theory will be further clarified.

4.1 What is the Status of the Theory?

One might wonder whether my theory of state consciousness is meant to express a *necessary* truth about what makes mental states conscious. A version of this objection can be stated as follows:

> The meaning of the expression 'conscious state' does not involve the notion of 'thoughts' at all. If that is so, then your theory can at best produce a contingent truth about what conscious mentality is in human beings and similar organisms. Why should we take your theory to express any necessary truths?

I do regard the claim that 'a conscious state is one that is accompanied by a meta-psychological thought that one is in that state' as expressing a necessary truth. However, this is not an analysis of the *meaning* of 'conscious state.' Without becoming unnecessarily involved in drawing the analytic-synthetic boundary, let us understand an 'analytic' sentence as one whose denial is explicitly contradictory. An analytic truth expresses some fact about the meaning of a term or expression. Synthetic truths are simply those truths that are not analytic. I agree that my so-called 'analysis' of state consciousness does not express an 'analytic' truth. The objection begins with this fact and it is one that I gladly acknowledge. The claim in question is synthetic: it is not *self-contradictory* to say that "I am in a conscious state which is not accompanied by a MET." It is just false.

The problem with the objection is the next step; namely, the idea that 'only analytic truths are genuine candidates for necessary truths' which is implied by the claim that 'synthetic truths can only be contingent.' A well-known example illustrates the falsity of this principle. It has been forcefully argued that water is necessarily composed of H_2O (see e.g. Kripke 1972) and so 'water is H_2O' expresses a necessary truth. But, of course, it is not analytic, although it cannot both be true that 'the stuff is water' *and* 'it is not composed of H_2O.' The same goes for 'heat is mean molecular kinetic energy.' There is no reason to restrict necessity to analytic truths. Moreover, that water is H_2O is known *a posteriori*. There are *a posteriori* necessary truths. If there is any controversy about whether synthetic *a posteriori* truths can be necessary, it is usually due the fact that they are *a posteriori*. My view of state consciousness avoids these worries because it puts forth an *a priori* truth. One comes to know that conscious states must be accompanied by a MET (of the right sort) *via a priori* reasoning, e.g. the reasoning used in the previous two chapters. That there are *a priori* necessary truths is surely not controversial. My theory, therefore, embodies a synthetic, *a priori*, and necessary truth. Other truths have been taken to enjoy such a status, e.g. Kant held that mathematical truths are of this kind and "every event has a cause" is commonly treated as such.

Nonetheless one might still demand some *positive* reason for my claim. It is one thing to show that synthetic truths *can* be necessary, but it is quite another to show that a particular one is. Why *should* one treat my theory as expressing a necessary truth?

I have already gone a long way in answering this question. I explained in section 2.1 that any reductionist explanation of state consciousness is limited in its ability to provide necessary conditions because of multiple realizability. Many kinds of meta-psychological states *could not* render mental states conscious (sections 3.1 and 3.2). Furthermore, 'the more direct Kantian approach' developed in sections 3.3 and 3.4 contains a positive explanation of the 'necessity' in question (which will be further developed throughout this chapter). One *must* conceptualize one's own conscious states. A conscious state must be presented to its owner in some way or other, i.e. thought of under some mode of presentation. A mental state is nonconscious when it is not occurrently thought about under some mode of presentation. I equate 'thinking of x under some mode of presentation' with 'x is being conceptualized in some way.' There *could not* be a conscious mental state which is presented to its owner devoid of all conceptualization. This amounts to denying that there could be a consciousness directed at an object in the purely material mode, i.e. one cannot have a purely demonstrative conscious state devoid of *all* conceptualization. The objects of one's conscious states (and the states themselves) must always be presented to one *qua* something or other, i.e. in the intentional mode. Any serious theory of conscious mentality will distinguish the representational content of a conscious state from its experiential content (see e.g. McGinn 1982: 37-8). The latter includes how the object is presented to or 'how it seems' to the conscious subject.

Thus, I see no reason to treat my theory as expressing anything less than a necessary truth. I identify the *properties* 'being in a conscious mental state' and 'being in a mental state accompanied by a MET (of the right kind) directed at it.' These are two ways of picking out the *same* property, and allows that such METs can be realized in very different physical structures.

4.2 A Kantian Objection

Perhaps I have too liberally interpreted some Kantian doctrines, e.g. on the permanent possibility of the 'I think' (section 3.4). My main concern is not with Kant exegesis. However, since I do rely on many of his insights in defending the theory, the following objection suggests itself:

> When Kant argues for the necessity of applying concepts to experience he is primarily concerned with the objects of 'outer sense' whereas you are speaking of conceptualizing your 'inner' states. Kant argues that in order to have conscious experience of *objects* or an *objective realm* one must apply certain concepts. It is these objects that must be conceptualized. You are exclusively speaking of the objects of 'inner sense' because you claim that it is your METs that apply concepts to mental states.

There are really two questions here. (1) Is it reasonable to extend Kant's thesis to the objects of inner sense? and (2) If so, why does state consciousness *always* involve the application of concepts to one's own states?

1. Kant was most often concerned with the objects of 'outer sense' in showing the necessity of conceptualizing one's experience. However, the reason for this emphasis throughout the *Critique* often resulted from his desire to distinguish his position from less plausible idealist alternatives (e.g. Berkeley's). Kant was often concerned with my type (1b) states, i.e. world-directed perceptual states. But, of course, there are objects of 'inner sense,' e.g. bodily sensations and emotions. As Kant himself emphasized, my mental states must be able to be the object of my self-consciousness. There is no

reason to restrict the thesis that 'one cannot have experience without some conceptualization' to the objects of outer sense. Bennett (1974: 30) agrees when he says that "...awareness of one's own states is awareness *that* one is in those states, and this involves the making of judgments." One cannot be aware of one's own mental states without making judgments about them, and the ability to judge that one is in a mental state involves some conceptualization. Inner objects are as answerable to the application of concepts as outer objects if they are to figure into conscious experience. Some lower order 'inner' state is being conceptualized *via* a higher-order judgment or thought. I construe Kant's 'judging' as my 'thinking'.

2. Thus far I have said only that *sometimes* the 'conceptualized' objects are 'inner.' But my theory says something much stronger; namely, in having conscious states one is always conceptualizing, and thinking about, one's inner states. I have argued at length for this view, but more ought to be said in this context.

First, I suggest that Kant held this stronger view. My textual evidence comes from the already discussed difference between the faculties of sensibility and understanding. The understanding actively operates on that which is passively received through the senses. That the understanding can 'operate on' anything at all presupposes that something 'inner' is present in the first place. There is a clear theme in Kant's theory of mind to the effect that the understanding operates on the (inner) passive states of sensibility in order to produce conscious experience. I suggest that such 'passive' states are the mental states which are rendered conscious by the higher-order 'thinkings' or 'judgings' of the understanding. Those states would be 'nothing to me' if they were not accompanied by the operations of the understanding. One has various internal states which are passively received through the senses and are rendered conscious by the conceptualizing activity of the understanding. This is not to say that nonconscious first-order states are passive in the sense that they cannot play a causal role in the production of behavior. They are passive in the sense that they are formed through the acquisition of information *via* 'the sensibility' or normal perceptual channels. It will be true that the information involved in such (nonconscious) states must also be categorized or organized in some way by the system, but I do not construe these abilities as sufficient for 'understanding' or 'conceptualization.' Kant was primarily concerned with how the understanding cooperated in producing *conscious* experience.

The picture that emerges, then, is that minds have various representational (and other) states which are rendered conscious when the understanding operates on them. Kant's 'understanding' plays a similar role to my METs. It is commonplace to speak of internal states 'representing' external objects without any reference to consciousness. A system might have various representational states in virtue of its causal relations to outer objects. It might have many 'passively received' representations of the external world which, in turn, play a causal role in the production of its behavior. The same presumably goes for human beings. My neural states have the representational content they do (partly) in virtue of the relations they bear to the external world. They are rendered conscious by the (higher-order) active faculty of thought or understanding. It would be odd to hold that only for bodily sensations (or hallucinations or illusions) does the understanding operate on some inner state. We ought to say that *whenever* one has a conscious perceptual or intentional state, the understanding operates on some passively received internal state. Of course, the activity of the understanding itself is not normally conscious. This is just to say that the MET is not itself conscious when one has a first-order conscious state, or that the application of concepts to one's inner states is normally a nonconscious activity.

4.3 Do the Mental States Cause the METs?

Must there be any causal connection between the mental states which are rendered conscious and the METs? Of course, there is nothing in principle objectionable to the idea of one mental state causing another. But must *we* postulate a causal connection between them? Do we need to hold that the relation between the mental state and the MET is much closer than some form of accompaniment? I do not think so.

First, mental states can be nonconscious, i.e. not accompanied by a MET. So a mental state cannot automatically cause the occurrence of a MET. Something must explain why the MET is sometimes present and sometimes not. The best answer is that some other state is at least partly responsible. The mental state cannot, by itself, cause the MET. It might have some causal role to play when there is a MET, but there is little reason to treat it as 'the cause' or 'the primary cause'.

Second, mere accompaniment would be sufficient to explain state consciousness. There is no reason to invite trouble unnecessarily by having the mental state at which a MET is directed as the main causal factor in the generation of the MET. For one thing, it is notoriously difficult to make sense of any necessary connection between causes and effects.

One possibility, however, is that there is a reliable 'tracking condition' which obtains between the conscious state and the MET directed at it. For example, it might be that the MET is not caused by the mental state itself, but rather by something else which signals the presence of or even causes the mental state. The lower-order state and its MET might have a common cause such that whenever the former is produced the latter is also (typically and reliably) caused as well. There could then be a reasonably reliable connection between their occurrence without positing any direct causal link.

Third, Rosenthal (1990: 46 fn.) considers the objection that some causal connection is needed to explain how the METs *refer* to the mental states they are about. He rightly responds that *if* causal ties are needed to explain reference in general, then they should figure in here as well. But it is also not clear that the causal theory of reference is correct, or that it applies in all cases. If there are any puzzles about how METs refer to mental states, they result from general problems about reference and do not cause any special difficulties for the HOT theory. In any event, even if there is the need for *some* causal connection, the lower-order state still need not be the *primary cause* of the MET.

More recently, Natsoulas (1993) has further pressed Rosenthal on this point asking how the MET "finds its target" among all of its possible causes. Rosenthal (1993b) virtually repeats the above response but, recalling the discussion of sections 2.3 and 2.4 (and Figures 1 and 2), we should at least note the following:

Both authors rightly recognize that this problem is far worse for Rosenthal's 'appendage' theory than for the WIV or the 'self-intimational' view put forth here. The reason is that the former treats the MET as a distinct state from the conscious state whereas the latter does not. Thus, the WIV need not concern itself with explaining any causal tie *between* distinct states. As even Rosenthal admits: "Our awareness of a state is intrinsic to that state on the self-intimational theory [= WIV]; so a causal tie between the two is irrelevant" (1993b: 159). We might of course take this as a further advantage of the WIV over Rosenthal's theory, and add it to those explained in section 2.4. However, we should remind ourselves that in the case of *introspection* there are two distinct states and the question of any causal connection between them remains (although it is better than having to explain the causal tie between *three* distinct states). So although the WIV has this advantage regarding first-order conscious states, the issue seems to be alive concerning *introspective* states. That is, we should be prepared to admit that even the WIV cannot escape this problem so easily.

4.4 The Circularity Objection

Another type of objection can be put as follows:

> You hold that a conscious system is always thinking about its own mental states. There is always meta-psychological 'thought awareness' involved in having conscious states. Don't you find this to be an awkward consequence? Moreover, if there is always such higher-order awareness, doesn't that make your theory circular? That is, aren't you guilty of using some form of consciousness (e.g. 'awareness') in explicating conscious mentality?

Conscious systems are always thinking about their own mental states. Conscious states are always accompanied by METs. I do not find it awkward that one always thinks about one's own (conscious) mental states. Indeed, if one did not have such meta-awareness, then (as Kant might say) one's intuitions would be blind. Recall that Armstrong also allows for a 'reflex' consciousness which accompanies all conscious states.

The HOT theory is not circular. It does not smuggle the notion of consciousness into the very explanation of state consciousness. If it did, then a vicious regress would result. If having a conscious state required the presence of a conscious MET, then there would have to be another (conscious) MET' which made the MET conscious, and so on *ad infinitum*. Conscious states would then be impossible. But METs need not be conscious.[23]

I have argued (in a Kantian spirit) that the role of my METs is to be understood partly in terms of the application of possessed concepts. But their application need not be, and usually is not, a conscious activity. One's perceptual experience of a dog is not typically accompanied by a *conscious* application of the concept 'dog.' One's consciousness can be world-directed while having occurrent, momentary METs. Simply because in normal (world-directed) conscious experience we are not aware of being in any such meta-psychological states, does not show that they are not present. Since they will typically be nonconscious METs, we should expect not to be aware of them. They can become conscious during introspection, but are usually not.

I suspect that circularity worries are often motivated by lingering reductionist desires (cf. section 2.1). Recall that I am not trying to explicate state consciousness in nonmental terms, but rather with the aid of related mental notions such as thought, awareness, concept, and mode of presentation. Though these concepts often can carry connotations of consciousness, they need not. In the nonintrospective case, there is nothing it is like to be in the relevant METs. We can steer clear of circularities without rendering consciousness utterly mysterious and inexplicable (à la Nagel).

An example may help to clarify just what is and is not conscious in experience. I walk daily from my residence to campus and, of course, have various conscious mental states along the way, e.g. conscious visual experiences of cars and buildings. We must distinguish the objects of my conscious states from *the way in which* they are presented to me or their 'mode of presentation.' The ways in which objects can be presented to a system I will call its 'conceptual point of view.' Every conscious system has a conceptual point of view from which it views inner and outer objects; without one it would be incapable of having conscious states. The way a system understands its world depends upon its conceptual apparatus (or point of view).

Back to my walk to campus. When I have conscious experiences, I am not aware of my conceptual point of view. My conceptual framework (or the relevant part) is not itself conscious. I am not consciously aware of *the way* that objects are presented to my conscious mind, but only of the objects. As Kant might say, my conceptual apparatus is *presupposed* in having those experiences. I can also have a yet higher-order awareness, i.e. I can reflect on the conceptual point of view itself during introspection. I can think about the way that I think or what is involved in having conscious states. This is partly what allows us to do philosophy of mind, and why dogs cannot. I can become consciously aware of my perceptual states and so can reflect on their very nature, i.e. on *the manner in which* objects are presented to me. It is little wonder that so few creatures are blessed (or, some might say, cursed) with such an ability.

The troublesome term 'subjective' can be useful here if we are careful. There are two types of subjective states.[24] Some states, which we might call 'Subj-F,' *feel* a certain way (e.g. pains) and should be construed in a *sensory* manner. When one has a first-order conscious state, the MET is *not* a Subj-F state but it is subjective in that it reflects one's conceptual point of view. These are more *cognitive* kinds of states and so we can call them 'Subj-C states.' METs are the cognitive states that must accompany any conscious state. The division between Subj-F and Subj-C states importantly mirrors the Kantian division between the sensory and intellectual. There is always something it is like to be in a Subj-F state, but there is often nothing it is like to be in Subj-C states. Subj-F states are those of which we normally say that 'there is something it is like' to be in them. However, it also seems that there is something it is like to have conscious thoughts of various kinds. But, of course, they are cognitive, and not sensory, states. Conscious thoughts are, therefore, rather special kinds of mental states. There is something it is like to be in them, but they are also Subj-C states. This helps to answer the circularity objection because it illustrates how certain kinds of subjective states (Subj-C) can render others conscious without themselves being conscious.

Much of the recent concern about the subjectivity of the mental has been with Subj-F states. For example, Jackson (1982) argues that the smell of a rose or the sensation of red cannot be captured in purely physicalistic terms, and that materialist accounts of mentality cannot therefore adequately explain Subj-F states.[25] On the other hand, some related arguments seem more concerned with Subj-C states. For example, Nagel explains that by "what it is *like*" he has in mind "how it is for the subject himself" (1974: 170, n. 6). This is ambiguous between "what it is like for the subject to conceptualize or understand C" and "what it is like for the subject to feel C," i.e. ambiguous between *the way* in which the subject experiences and *how it feels* for the subject. Nagel is often more concerned with the former, and so with Subj-C states, especially when he speaks of an organism's 'point of view' and emphasizes that we cannot understand *the way* that bats experience the world. The point of view in question "is not one accessible only to a single individual...it is a *type*." (Nagel 1974: 171) Clearly, one ought not to identify 'types' with 'species,' but Nagel never explains how to individuate them. I suggest that we should do so on the basis of differing *conceptual* points of view. Organisms share conceptual points of view to varying degrees. The degree to which two organisms share a point of view is the degree to which they are of the same type. Two organisms are of the same type if they share — to some significant extent — conceptual points of view.[26]

The conceptual framework or 'point of view' is usually what we have in mind by a 'subjective perspective.' A conscious system not only has conscious states, but also has a perspective on the world of which it is part. It is natural to identify it with one's conceptual point of view. Nagel is most often concerned with an organism's subjective perspective on the world, especially when he argues that it cannot adequately be captured in a purely objective or scientific world-view. It is impossible for creatures with a 'subjective view' to attain a purely objective 'view from nowhere' (Nagel 1986). My point here is that conscious systems have a subjective perspective which is often not itself conscious and goes beyond having momentary conscious mental states. Having a conceptual point of view is a quite general nonconscious capacity and is, in turn, what makes conscious mental states possible.

I do not mean to suggest that these two types of states can be so neatly separated in practice. Although Jackson often seems more concerned with Subj-F states (e.g. the sensation of red), he also uses the very cognitive notions of 'grasping mental facts' and 'acquiring nonphysical information.' Nonetheless, it is useful to make this distinction for the same reason that Kant separated the sensible from the more cognitive features of mind, i.e. in doing so we see that conscious experience only arises through their cooperation.

4.5 The Content Objection

Since some have even tried to deduce the unlikelyhood of brute *pain* from the HOT theory (e.g. Carruthers 1989), more must be said by way of defending the theory against one natural type of objection.[27] Recall that a HOT is an indexical thought, i.e. the thought 'that *I* am in M.' What exactly is its content? Of course, it involves reference to a subject ('I') and to a mental state ('M'). One might thereby object that the HOTs are too sophisticated to be had by all conscious animals:

> Thoughts with content involving reference to 'oneself' and to 'mental states' seem to be lacking in many conscious creatures. One surely can have at least some primitive conscious states without having the kinds of thoughts required. If so, then HOTs are *not necessary* for having conscious states.

Any creature with conscious states — no matter how primitive — can have the thoughts in question because the content of the HOTs need not be as sophisticated as one might initially suspect. Possible contents of a thought that

'I am in M' can be generated by considering different self-concepts (or concepts of 'I'), and various concepts of mental state ('M'). Consider the following types of self-concept:

1. I *qua* thinker among other thinkers.
2. I *qua* enduring thinking being.
3. I *qua* experiencer of mental states.
4. I *qua* this thing, as opposed to other physical things (where 'this thing' refers to one's body as distinct from other bodies).

A type (1) concept obviously cannot always figure into our HOTs. It is a sophisticated concept of oneself which perhaps only humans have, and so should not be *required* for conscious mentality. I have argued elsewhere that any conscious system must be able to think of itself as a temporally enduring subject with a past, and so must have the type (2) concept, but I do not wish to rely on it here.[28] It should be noted, however, that even if all conscious systems have the type (2) concept, there would still be significant degrees *within* this level of concept (as is the case for all four concept-types). The robustness of one's type (2) concept depends on the degree to which one can grasp the crucially contained *temporal* notion, and on how far back one's episodic memory can reach. The conscious lion will not think of itself as temporally enduring in the same sophisticated way that we do.

In any case, we can begin by supposing that the HOTs need not require a concept more sophisticated than type (4). A system must at least be able to differentiate itself from other physical things, and, of course, may do so by virtue of different 'body concepts' naming various physical properties. Once again, there are levels of sophistication within the type (4) concept, and so it is surely a rudimentary ability that even the lowest animals possess (e.g. mice and squirrels). A system can have a type (4) concept without, for example, it thinking of itself *qua* thinking thing. However, as Davis (1989) points out, just because a system doesn't consciously think of itself as having mental states, it does not follow that it is not *aware* of its mental states. Naturally, some creatures (e.g. flies and worms) probably do not even possess type (4) self-concepts, but then it also seems unlikely that they have any conscious states.

It is useful to consider why the 'I' must be included in the HOTs at all. Why can't they just be thoughts 'that *there is* an M?' There are two general reasons:

1. Kant urged, as Van Gulick (1989: 226) notes, that "the notions of subject and object are interdependent correlatives within the structure of experience." The idea is that when one has a conscious thought about (or experience of) an external object, one must also have an implicit thought of the form 'the object seems to *me* to be such-and-such.' One cannot just think about the external world without thinking of oneself as related to it. At minimum, one must be able to differentiate oneself from the outer world in order to have conscious experience. Experience is of an 'objective realm' of objects in the sense that they can be distinguished from oneself. Thus, having "I-thoughts" are presupposed in experience itself. In order to have thoughts about external objects one must be able to differentiate them from oneself, but 'oneself' must include one's *mental states*. Having concepts of objects presupposes an implicit grasp of the objective/subjective contrast, which involves distinguishing such objects from one's fleeting subjective mental states. If one did not implicitly distinguish (outer) objects from one's mental states, then one would treat the enduring objects of experience as merely momentary fleeting subjective states which, in turn, would make objective experience impossible. Having objective experience presupposes grasping that objects 'seem' or 'appear' to me to be a certain way at different points in time, and having concepts such as 'appearing' and 'seeming' surely imply having some kind of self-concept, e.g. the type (3) concept. (For more on this Kantian theme, see Bennett 1966: chapters eight and nine; Strawson 1966: 72-117; and Gennaro 1992.)

2. A related reason has to do with psychological explanation. If one is trying to explain the behavior of a deer avoiding a lion which had previously chased it, it is not enough to attribute (to the deer) the thought that 'the lion chased *some* creature in the past.' Such mental attributions do not seem sufficient to explain its highly motivated behavior in running away, or in remaining carefully hidden, from the lion. The deer must also have the indexical first-person thought that 'it was *me* that the lion chased.' Having some kind of self-concept seems essential in explaining the behavior, and especially the highly *motivated* behavior, of organisms. The deer does not merely think that *there is* something dangerous out there, but rather that there is a lion *related to me* or that there is something dangerous near *me*. A good explanation of how conscious states motivate the way they do is that they are intentionally (and implicitly) represented as one's own in the HOTs accompanying those states. This somewhat Kantian view has been interestingly revived in the recent

literature on *de se* attitudes (Perry 1977, Lewis 1979). Thus, there are good reasons to attribute indexical thoughts to any conscious creature, which, at least very often, involves having first-person thoughts.

There is, of course, the much larger general issue of what sort of behavioral third-person evidence would show that a brute has meta-psychological thoughts. My emphasis has not been on this approach: I have instead looked at more theoretical and conceptual concerns regarding brute experience within the framework of the HOT theory. However, it is worth mentioning that this question is raised in two distinct ways: whether a creature can have thoughts about *itself*, and whether one can have thoughts about the mental states *of others*. Of course, the HOT theory demands that any conscious creature be capable of thoughts in the former sense, but, despite results from experiments involving placing a large mirror near the cages of chimpanzees, monkeys, pigeons, and other animals, it is not clear how the evidence gathered from observing such non-linguistic behavior can help confirm or deny the existence of HOTs. For one thing, it is not clear how such thoughts can be reliably manifested in the way that an animal behaves in front of a mirror (see Bennett 1988: 207-209). Moreover, many of these "I-thoughts" seem more to concern "thoughts about its own *body*," which leaves open the question of thoughts about *thoughts*. That is, such experiments seem better suited to uncovering the presence of various type (4) concepts, leaving open whether or not the brute has any higher grade of self-concept.

On the other hand, many ethologists and psychologists test for the ability to have thoughts about the mental states *of others*. This is not the place for a thorough discussion of the relevant literature, but it is worth noting that some have argued that apes and chimpanzees (but not vervet monkeys) can attribute mental states to others, i.e. think of others as subjects with mental states.[29] For example, Seyfarth and Cheney (1992: 29) report evidence that "chimpanzees may actively teach their infants how to crack open palm nuts, suggesting that mothers recognize and attempt to rectify their infants' ignorance." This suggests that at least some higher mammals can even have type (1) concepts, i.e. I *qua* thinker among other thinkers. Once again, however, there are degrees of the type (1) concept depending upon the overall conceptual capacities of the animal. Humans can attribute certain mental states to others (e.g. grief and sorrow), whereas even apes do not seem capable of such empathy.

What about the 'M' in 'I am in M'? Again, there will be many degrees of sophistication. Some conscious beings will have the concept of a *type* of mental state, i.e. the concept of 'M' *qua* type-M. Humans can grasp the property 'being in pain' or 'having a desire.' When I am in some mental state token M I am capable of understanding it as a token of type-M. I can be aware of my mental state *qua* token of a mental type. But such a concept is far too sophisticated to build into the HOTs of any conscious animal since many brutes clearly do not possess it, and even *we* do not always employ it when in a conscious state.

However, one can still be aware of a token mental state M without being aware of it *qua* type-M. An animal can be aware of its desire to eat without being aware of it *qua* desire, which is partly to say that a system can be aware of a mental state without having the concept of that *type* of state. It can be aware *of* M without being aware *that* it is a type-M state. When the lion is chasing the deer it is aware of its desire to eat, but it does not have the concept 'desire.' It can be aware of its hunger without recognizing it, or thinking of it, as an instance of hunger. An infant can be aware of a VCR without recognizing it *as* a VCR, i.e. without having the concept 'VCR.' This is not to say that one can be aware of an object *completely devoid of any conceptualization.* It is difficult to understand what such a purely demonstrative awareness or thought could amount to. Having a thought about (or an awareness of) x must surely involve x presented to the subject in some conceptualized way. Thus, there is little reason to allow the possibility of being aware of M in the purely 'material mode,' i.e. where there is no conceptualization at all. Like awareness of external objects, one must be aware of mental states in the intentional mode, i.e. *qua* something or other. But, of course, this leaves open what is involved in the 'something or other.' Thus far I have only only ruled out that the HOTs require having concepts of mental types.

The degree of sophistication with which one can conceptualize one's token mental states will naturally depend upon one's conceptual resources. Some creatures will be able to conceptualize, and so be aware of, their mental states *qua* their differences from other mental states. One might just be aware of a token-M as *different* from M,' M',' and so on. This is the inner analogue of being able to discriminate amongst external objects. The richer one's stock of concepts, the wider the range of possible conscious states. Having more fine-grained conceptual capacities allows one to recognize finer grained differences amongst the objects of outer and inner sense. We may not even be able to understand the more coarse-grained way in which some cognitively deficient creatures conceptualize the world and their inner states, let alone be able to capture it in our language. But all we require is that they do so *in some way or other*.

What is important is only that one be able to discriminate amongst the objects of outer and inner sense in virtue of *some* property or properties. The infant is aware of the VCR (and not something else) because it can think of it *qua* some of its properties. The infant has the concept 'rectangular' or 'black' and so at least recognizes it *qua* those properties. Similarly, when one is aware of a mental token-M one must be able to recognize it *qua* some mental property, and surely even the most primitive forms of consciousness are capable of this sort of recognition. If we think that a system has conscious states, then we must *already* be prepared to attribute to it some set of concepts. Of course, some may be very rudimentary concepts such as 'red,' 'different,' 'hurt,' 'dislike,' 'yearn,' 'like,' 'danger,' 'large,' and 'darker.' They might also be far more coarse-grained than any of ours. But whatever concepts it does have can figure into its HOTs, i.e. into the way that it apprehends *inner* reality. The greater one's stock of concepts, the greater one's ability to grasp and discriminate within inner and outer reality.

Thus, one can be aware of one's own mental states without having a very sophisticated self-concept. Any conscious creature will at least have some crude set of mental concepts that enable it to apprehend inner reality, and allow it to differentiate amongst its mental states. Our inquiry concerning both the 'I' and 'M' concepts shows that a conscious creature should at least be able to *think* of itself as having mental states *qua* at least some mental property, since it can be *aware* of them. It can think of itself as having mental states which seems closest to the type (3) self-concept (i.e. I *qua* experiencer of mental states). One can possess a type (3) concept without having type (1) or (perhaps even) type (2) concepts, and without having concepts of mental types.

Thus, there is good reason to suppose that any conscious system can have the HOTs so construed. They need not be very sophisticated thoughts, but sometimes can be. Any conscious creature can think that it is in a mental state since it will be able to conceptualize (in some way or other) the object of thought. When a creature lacks even the most primitive 'I' and 'M' concepts, then we ought seriously to doubt whether it has conscious states at all. Flies, and presumably worms and snails, do not have the requisite concepts. The HOT theory has the virtue of explaining why they do not have conscious states: they cannot form the conscious rendering HOTs. Conversely, if we are already inclined to think that a creature has conscious states, then the HOT theory urges that the reason for any general agreement is that it has the relevant 'I' and 'M' concepts.

The notions of indexicality and self-reference have also played a prominent role in the recent literature.[30] There is an important connection between indexical thoughts and modes of presentation. McGinn (1983: 17) closely links them when he says that:

> ...it is the *perspectival* character of indexical modes of presentation that stands out — the way they incorporate and reflect a 'point of view' on the world. This perspective is something possessed by a psychological subject....

Having indexical thoughts essentially involves having a point of view on the world because they involve viewing oneself as related to objects in the world. But it is not merely my perspective *on the world* which is involved in having I-thoughts. The way that I represent the world is also present in having such thoughts. One's subjective perspective is implicitly represented in one's ability to have indexical thoughts. McGinn (1983: 17) goes on:

> ...all the indexicals are linked with *I*, and the I mode of presentation is subjective in character because it comprises the special perspective a person has on himself. Very roughly, we can say that to think of something indexically is to think of it in relation to *me*, as I am presented to myself in self-consciousness...

Self-consciousness involves a 'conceptual point of view' and indexical thoughts. Items are not just presented to my conscious thought but to me 'as I am presented to myself in self-consciousness'.

4.6 The Straight Denial Objection

This objection simply denies that a state is conscious when a MET of the right kind is directed at it, i.e. it urges that a MET is *not sufficient* for having a conscious state. One way to formulate the straight denial objection is as follows:

> Can't I just think that I am in some mental state and not be in it, let alone have it be conscious? If I can have a MET that I am in M and not be in a conscious M, then doesn't that refute your theory?

One can, for example, think that one has a desire that p without having a conscious desire that p. One might not even have the desire at all. There are two ways to reply to the objection.

1. Recall that the MET must be an assertoric state, i.e. an affirmative thought that one is in a mental state. The objection is far from decisive. For one thing, it seems to imply that the HOT theory presupposes a radical kind of infallibility. The objection could be taken as attacking my view on the grounds that 'whenever one has a MET that one is in M, one has a (conscious) M,' but I hold no such view. One can have all kinds of thoughts which purport to be about one's own mental states, but just be mistaken. I can affirmatively think 'that I am angry' or 'that I have a desire to kill my mother' and just be wrong. We allow for the fallibility of introspective states. The mere presence of a MET that I am in M does not *guarantee* that I am in M in the first place, let alone that M is a conscious state of mine.

2. What makes a mental state conscious is the presence of a MET directed at that state, but a MET cannot bring about a conscious mental state if the state does not exist in the first place. Many different kinds of nonconscious mental states can exist independently of their conscious counterparts. They are best identified by way of their causal connections with behavior, stimuli, and other mental states, i.e. by way of their behavioral-functional roles (cf. section 1.4). If a system *has* a mental state M, then a MET directed at *it* will render it conscious. But M must already be present. Once again, in order for the understanding to 'operate on' anything, something must be there in the first place (see sections 3.3 and 4.2).

The straight denial objection, thus, might try to infer the falsity of the HOT theory from the fact that I can have a MET that I am in M without being in a conscious M. One way to refute it is to emphasize that there first must be the mental state which the MET is directed at, although a MET can occur when the mental state referred to in its content does not exist. I might be acting and have a thought that I am in pain or that I am angry at my mother. Such thoughts do not guarantee the existence of their objects. There are also many pathological cases where the subject thinks that he is in M, but is simply not in M at all.

The straight denial objection could be modified in the following way:

> Suppose that you *are* in a nonconscious mental state, e.g. you really are angry at your mother or have a desire to kill your boss. Suppose further that your psychiatrist and others who observe your behavior over time tell you

> that you are in such states. You believe them because you trust their opinion or professional judgment. You come to have a MET to the effect that you are angry at your mother or 'that you want to kill your boss.' In this case, you *really do* have the mental state which is referred to in the content of your MET. But you are not consciously experiencing the anger or desire, i.e. you do not *feel* angry or presently *yearn* to kill your boss. You simply have an affirmative thought that you are in such states. You might even be somewhat surprised to find out that you have those mental states. This seems possible and so your account is clearly defective.

We might reply by insisting that the anger or desire does become conscious in the case described. After all, the whole point of the psychiatrist telling you about your anger is to 'bring it to consciousness.' Your anger is the object of your conscious thought and, in *that* sense, it has become conscious. However, one should rightly counter that this does not fully answer the modified objection because one still might not consciously *feel* the anger or yearn to kill one's boss. This is the heart of the objection. An ambiguity in the expression 'the anger (or desire) is conscious' must be addressed. We can distinguish between 'being conscious of one's anger' and 'being consciously angry.' There is a difference in the way that M is conscious depending upon whether or not the MET is conscious, i.e. depending upon whether M is the *object* of one's consciousness. When a desire is the object of one's consciousness in introspection, it may not be accompanied by its characteristic 'feel.' The 'anger' is not *consciously directed at* anything, but instead is the object of consciousness. This explains why we are sometimes reluctant to treat the anger or desire as conscious in the introspective case. In the nonintrospective case, the conscious anger or desire is directed at its outer object whereas, in introspection, it is the object of a conscious MET. Thus, I prefer to say that states can be rendered conscious in different ways depending upon the nature of the MET, i.e. depending upon whether or not the MET is itself conscious. One can have a conscious MET directed at a desire without necessarily *feeling* that desire. Nonetheless, the desire will become conscious: it is the object of one's conscious thought.

There is another important way to explain why (in some cases) the anger does not become consciously felt when I think about it after my session with the psychiatrist. A MET can be caused in many ways, and I hold that it must not arise *via inference*, or as a result of indirect evidence. In the above case, the psychiatrist explains to me that I behave in certain ways and so I must have a desire to kill my boss. I trust his judgment and so come to have a MET that I want to kill my boss. The MET has arisen *via* inference, i.e. I infer that

I have M on the basis of certain information or evidence. But we should hold that a MET must be noninferentially caused if it is to yield a conscious state. No inference can figure into one's becoming aware of one's mental state. It is natural to treat all such inferences as *conscious*, although perhaps there can be nonconscious inferences as well (see e.g. Rock 1983: 240-282). If so, it is not clear that the HOT theory must rule these out. This is the 'noninferentiality condition.' At the least, then, there can be no conscious inference running from the mental state to the MET about that state.

There is a different kind of noninferentiality condition which is also needed. For reasons expressed earlier, I have treated the relation *from* the MET *to* the mental state as one of 'awareness.' It is the kind of awareness I have called 'thought awareness' and can be understood as a 'quasi-perceptual' state directed at an inner mental item.[31] My thought awareness that I am in M is an *immediate awareness* which also is noninferential, i.e. I am not aware of M in virtue of being aware of anything else. If I am aware of my anger in virtue of being aware of my behavior or something else, then it may not be consciously felt.

Although the straight denial objection presents one of the more serious objections to the theory, it is also restricted to introspective cases, i.e. it always treats the MET as a conscious MET. This is what generates the worry that the anger is not really felt in certain cases. It is based on the premise that there can be *conscious* METs which do not render their (putative) objects conscious. In doing so, the objection disregards the large majority of conscious states.[32]

4.7 Dennett's Objection

Daniel Dennett has recently posed the following challenge to the HOT theory:

> ...imagine [a] complex zombie, which monitors its own activities, including even its own internal activites, in an indefinite upward spiral of reflexivity. I will call such a reflective entity a *zimbo*....what we have succeeded in imagining, it seems, is an unconscious being that nevertheless has the capability for higher-order thoughts. But, according to Rosenthal, when a mental state is accompanied by a conscious or unconscious higher-order thought to the effect that one has it, this *ipso facto* guarantees that the mental state is a conscious state! Does our thought experiment discredit Rosenthal's analysis...? (Dennett 1991: 310-11)

The answer is NO. The primary reason should be clear in light of the last chapter and the reply to the previous objection, but a few remarks are in order. The main problem with Dennett's objection is the lack of explanation as to just what the higher-order states are supposed to be. The HOT theorist can, of course, deny that *any* higher-order state will be sufficient to render the lower-order state conscious. Indeed, much of the previous chapter was devoted to showing why the MET could not be a *belief* and must be a *thought* in the carefully described senses. Furthermore, the reply to the straight denial objection showed the additional need to clarify the status of the conscious rendering MET. Not just any old "higher-order monitoring" will do, and a large part of this project has been to show why (with more to come in chapters five and seven). So we must expect any serious critic to recognize this fact about the HOT theory. Zimbo is clearly not the kind of "reflective entity" which has what I mean by "thoughts." Moreover, Dennett does not explain what he means by his terms, and he plays on the crucial ambiguity in terminology, e.g. between "informational states" and "thoughts." This lack of precision can be seen in the following series of claims (my emphases):

1. "...zimbo...has internal (but unconscious) higher-order *informational states* that are about its other, lower-order *informational states*." (Dennett 1991: 310)
2. "...zimbo would (unconsciously) *believe* that it was in various mental states..." (1991: 311)
3. "It would *think* it was conscious even if it wasn't." (1991: 311)

First, we have seen the need to distinguish beliefs and thoughts whereas Dennett seems to use them interchangeably. But we even can agreee that zimbo has meta-psychological *beliefs* without having any conscious mental states, but this does not tell against the HOT theory (much like Rey's Recursive Believer System). Only meta-psychological *thoughts* are sufficient to render a mental state conscious. Therefore, much of the last two chapters have been devoted to showing that (2) is possible without conscious mentality, but that (3) would have to be false.

Second, claim (1) seems not even to be in the game. The issue is what makes a *mental state* a conscious one, but presumably "informational states" do not even qualify as genuinely mental in the first place. Or, if they are supposed to be a kind of mental state, it is not clear how they are, what kind they are, and how they differ from other (presumably) more sophisticated types of states. Moreover, if meta-psychological *beliefs* cannot render states conscious, then there is even less reason to suppose that mere "informational states" are up to the task. Again, the HOT theorist need not suppose that any higher-order state will do.

Perhaps we cannot blame Dennett for his more casual use of the language given the context he is writing in, but it seems to me that we have the ammunition for an adequate reply and that any serious critic should take note. However, we can still wonder if Dennett really does mean to use the above terms synonymously. If so, then we must point out the differences that a mature HOT theory should make and reply as I have. But if not, then he owes us an explanation as to any differences between them, and why *all three* types of states are not sufficient for rendering a state conscious.

4.8 The Complexity Objection

Another kind of objection might go as follows:

> In many typical conscious experiences, e.g. a visual experience, the subject is conscious of numerous aspects of and items in one's visual field. Even if you succeed in rebutting the content objection which concerns the sophistication of the concepts in the METs, there is still a problem about their complexity. The METs would seem to be very complex states because they would have to include mention of numerous items involved in the experience and so would contain an incredibly large number of concepts. Isn't it unrealistic to suppose that we are continuously having thoughts of such a complex nature?

First, it is true that we are aware (in some sense) of many items in our visual field in, for example, a typical perceptual experience. However, much of this awareness is nonconscious 'thought awareness,' i.e. most of the items represented in one's visual field are not consciously perceived or attended to. When I look around the room, I am only consciously aware of a relatively small percentage of items at any given time. Thus, the MET I have at any time need not be as complex as one might suspect since it only contains the concepts involved in the *conscious* mental state. The METs need not therefore contain such "an incredibly large number of concepts." The MET is only as complex as that relatively small conscious portion of one's visual field. The lower-order representational state will actually often be much more complex than the MET.

Second, even if the METs are fairly complex, that poses no special problem for the HOT theory especially since they are nonconscious METs in the typical case of world-directed perception. It only seems like a problem when it is assumed that those thoughts are themselves conscious and so wouldn't "leave room" for our ordinary conscious experience and intrude upon our stream of consciousness. But we needn't worry that the complex METs invade our consciousness since they are not themselves conscious in these cases. A similar point is made by Rosenthal (1993a: 209) in response to a related (but not identical) objection, which challenges the HOT theory on the grounds that we are at any given time usually "in a multitude of conscious states; it seems extravagant to posit a distinct higher-order thought for each of those conscious states." Rosenthal replies to what we might call the "multiplicity objection" by pointing out that

> [t]he worry about positing too many higher-order thoughts comes from thinking that these thoughts would fill up our conscious capacity, and then some; we would have no room in consciousness for anything else. But this is a real worry only on the assumption that all thoughts are automatically conscious thoughts." (1993a: 209)

Thus, Rosenthal's reply to the multiplicity objection can help us answer the complexity objection, but it is worth emphasizing the difference between them. Our initial objection concerns the complexity of a *single* MET, whereas the multiplicity objection stresses that we must have *many distinct* METs at any given time. Although it seems that Rosenthal's reply to the latter helps answer the former, it is worth asking whether the HOT theorist is forced to make a choice about the number and nature of METs at a given time, especially when one is having complex conscious perceptual experiences. The question is: Does one always just have a single, and so often rather complex, MET at any given time, or does one (at least sometimes) have many distinct METs directed at presumably different aspects of a conscious state? This is a difficult question partly because it is unclear what theoretical advantages one answer has over the other. What is clear is that the objection associated with either option can be handled in a similar way.

It seems wisest to suppose that many METs do simultaneously occur when one has a fairly complex perceptual state, especially those involving multi-sensory channels. The natural way to individuate the METs would be in terms of the different sensory modalities involved. For example, one may have a conscious state which combines the visual image of the waves on a beach, the feel of the water, and the sound of the waves crashing. It seems natural to allow for a different MET associated with each of the sensory modalitites. Indeed, this option takes even more of the sting out of the complexity objection because it lessens the need for a single complex MET, although it does so only by positing a larger number of METs. One advantage it has is that it can help accomodate the idea that conscious states are likely to have a global representation in the brain. We may suppose that different cortical areas associated with different sensory modalities simultaneously 'think' about differing aspects of incoming representations.

4.9 Animal Brains and the Higher-Order Thought Theory

What more can be said in a positive manner? In this section, I wish to focus on how the HOT theory might be realized in the brain. As I mentioned in section 4.5, some have even denied that most animals feel pains (Carruthers 1989, Harrison 1991). Thus, let us look more closely at brute pain in particular and assume that since a HOT is necessary for having a conscious state, some 'more cognitive' area of the brain must be involved. For example, when one has a conscious pain, one will have a lower-order state (e.g. some neural firing in a primitive part of the brain) accompanied by a thought about it. Presumably, such thoughts occur in brain areas responsible for relatively higher cognitive functioning (e.g. the cortex), whereas the 'lower-order' state might be in the thalamus or hippocampus. We might associate some of the brute behavioral-functional role of pains to the 'lower' structures that we share with many animals, but a HOT is required to *feel* pains.

An obvious question is: Which animals share with us enough of the relevant brain structure required for conscious pains in us? We should, of course, always be cautious when inferring mental capacities from the presence or absence of brain structures, but surely having them can serve as reasonably good evidence for the presence of conscious pains. For the sake of argument, then, let us suppose that some kind of cortical structure provides good evidence for the capacity to have conscious pains (visual experiences, desires, etc.). If we restrict ourselves to the *neo*cortex, then it seems only mammals have conscious pains, since the neocortex is often just defined in terms of a layered structure in the mammalian telencephalon (Sarnat and Netsky 1974: 249; Bullock *et. al.* 1977: 485). But even this restriction would allow for conscious pains to be had by many of the creatures Carruthers mentions (e.g. dogs, cats, cattle); not to mention rodents (e.g. rats and mice), monotremes (e.g. the platypus), and marsupials. Indeed, the Echidna (which is a kind of monotreme) is well-known to "have an unusually extensive and fissured cerebral neocortex" (Ebbesson 1980: 453). There is also neocortex in infants, and even layers of it in the late human fetus (Sarnat and Netsky 1974: 244, 252). It is thus incorrect to suggest (Nelkin 1986: 137; Harrison 1991: 28) that we share a neocortex primarily with the primates. It is also worth noting that many scientists would like to see the criteria for what counts as a neocortex reexamined (Sarnat and Netsky 1974: 245, 249; Bullock et al. 1977: 485).

Obviously, many of these creatures are not blessed with our advanced kind of neocortex, and so we can have more sophisticated attitudes toward our pains. Dogs do not have the conceptual apparatus that humans do, and so the degree to which various concepts figure into their HOTs will be the degree to which dogs can have pains like ours. The concepts which figure into one's HOTs will color and shape one's conscious states (as is well-known to occur, for example, in "wine-tasting" and "music-listening" experiences). The conscious pains of brutes might not feel exactly like ours, but so what? As was argued earlier, we can grant that lower-animals cannot have the same kinds of attitudes toward their pains, but all we require is that they have some kind of HOT (even if very conceptually primitive). Surely, the 'higher-order' brain structures that animals and infants *do have* are up to the task. After all, these are the same creatures that we credit with emotions, visual perception, and olfactory and auditory experiences of considerable complexity.

It is probably true that most insects, and some birds and fish, do not have conscious pains, but I trust that whether or not they feel pain is not what usually causes us to take issue with the aforementioned moral position. The fact that many animals share certain brain structures with us is at least some evidence that they feel pains on the HOT theory. Those who do not hold the HOT theory should even have an easier time defending conscious brute experience, since this theory demands the presence of the more 'cognitive' and second-order HOT. Nevertheless, the HOT theorist also need not deny consciousness to most lower animals. We can therefore agree with Nelkin (1986: 137) that "there is a large *cognitive* element in our very *feeling* of pain," and even hold that an intentional *attitude* is necessary for conscious pains (since HOTs are necessary for conscious states generally). But we need not agree that "pain *is* an attitude, not a sensation" (Nelkin 1986: 148, my emphasis). It is one thing to hold that having a conscious pain requires having an intentional attitude, but quite another to *identify* conscious pains with the attitude.[33]

It should be pointed out that *lacking* such cortical structures would not even *prove* that brutes do not have conscious states (just like having them does not *prove* that they do). It might be that certain cognitive functions are generated by different structures *in them*. Most identity theorists will happily acknowledge that different kinds of neural states can underlie the same mental type. So even though various cortical structures might be identified with the HOTs *in us*, different structures could be responsible for HOTs *in them*.

Moreover, it seems that many *non-mammal* vertebrates do have some kind of cortex, which should force us to reconsider our restriction to the mammalian 'neocortex,' especially since pain is only slightly influenced by cortex lesions and the "stimulation of the cortex does not give rise to clear cut pain experiences" (Bullock et al. 1977: 476). In any event, cells in reptiles have a tendency to migrate outward "to produce a clearly superficial layer of gray matter — a primitive cortex," (1977: 476) and the same seems true for many birds which have a homolog of a neocortex (1977: 485). Ann Butler reports (in Ebbesson 1980: 307-8, 321) that there are cortical zones in turtles, snakes and birds, and the dorsal cortex of lizards is homologous to the mammalian neocortex. Thus, although the 'neocortex' is usually defined in terms of a mammalian structure, "a homologous primordium of neocortex may comprise part of the forebrain of all vertebrates...[the] primordial neocortex [is] a formation between the hippocampus (archicortex) and the piriform cortex (paleocortex) [and] is first recognized in reptiles". (Sarnat and Netsky 1974: 249). The so-called 'mesocortex,' which is transitional between the archi- and neocortex, is "present in all mammals, but cannot be distinguished from the primordial neocortex in reptiles" (1974: 245).

It is obvious, then, that things are not even so simple regarding the presence of cortex in animals. We can conclude, first, that even if 'a *neo*cortex is required for conscious pain,' many primitive mammals (e.g. mice and Echidnas) pass the test. Secondly, many non-mammals (e.g. reptiles and birds) also seem to fit the bill since they do have a primitive form of neocortex. Third, if we only require *some form of cortex* for having conscious pains, then the case grows even stronger for non-mammal vertebrates. Together with other similarities to us (e.g. behavioral and evolutionary), it is most reasonable to suppose that the large majority of lower animals have conscious pains. Harrison (1991) rightly notices that three distinct arguments are often intertwined: behavioral similarity, one deriving from evolutionary considerations, and brain structure. While he rightly points out difficulties in *proving* that brutes have pains from each argument *individually*, the fact remains that the three *taken together* carry a great deal of *evidential* weight. Of course, my main concern in this section has been with 'the argument from brain structure'.

One further piece of evidence is worth mentioning. There are individuals with hydrocephalus, a condition which results in having virtually no cerebral cortex (see Paterson 1980). Such patients often have only a thin layer of brain tissue attached to the skull wall. Nonetheless some of them are relatively normal, and one is even a mathematician with a 126 I.Q. No visual cortex is evident despite many of them having above average visual perception. Harrison (1991: 29) correctly notes that it "is likely that the functions which would normally have taken place in the missing cerebral cortex had been taken over by other structures." The human brain can show remarkable functional plasticity, but since there are virtually no 'other structures' to do the 'taking over,' we should more generally conclude that one can have a wide range of conscious experiences in the absence of large portions of one's brain. Similarly, it is highly likely that many lower animals have conscious experiences (and especially pains) despite a comparative lack of cortical brain structure. Very little seems necessary given what we know about these 'thin-brain' cases.

However, none of this should be taken to imply that are no nonconscious pains — I think there are. A creature might behave in certain ways suggesting the presence of a pain without feeling it. That is, pains have a typical functional-behavioral role which might be manifested in the absence of the subject feeling the pain (recall section 1.4). Nonconscious mental states can be, as Carruthers urges, "those which help to control behavior without being felt by the conscious subject" (1989: 259). So I do not simply wish to endorse the relatively commonly held view that 'pains are essentially conscious.' However, it is one thing to hold (as I do) that creatures can have *some* particular nonconscious pains, but quite another to think that *all* of a creature's pains are nonconscious. Indeed, it seems nonsensical to say that a creature can have nonconscious pains *without even being capable of having any conscious pains*. When we attribute a (nonconscious) pain to another creature, we do so (partly) on the grounds that it can have conscious pains of that type. Otherwise, why even call it a nonconscious *pain*? When we are sure that a system does not have conscious pains (e.g. present day robots), we do not claim that it has pains which are all nonconscious no matter how sophisticated its behavior (cf. section 1.4).

Despite the argument of this section (and 4.5), one might still believe that it is morally permissible to kill animals, and even to make them suffer, for various reasons. For example, animal experimentation can serve important and worthwhile purposes. Even Singer (1980: 374) admits that some experiments can "lead to significant gains in our knowledge of biological processes and the prevention and treatment of disease," and so are morally justifiable when we do our best to avoid causing unnecessary pain, alternative techniques have been exhausted, and there is significant knowledge to be gained. Perhaps less of a case can be made for raising animals for food (as Singer believes). I remain unconvinced that eating animals is morally wrong for reasons which go well beyond the scope of this work, although certainly more care should be taken in how they are treated since unnecessary *cruelty* always seems wrong. Thus, there is still significant room for disagreement on many related moral issues even once we agree that animals feel pain. I do not consider myself to be an "animal rights activist" in any sense. However, we must at least be sure to recognize that animals really do feel pains, even if we disagree about what might follow from that fact.

4.10 Inner Sense and The Perceptual Model

One last aspect of the theory needs to be explored. In discussing self-consciousness (of any type) I have often spoken of 'inner awareness,' 'meta-awareness,' 'thought awareness,' and sometimes 'inner sense.' Kant is, of course, well-known for the view that inner sense is best understood on the analogy with outer sense or outer *perception*. Armstrong follows Kant and treats self-consciousness as literally 'inner perception'.[34] This is certainly a *prima facie* reasonable model and I am somewhat sympathetic to it. On the other hand, 'perceiving x' is often viewed as quite different than 'thinking (about) x.' Perceiving is often contrasted with thinking, and so those who oppose the 'inner sense' model favor one based on 'inner thinking.' Given my reliance on meta-psychological *thoughts*, we need to be clear about the two models. My view is that the difference in question is often highly exaggerated (if there is an interesting one at all), and there is little reason to prefer one model over the other in the context of the HOT theory.

There are clearly two respects in which inner perception is unlike outer sense. They are two of the reasons that I have called the meta-awareness '*quasi*-perceptual.' First, the objects of inner sense are obviously not apprehended by means of any of the familiar five senses. Second, there is no *organ* of introspection. But, of course, no proponent of the inner sense model must deny either of these claims, although perhaps we could treat the brain itself (or some part of it) as the organ in question.

But granting that inner sense is different from outer sense in these respects, it is natural to look for another model. But if one adopts the 'inner thinking' model, then one needs to put forth some further interesting and important differences between them. What could they be and why would they matter?

One answer is that thinking exhibits a characteristic 'directness' which is lacking in perception. When I think about x, I am somehow more directly acquainted with x than when I perceive x. Presumably this should go for any value of 'x.' One is in a better epistemic position with respect to x when having thoughts about x.

But this line of argument is unconvincing since our sensory modalities often exhibit a similar kind of 'directness.' It is difficult to see why tasting x or even seeing x (in some cases) cannot be as direct as thinking about x. The proponent of inner sense would do well to claim that perception of one's own inner states is precisely the case where there is the *most* 'directness' between the perception and its object. There certainly can be a very high degree of *epistemic immediacy* in perception. Indeed, many epistemologists treat basic *perceptual* states and beliefs as the foundation for a theory of knowledge. They enjoy a privileged epistemic status. Perceiving x can be just as unmediated as thinking about x and, again, we might urge that such epistemic priority is simply *best* seen in inner sense. For one thing, the perceptual state is more intimately related to the object of perception, i.e. they are both internal items or brain states. Epistemic priority or immediacy is, in part, a function of the spatial proximity between a perceptual state and its object. Nonetheless, we have seen that one can be mistaken about the contents of one's own mind, but fallibility can be found both in thinking and perceiving.

Moreover, it is not always clear that a conscious perceptual state directed at x is importantly different than a conscious thought about x. Suppose x is an external object. I am now having a conscious perception of my computer. It is not obvious that my psychological state significantly changes when I 'switch' to a conscious thought about it. Am I somehow more 'directly aware' of it? Does my qualitative state change in any significant way? I am inclined not to think so, and the same would seem to hold if x is an inner state. At the least, thinking about a present existing object involves perceiving it and perceiving involves thinking. Even if there are *some* differences, they do not lead to preferring one model over the other.

Here is a general difference between thinking and perceiving: the objects of the former are not guaranteed whereas genuine perception arguably requires the existence of the object. One can have thoughts about non-existent objects, or think about some non-actual state of affairs. On the other hand, genuinely perceiving x requires the presence of x (even though it may not guarantee that x has all of its perceived *properties*). Some mark this difference by treating 'to perceive' as a success verb, or by understanding perceptual awareness as 'factive'.

I agree that there is this difference, but I fail to see how it gives us any reason to prefer one model over the other. On the one hand, one can have a MET about a non-existent mental state. This is just to deny the infallibility thesis and seems to favor the 'thought' model of self-awareness. On the other hand, I have argued that if a mental state is to be rendered conscious by an appropriate MET, there must already be something there in the first place. This seems to favor the inner sense or 'perceptual' model because a genuine conscious rendering MET requires that its object be present. Having a MET directed at M is factive in the way that perception is, i.e. the existence of M is guaranteed. The object of inner sense is already present and then a meta-awareness 'scans' or 'becomes perceptually aware of' it. Armstrong (1968) explicitly endorses this kind of 'scanner model' approach.

Rosenthal (1990: 32-37) argues in favor of the 'thought' model. I am generally unconvinced by his arguments for some of the above reasons, but here is one of his attempts:

> Perceiving something involves a sensory quality, which in standard circumstances signals the presence of that thing. If a mental states being conscious were like perceiving that state, there would be a mental quality associated with being in that state; otherwise the comparison with perception would be idle. (Rosenthal 1990: 34)

I am not sure what to make of this purported disanalogy and why Rosenthal thinks that it tells against the perceptual model. It is true that when we perceive x we do so in virtue of certain sensory qualities. Rosenthal rightly notes that there then ought to be some mental quality associated with the objects of inner sense if the comparison is to be justified. But, of course, *there is* such a mental quality in any conscious state. Rosenthal even recognizes that "[in the case of] sensory states, there is a natural candidate for that quality: the qualities of the sensory states themselves" (1990: 34). Such qualities are, of course, different from the qualities of outer objects, but that is to be expected. The only other reason Rosenthal offers in favor of the thought model is based on his ill motivated view that consciousness is an extrinsic property of conscious states (cf. sections 2.3 and 2.4). For some obscure reason, he thinks that the perceptual model entails that consciousness is intrinsic to mental states. If so, so much the better.[35]

Perhaps the most interesting way to distinguish the two models involves talk of "awareness *of*" as opposed to "thoughts *that*." We might even put it as an objection and relate it to back to the discussion in section 4.5:

> When analyzing the content of METs and urging that they needn't be so sophisticated, you exploited an important ambiguity between thoughts about mental states and awareness of them. For example, you argued that having the relevant METs need not imply having the concept of M. But surely one cannot have the thought *that* one is in M without having the concept of M, whereas one can be aware *of* M without having the concept of M. Generally, awareness of x does not imply having the concept of x whereas having the thought that x does. Doesn't this cause problems for the HOT theory? and Doesn't this give us a good way to distinguish the inner sense and thought models?[36]

There are two questions here, but the answer is no to both. First, even if a sharp distinction could be made in this way, it would at most show that the HOT theorist should adopt something more like the perceptual model, and perhaps no longer use the misleading 'thought that' locution in characterizing the METs which render the lower-order states conscious. All other virtues of the theory remain and the HOT theorist need not be so wedded to the thought model. Of course, since Rosenthal explicitly rejects the perceptual model, this could be a more serious problem for him.

But, second, there is the general problem of when we come to possess a concept: When does an awareness 'of x' turn into a thought 'that x' which involves having the concept of x? This is a deep problem which is not specific to the HOT theory. When does the child who is aware of the VCR come to have the concept of a VCR? Recall that the child must have some differentiating concepts (e.g. rectangular, black), but what does it take to have the concept 'VCR'? When does a lion's awareness of his desire to kill the antelope become such as to credit him with the thought *that* it has the desire?

When does it come to have the concept 'desire' over and above mere awareness? Surely we cannot expect it to have, for example, a theoretical understanding of its functional role or knowledge of various general truths about desires. Otherwise, no child could even have the concept 'desire.' No doubt there are many degrees of grasping concepts and finding a satisfactory line to draw between any minimal notion and the most robust sense is a difficult chore at best. If the lion is at least aware of a strong 'yearning,' then why doesn't that suffice for having the concept of desire in a way that would allow us to attribute to it the thought *that* he is desiring to kill the antelope? Many different answers have been given and defended, but it is hardly a problem specific to the HOT theory. I urge that we have an answer either way. On the one hand, if one wants to build in a very rich notion of concept possession, then perhaps the HOT theorist should simply adopt the perceptual model. On the other hand, if one accepts a more modest criterion of concept possession, then it is no longer clear that we should abandon the 'thought that' way of characterizing the higher-order states.

Third, there is the problem that the 'that/of' distinction cuts across the 'awareness/thought' distinction. At least linguistically, there is "awareness that" *and* "awareness of;" and "thoughts that" *and* "thoughts about." These each roughly correspond to the so-called '*de dicto*/*de re*' distinction where it is often suggested that only the former entails concept possession of the intentional object, but this is highly controversial in its own right.[37] My point here is only that even *within* talk of 'thoughts,' there is arguably the distinction between a thought *that* one is in M and the thought *about* M. If this can be sustained at all, then the HOT theorist can retain the thought model so long as the thoughts are construed in a more *de re* way.

Interestingly, some of this can be used in response to Dretske's (1993a) discussion which, in part, objects to the HOT theory. He first rightly distinguishes between the perceptual experience of x and a perceptual belief or thought about x. Similarly, he distinguishes consciousness of things and consciousness of facts, and explains that the latter "implies a deployment of concepts. If S is aware that x is F, then S has the concept F and uses (applies) it in his awareness of x" (Dretske 1993a: 265). On the other hand, "S is conscious of x" does not imply that "S is conscious that x is F." Dretske goes on to argue that the HOT theory does not properly recognize this, and so "it cannot be a person's awareness of a mental state that makes the state conscious" (1993a: 278). While I do not wish to critique Dretske's entire argument, some observations are in order:

1. Dretske acknowledges that, even if his argument goes through, one can still opt for the inner sense model, i.e. "[w]hat makes an experience conscious is not one's (fact) awareness that one is having it, but one's (thing) awareness of it." (1993a: 279) But he rejects this mainly relying on Rosenthal's objections (1990: 34ff) which we have already called into question. The point again is simply that the HOT theorist can still use the inner sense model.

2. In defending the idea that "S is conscious of x" does not imply "S is conscious that x is F," Dretske (1993a: 267) notices the "tricky" point that being conscious of "the difference between A and B is to see (be conscious) *that* they differ." This echoes the spirit behind the above point and the idea from section 4.5 that being aware of something at least implies differentiating it from other things in virtue of some properties (and the subject must at least have concepts of those properties). But then it seems that any awareness of x *does* indeed involve having some thoughts that x is F. I fail to see how Dretske avoids this problem especially since he wants to conclude that "awareness of things (x) requires no fact-awareness...of those things" (1993a: 269). It may not require having any particular kind of F-concept or the x-concept, but surely thing-awareness requires having some differentiating F-concepts and therefore at least some fact-awareness. The lion's awareness of its desire (x) requires at least having some thoughts that x is F. F need not stand for the type-concept 'desire,' but perhaps only for some other concepts which serve to differentiate x from other states. Similarly, one can be aware of an armadillo (x) without having the thought that x is an armadillo, but surely one must at least have some thoughts that x is an F of some kind. One cannot have thing-awareness completely devoid of conceptualization and so whatever concepts are used in the awareness can also figure into one's thought that the object is F.

I also remind the reader of Bennett's (1974: 30) point which was quoted in section 4.2 in a Kantian context: "...awareness of one's own states is awareness *that* one is in those states, and this involves the making of judgments." One cannot be aware of one's own mental states without making judgments about them, and the ability to judge that one is in a mental state involves some conceptualization.

3. Once again, exactly when one has enough F-concepts to have the concept of x is a significant problem. As we saw earlier, when one comes to possess a concept is a larger problem not specific to the HOT theory. When exactly

does one acquire the concept 'armadillo' or 'desire'? This is not adequately addressed by Dretske though he is keenly aware of the problem (1993a: 277-8). But in order to criticize the HOT theory on these grounds, one ought to be prepared to answer the question: when does a creature go from thing-awareness of x to being fact-aware that x (in a way that involves having the concept of x)?

I conclude that although there are some differences between thinking and perceiving, they do not force us to favor one model over the other. I am generally sympathetic to the perceptual or 'scanner' model for some of the above reasons, and also because I view the meta-awareness as momentary and (inferentially) isolated states of mind. This favors the perceptual model because when one has a sequence of perceptions, $P_1...P_n$, they are inferentially isolated *from one another*. P_1 might be a perception of a cup and P_2 the perception of a computer. There is no direct causal or inferential connection *between* P_1 and P_2 which is also true of the meta-awareness involved in the theory, i.e. there are no direct inferential or causal connections *amongst* the METs (when one is having first-order conscious states). Thinking often does involve inferential connectedness (e.g. in 'trains of thought'), though it need not. Just as a creature can have sequences of causally isolated perceptions about the external world so can it have similar inner thought-awareness. The defining feature of thinking or thoughts is not inferential promiscuity, but rather the momentary exercise and application of concepts. This is what ultimately justifies treating the conscious rendering meta-psychological states as 'thoughts'.

4.11 The Final Account

My final account of state consciousness, then, can be summarized as follows:

> A system S has a conscious mental state C at time t if and only if C is accompanied by a MET at t, and S is aware of that (token) C-state such that:
>
> a. C involves being conceptualized in some way,
> b. the MET need not itself be conscious,
> c. the MET does not arise in an inferential manner, and
> d. the meta-awareness of C is direct or *immediate*, i.e. S is not aware of C in virtue of being aware of some other state.

I think I have shown in the first four chapters that self-consciousness is necessary for state consciousness. Having conscious mental states entails the actual presence of self-consciousness as a thorough defense of the HOT theory reveals.

CHAPTER 5

Does Mentality Require Consciousness?

There is an enormous literature on the nature of intentional states and increasing work on the problem of consciousness. But few have written on both topics, and no systematic treatment of the relation between them has yet been offered. The aim of this chapter is partly to remedy that situation. Of course, the claim that mentality requires consciousness is highly ambiguous and so admits of many interpretations, some more plausible than others. I will examine several interpretations and explore various reasons for denying and affirming each. I do not claim that my list is exhaustive.

Aside from the obvious independent value and interest, this topic is especially important for us because *if* mentality *per se* does entail consciousness, then, by my main thesis, it would also entail self-consciousness.

5.1 The Austere Interpretations

Let us begin by briefly mentioning three of the stronger, and so least plausible, interpretations:

(MEC1) All desires must be conscious.

There is widespread acceptance of nonconscious mental states. In the post-Freudian era, we have grown accustomed to talk of nonconscious desires, motives, and beliefs. Given our post-Freudean acceptance of unconscious motives and desires, MEC1 is clearly false.

(MEC2) All thoughts must be conscious.[38]

Nonconscious thoughts or 'thought processes' have also been widely accepted. One can also have nonconscious thoughts, e.g. about objects in one's peripheral visual field (recall section 1.3). Thus, MEC2 seems equally implausible and is widely regarded as such.

(MEC3) Mental states are essentially conscious.[39]

MEC3 says that in order for a mental state *to be* a mental state, it must be conscious. As the strongest interpretation of "mentality entails consciousness," it is also the least plausible. The falsity of either MEC1 or MEC2 entails the falsity of MEC3. I mention it here for two reasons. First, it is the limiting case of MEC-interpretations. It says not merely that certain (kinds of) mental states are essentially conscious, but that mental states *per se* are essentially conscious. Second, some philosophers (e.g. Rosenthal 1986) are still primarily concerned to attack this "radical Cartesian" concept of consciousness. He is right in thinking it false and unable to yield an informative theory of consciousness. But, as I have shown in chapter two, he is guilty of setting up a false dilemma.

Another common interpretation which is at least *prima facie* more plausible than MEC1-MEC3 is:

(MEC4) All phenomenal states must be conscious.[40]

However, the idea that there are even nonconscious phenomenal states has been gaining support in recent years.[41] I have also argued at considerable length against MEC4 in section 1.4 with respect to nonconscious pains and the same goes for any type of phenomenal state. There is no reason to repeat those points here. I will simply remind the reader in a summary fashion of the following:

A phenomenal state need not be accompanied by its characteristic qualitative properties. A nonconscious phenomenal state is a phenomenal state without its qualitative property. Phenomenal states *typically* have their qualitative properties, but need not. Any *particular* phenomenal state need not have its typical felt quality, and so one can have particular nonconscious phenomenal states in virtue of having a mental state which plays the relevant functional-behavioral role. However, what justifies us in treating it as a nonconscious *phenomenal state* is (a) that the behavior of the system exhibits the typical FB role associated with that type of state, *and* (b) the system is capable of conscious phenomenal states of that type.

5.2 The Belief Interpretations

The most common stage on which this issue is played out is one that involves beliefs and belief attribution.[42] Thus, let us take an extensive look at ways in which having beliefs might involve consciousness.

(MEC5) Having beliefs requires having conscious desires.

MEC5 exploits the acknowledged connection between beliefs and desires, i.e. they must be attributed in tandem if they are to explain behavior. For example, in order to explain adequately why someone takes his umbrella with him, we need to attribute to him *both* the belief that it is (or will be) raining *and* the desire to keep dry. So far so good, but MEC5 claims that the desires must be conscious. We saw that MEC1 is false, but the term 'desire' does often carry connotations of consciousness. For example, one might 'crave' a thing or 'yearn' to do something. We can even admit that desires typically involve phenomenolgical features, but since they clearly need not always involve consciousness, it is difficult to see why there couldn't be a system with beliefs and only nonconscious desires.

One might reasonably respond that a system cannot have *all* nonconscious desires and so having any desires will ultimately invoke consciousness, but then we ought to distinguish 'desires' from 'goals.' Perhaps desires ultimately carry a commitment to consciousness, but they are only one kind of "goal-directed" attitude which generally need not carry any such commitment. Desires are a special kind of "goal-state" which direct a system's behavior toward the accomplishment of a goal. On a standard account, a goal directed system is one that exhibits a persistent and diverse range of behaviors in pursuing a given state of affairs such that there is no simple causal connection between the disturbing influences and the system's responses to them (see Nagel 1977, Bennett 1976, and Van Gulick 1980). Thus, MEC5 is still false because it seems there could be a system which has beliefs and *only* (nonconscious) goal-states, and explaining its behavior need not make reference to anything more. I do not wish to rule out the possibility of a system behaviorally complex enough to have beliefs and (at least some rather primitive) goal-states.

There is a related way to argue that having beliefs entails consciousness. It is motivated by the idea that reference must be made to the system's *input* in specifying belief content, which is a familiar theme to functionalists and behaviorists alike. One might further urge that the most natural way to construe the input is in terms of conscious sensory experiences (e.g. visual sensory states). The idea would then be:

(MEC6) Having beliefs requires that the system have at least some conscious sensory 'input' (see Peacocke 1983).

But must the functionalist *require* that the input be conscious? A behaviorally complex system may have 'sensors' which brings in input by picking up on various features of the environment (e.g. sound waves and light). The input plays a key role in the production of inner states which, in turn, bring about behavioral output. Such a system has "perceptual states" in the sense that it processes incoming environmental information. It, of course, does not have perceptual *experiences* since that implies having conscious states. In any case, it at least seems possible for there to be a system capable of beliefs which has all nonconscious input, i.e. there is nothing it is like for it to be in those "perceptual states." It would be rather presumptuous to rule it out *a priori* and without argument.

Perhaps beliefs require sensory experiences because they require having some other mental states with *both* intentional and qualitative features (e.g. visual experiences). Thus, we have the following:

> (MEC7) Having a belief requires having at least some other mental states with both intentional and qualitative features.

I only mention this as another possible MEC-interpretation. It is difficult to see what could motivate MEC7 independently of an attempt to support MEC5 and MEC6, but it is worth mentioning for this reason alone.

It has long been recognized that semantic opacity is a distinguishing mark of intentionality. Intentionality generates opaque contexts, i.e. contexts in which sameness of reference does not guarantee sameness of intentional content. Substitution of co-referential terms does not preserve the truth value of the containing sentence. A child might believe that there is water in the sink, but not believe that there is H_2O in the sink. Inten*t*ional contexts are inten*s*ional. While it may sometimes be useful to individuate beliefs in a non-opaque or 'transparent' way, no system would count as having beliefs or desires unless they are individuatable in an opaque manner.

John Searle uses this fact to argue for a necessary connection between intentionality and consciousness. He had earlier only tentatively claimed that "...only beings capable of conscious states are capable of intentional states" (1979: 92). More recently, he argues (1989) that if a state has intentional content, then it has, or potentially has, "aspectual features" or "an aspectual shape," which must "seem a certain way to the agent" and so incorporates a subjective point of view. Presumably, such subjectivity involves consciousness (although Searle doesn't specify exactly how or in what sense). This is meant to support the more general claim that "the notion of an unconscious intentional state is the notion of a state which is a possible conscious thought or experience" (Searle 1989: 202). The idea of an unconscious intentional state, then, is parasitic on the conscious variety. What distinguishes an unconscious *mental* state from other neural happenings is that it is potentially conscious. Thus, there is a sense in which intentional states (conscious or not) are irreducibly subjective.

I wish to focus on the key idea that in having beliefs and desires the subject must be able to *think* about the objects at which those states are directed. For example, Searle (1989: 199) explains that what makes my desire a desire for water and not for H_2O is that "...I can *think* of it *as* water without *thinking* of it *as* H_2O." McGinn (1983: 19) echoes this sentiment when he says that "...whenever you have a belief about an object you *think* of that object as standing in relation to yourself." Such thoughts obviously must be conscious if they are to "matter to the agent" or incorporate a subjective point of view. The idea, then, is:

> (MEC8) Having beliefs (and desires) requires that a system have conscious thoughts about the objects that figure into their content.

One can appreciate the force of MEC8 and agree that intentionality requires opacity in the sense explained, but still not adopt it as it stands. In belief attribution we often ask ourselves "How is the system able to think about the objects in question?" For example, we might wonder whether a dog has the belief that its master has just entered the house. Many of us are inclined to think so. But because of the opaque context we might then wonder whether the dog has many other beliefs which differ only in the substitution of a co-referential expression or term. Does the dog believe that a 6'2" person with a red shirt just entered the house? Does it believe that the president of General Motors just entered the house? One way to try to answer these questions is by searching our intuitions about the dog's (conscious) capacity *to think* about his master *qua* person with a red shirt or *qua* president of General Motors. We wonder, for example, whether the dog has the *concepts* 'person,' 'shirt,' 'president' and 'General Motors.' It then becomes natural to move inside the dog's head and ask if it is capable of having thoughts containing such concepts. We are thus faced with "conceptual points of view" and "subjective perspectives" in attempting to sort out which beliefs Fido has. It is true that we often follow this procedure *as a matter of fact*, but we will see that that does not entail the truth of MEC8. Searle rightly notices, however, that many contemporary philosophers, psychologists and cognitive scientists ignore the importance of consciousness in offering a theory of mind. Nonetheless, his position faces several difficulties.

1. There is a significant gap in his argument. It concerns his move from opacity to the possession of aspectual features. We *often* explain opacity in terms of a subjective point of view, but that is not enough for it to be a *necessary condition* for having beliefs and desires. Searle's claim is very strong; namely, that *all* belief-desire possession presupposes a subjective point of view. One might agree with the weaker claim that in determining whether or not a system has *some* beliefs or desires it *may* be necessary to look to a subjective perspective. But there are also cases of opacity from mere behavioral discrimination. For example, some systems will show behavioral sensitivity to certain features of their environment at the expense of others, which might be enough to determine whether or not they have one among many (referentially) equivalent beliefs. We often base judgments about another's stock of beliefs on only this type of evidence. Moreover, it seems that there *could* be systems behaviorally complex enough to warrant belief-goal attributions, but which lack a subjective point of view. I find little reason to rule out this possibility *a priori*, although I do not pretend to have *proven* it either.[43] Clearly *in the actual world* it does seem that any creature with beliefs also has conscious mental states, but, of course, that does not show that consciousness is a *necessary condition* for having beliefs.

Searle uses the example of a desire for water and a desire for H_2O. He seems to think that no 'third-person evidence' can be adduced to justify attribution of one at the expense of the other. The behavior of a system desiring water would be indistinguishable from one that desires H_2O. But that is false. As Van Gulick points out,[44] "...there would likely be differences in [its] behavior as well, e.g. in [its] likelihood of drinking the liquid in a bottle labeled 'H_2O'." Even Searle seems to allow this when he says

> It is...from my point of view that there can be a difference for me between my wanting water and my wanting H_2O, even though the external behavior that corresponds to these desires *may be identical* in each case. (1989: 199, my emphasis)

If they "may be identical," then they also *may not* be identical; that is, sometimes one's overt behavior can provide sufficient evidence for having a desire for water but not for H_2O. *One way* to explain the difference is to invoke a point of view, but that is not the only way. If there were a complex robot with the capacity to clean my apartment and perform the functions of a maid, it would be a *prima facie* candidate for ascriptions of mentality. This would, of course, partly depend on just how complex its behavior is. It might be sensitive to certain features of its environment (e.g. water) and not others (e.g. bottles labeled 'H_2O'). It seems possible for its behavior to provide good enough evidence *at least some of the time* for the way that it sorts out different features of its environment. Searle presumably does not think that there *could* be such a system, but more argument is needed to shun this possibility. I wish to leave it open. Van Gulick captures the spirit of this general point as follows:

> What is at issue is the extent and respects in which the states posited by one or another psychological theory can differ from the paradigmatically mental states of conscious experience and still be counted as genuinely mental....we may better understand the familiar mental states of our first person experience by coming to see them as an especially interesting subset of states within a larger theoretical framework. Indeed that is pretty much what I think has already begun to happen. Such a [procedure] need not be a mere metaphoric or "as-if" use of mental talk as long as we can provide a good theoretical explanation of the features that such...states share with conscious states to justify us in treating them as literally mental.[45]

Searle, of course, does admit the existence of nonconscious mental states, but insists that what makes them mental is that they have, or at least potentially have, an aspectual shape.

2. At this point, Searle might raise questions about indeterminacy of intentional content. One reason he rejects the above approach is that "third person evidence always leaves the aspectual features underdetermined" (1989: 200). But, first, we have already seen that it need not *always* underdetermine the aspectual features. Searle points out that a Quinean indeterminacy will ensue if all of the facts about meaning are third-person facts, but it is not clear that *every* belief or desire attributed to a system based on third-person evidence must suffer from such indeterminacy. Second, and more importantly, the mere possibility of indeterminacy is not, by itself, enough reason to adopt an alternative approach. Some of us are not uncomfortable with a theory of content which involves some degree of indeterminacy if it has other theoretical advantages. Perhaps it should simply be viewed as a natural and unavoidable consequence. Why should we expect that a theory of intentionality will *always* be able to fix the content of its states in an unproblematically deter-

mined way? Searle seems to think that determinacy can be gained in a straightforward manner once we incorporate a first-person point of view. He says (1989: 200-1) that "...it is obvious from my own case that there are determinate aspectual facts..." (see also Searle 1987). But is it so obvious? The first-person perspective might help to determine some aspectual facts, but it is far from clear that it will always do so. The real force behind Quine's (1960) position is that even the first-person point of view does not always fix what we mean by a term or concept. It is not obvious that *I* always know what *I* mean by 'rabbit' or any other term. Appealing to introspective evidence to settle meaning indeterminacy is also problematic and so using it to support MEC8 is less than convincing.

3. Searle's ultimate point is that "...any intentional state is either actually or potentially conscious" (1989: 194). Later he says that what makes non-conscious mental states genuinely *mental* is that "they are possible contents of consciousness" (202). He does not explain what is involved in having a conscious intentional state and so it is not always clear what these claims amount to. Perhaps they are only meant as re-statements of MEC8. However, Searle sometimes seems to be claiming that the intentional state *itself* "is a possible content of consciousness," e.g. if the 'they' in the quote above refers back to the 'mental states.' It is one thing to say that the *content* of one's intentional states must be a possible object of one's conscious thoughts (as in MEC8), but it is quite another to say that the *mental state itself* must be. The former only invokes first-order mentality in an attempt to link intentionality with consciousness. The latter involves iteration, i.e. a mental state directed at another mental state (e.g. a thought about a belief). This is stronger than MEC8 because it invokes second-order conscious thoughts, or, we might say, introspection. Thus, we can treat this alternative as follows:

> (MEC9) Having beliefs (and desires) requires that the system be able to have conscious thoughts *about them* (i.e. introspect them).

If one thinks that MEC8 is false, then one will also naturally deny MEC9. If having beliefs does not even require having *first-order* conscious thoughts, then they do not require having *second-order* conscious thoughts. But even a supporter of MEC8 might hold that MEC9 is false, because it links having beliefs with the more sophisticated introspective capacity. Many of us think that dogs have beliefs. There are, perhaps, good reasons to think otherwise, but one of them does *not* seem to be that dogs cannot introspect their beliefs. Many (actual and possible) creatures have beliefs and desires and are unable to have second-order conscious thoughts about them. It seems possible for a creature to have first-order intentional states without being able to introspect any of their mental states.

However, it is worth briefly discussing how some have tried to link belief possession with higher-order capacities (e.g. self-consciousness). Davidson (1984, 1985) and McGinn (1982) both argue, in somewhat different ways, that having beliefs requires that the subject have a higher-order rational grasp of them.[46] This is perhaps a somewhat different way of supporting MEC9 and can be put as follows:

> (MEC10) Having beliefs requires that the system be able to rationally revise them.

Davidson's reasoning proceeds from an emphasis on the objective-subjective and the truth-error contrast. He argues, for example, that having beliefs requires understanding the possibility of being mistaken which, in turn, involves grasping the difference between truth and error (1984: 170). Similarly, he claims that having beliefs requires having the concept of belief which, in turn, entails grasping the objective-subjective contrast and therefore the concept of objective truth (1985: 480). One revises one's stock of beliefs in light of recognizing mistaken beliefs. Two points are worth noting here:

First, it is not clear that believing something presupposes *consciously* understanding the difference between believing truly and believing falsely. A system might nonconsciously understand *when* its beliefs are false in light of certain encounters with the world and adjust them accordingly. It might have been fed misinformation which led to the production of false beliefs. Various other kinds of input could then lead it to stop behaving as if those beliefs are true.

Second, it is far from obvious that having beliefs requires having the concept of belief (on just about any construal of 'concept possession'), which should already be clear from our discussion of MEC8 and MEC9. Moreover, consider a three year old child. We do not doubt that she has beliefs, but why suppose that she has even a minimal concept of belief? Davidson seems to equate 'having the concept of belief' with 'having beliefs about beliefs.' I am not convinced that a three year old has conscious meta-psychological beliefs, but even if she does, it seems *possible* for there to be a creature with only first-order beliefs. Once again, a system might (nonconsciously) understand when it is mistaken and thus alter its set of beliefs without consciously doing so or having the concept of belief.

Mandelker (1991) has recently argued that intentionality requires conscious experience as part of an attempt to show that intentionality cannot be captured purely in terms of relations between a system and its environment. He utilizes several Davidsonian theses and argues as follows:

(1) Having Beliefs Requires Understanding a Language.
(2) Understanding a Language Requires Conscious Experience.

Therefore,

(3) Having Beliefs (and all intentionality) Requires Consciousness.

However, Mandelker's discussion invites objections on several key points.

For example, in supporting premise (1), he relies heavily on the aforementioned claims concerning grasping or understanding the subjective-objective and truth-error contrast. But, as we saw above, further argument is needed if he is to be entirely successful. More specifically, some reason must be given for why having beliefs requires *consciously* understanding a language. Perfectly good sense can be made of a system understanding a language or some set of concepts in a nonconscious way. Even some present day computers can understand a language in the sense that very sophisticated communication is possible between it and a user. A great deal of research in cognitive science is devoted precisely to this endeavor. The problem for Mandelker is that the plausibility and force of both premises depends greatly on how one interprets the phrase "understands a language." Premise (1) is probably true, but it also admits of many interpretations. That is, if a system truly has beliefs, it probably must be able to understand a language *in some sense*, but the issue is whether it needs to be in a *conscious* sense.

This general point has been raised by Van Gulick (1988) who urges that understanding is best characterized as a matter of degree, and not as an all-or-nothing matter. Systems understand the symbols they process to varying degrees. At the highest end of the continuum are systems (like us) which can understand concepts in a sophisticated conscious way, whereas systems at the other end of the continuum possess understanding in a more limited and even nonconscious way. Thus, "semantic self-understanding need not involve any subjective experience or understanding," (1988: 94) although it often does.

Mandelker treats "understanding" in an all-or-nothing way: if you don't consciously understand, then you really do not understand. But if Van Gulick is right, then premise (2) is also false, or at least in need of further clarification. Understanding a language does not always involve qualitative experience since genuine, though limited, understanding can be achieved in a nonconscious way.

Mandelker would no doubt reply with his argument to the effect that any genuine understanding of the meanings of terms must ultimately involve reference to conscious experience (partly because of the holistic character of language). Of course, it may be that the meaning of many terms (e.g. red, lust, hatred) involves such reference. However, it is not clear that any and all concepts are so closely tied to consciousness, but that is what Mandelker needs to show in order to prove premise (2). Further argument is needed to rule out the possibility that a nonconscious system can have a genuine set of concepts (e.g. above, tall, question) in the absence of conscious experience. It is difficult to see how such an argument could be successfully offered. Indeed, perhaps some present day computers and robots already understand sets of concepts or a language, even if not in the sophisticated conscious way that we do.

Mandelker (1991: 375-6) makes another general, but critical, mistake when he announces that "[s]ince apprehending an intentional state from a first-person perspective involves qualitatively experiencing being in that state, a system must be capable of qualitative experience in order to have intentional states." This bit of reasoning contains an obvious error conflating first-order and second-order intentionality. When I "apprehend an intentional state from the first-person perspective," I am presumably consciously aware that I am in that intentional state. So I am having a higher-order thought about that state, which (not surprisingly) would involve consciousness.

His reasoning, then, seems to be that having second-order intentional states (e.g. a thought about one of my beliefs) requires consciousness; *therefore*, having intentional states requires consciousness. This argument is clearly invalid. Even if the premise is true, the conclusion does not follow partly because there remains the crucial possibility that a system could have *first-order* intentional states without conscious experience. As I have argued (and will again in the next section), such a possibility must be taken very seriously and has significant merit. But even if one wishes to deny that possibility, Mandelker's conclusion still does not follow from his premise.

Just because second-order intentionality requires consciousness, it does not follow that intentionality *of any kind* does unless it could also be shown that having first-order intentionality *entails* having second-order conscious intentional states. But, as we have seen, this is not so easily done.

McGinn (1982), however, also claims that there is a necessary connection between (first-order) intentionality and self-consciousness. He says that:

> ...[having] propositional attitudes requires self-consciousness: for the possession of propositional attitudes requires sensitivity to principles of rationality, and such sensitivity in turn depends upon awareness of one's attitudes. (McGinn 1982: 21)

The idea is that having beliefs involves being able to rationally adjust or revise them which, in turn, involves self-consciousness or some kind of self-awareness. Assuming that McGinn understands 'self-consciousness' and 'awareness' in a reasonably robust sense, the problem (again) is that it seems possible for a system to rationally adjust its beliefs without being consciously aware of them. There are many ways for a system to rationally revise its beliefs — only one of which involves doing so by becoming conscious of them. Do *we* even always adjust our beliefs in such a consciously reflective way? It does not seem so. It may still be true that "possession of propositional attitudes requires sensitivity to principles of rationality," but I doubt whether embodying such principles requires self-consciousness. One might, for example, have a learning mechanism which takes in new (and perhaps disconfirming) information and adjusts its lower-order states accordingly. Even a relatively simple computer can search for and dissolve any inconsistencies it might embody. A system can act *in accordance with* principles of rationality without being consciously aware that it is doing so, although it may only be able to do so efficiently after many years of natural selection or constant revision. Thus, MEC10 faces serious difficulties provided that "being able to rationally revise one's beliefs" is meant to involve a reasonably rich notion of self-consciousness.

5.3 The System Interpretations

Thus far I have examined various interpretations and have offered reasons for thinking that they are all false. We should now wonder whether *a system* can have certain kinds of mental states which are all nonconscious. For example, consider the following claim:

> (MEC11) A system cannot have intentional states which are all nonconscious.

MEC11 is natural to hold if one is tempted by any of the belief interpretations. But if having beliefs and goals does not *require* having conscious states (as I have urged in the last section), then it seems there could be a system which has all nonconscious beliefs and goals. I do not claim to have proven this possibility, but merely to have given some reason not to rule it out (recall the discussion of MEC8). At this point, however, I wish to discuss one strategy that could be used against MEC11.

Recall that beliefs are, first and foremost, dispositions to behave in certain ways under certain conditions. As such, they do not carry any immediate commitment to consciousness. Perhaps some dispositions to behave must be accompanied by inner conscious thinkings or phenomenal states, but not all of them do. Dennett argues that a key feature of beliefs and goal-states is their pragmatic value in predicting another's behavior. This "intentional strategy" is "third-person" in spirit and

> ...consists of treating the [system] whose behavior you want to predict as a rational agent with beliefs and [goals]...What it is to be a true believer is to be an *intentional system*, a system whose behavior is reliably and voluminously predictable via the intentional strategy. (Dennett 1987: 15)

Let us first assume that being a "rational agent" need not involve *consciously* rationally revising one's stock of mental states (MEC10). Second, one can be generally sympathetic with Dennett's strategy without thereby *equating* having beliefs with being predictable in such a way. That is, one need not concede that "...*all there is* to really and truly believing that p (for any proposition p) is being an intentional system for which p occurs as a belief in the best (most predictive) interpretation" (1987: 29). I hesitate to endorse such an equation mainly because it threatens beliefs into non-existence. This is a kind of anti-realism about beliefs that one need not endorse, even if one is also not sympathetic with more extreme realist views (e.g Fodor 1975, 1981).[47] In any event, it is perhaps wisest *to interpret* some inner states of a system as representing the beliefs in question rather than merely adopting an "intentional stance" toward systems whose behavior is complex enough to warrant mental ascriptions. The "intentional strategy" works thus:

> ...first you decide to treat the object whose behavior is to be predicted as a rational agent; then you figure out what beliefs [it] ought to have, given its place in the world and its purpose. Then you figure out what [goals] it ought to have, on the same considerations, and finally you predict that [it] will act to further its goals in light of its beliefs... (Dennett 1987: 17)

This way of thinking about beliefs and goals is neutral with respect to whether the system has conscious states (cf. Bennett 1976). The intentional strategy could apparently work for many systems not capable of having conscious states. Perhaps a suitably complex robot could fit the bill, or imagine through space travel we encounter life-forms whose behavior invites intentional ascriptions, i.e. belief-goal attribution turns out to be of great predictive value. Even if we become convinced over time that they are conscious beings, it is not *that fact* which is necessary for them to have beliefs and goals. Obviously, Searle and others would disagree. They might object by claiming that it is impossible for a system to display the requisite behavioral complexity devoid of any conscious experiences. But that is a very strong claim, and certainly one that requires further argument. It may be that no (known) *actual* person or creature exhibits such behavioral complexity without consciousness, but additional argument is needed to support the stronger claim that consciousness is a *necessary condition* for intentionality. Three related issues need to be briefly addressed.

1. As was discussed in connection with MEC8, adopting this kind of approach comes with a price: a certain degree of indeterminacy of content. Dennett (1987: 40) is well aware of this when he says that "...it is always possible in principle for rival intentional stance interpretations of those [behavioral] patterns to tie for first place, so that no further fact could settle what the intentional system in question *really* believed" (cf. 83-6; 104-5).

Once again, we should be willing to pay this price. Determining meaning or content in even the most familiar scenario is not an easy chore, although a more realist attitude about the existence of beliefs (in terms of inner representations) might help to resolve some of these worries. Dennett, of course, insists that he is a "sort of realist" insofar as the patterns of behavior to be explained are real objective features of the world (1987: 37-42; and Dennett 1991).

2. Another complicating issue is how to decide which objects are intentional systems. One can always adopt a purely "physical stance" toward anything and, on the other hand, any object could apparently be treated as an inten-

tional system. The deciding factor is presumably the pragmatic value of explaining the system's behavior. When purely physicalistic explanations outlive their usefulness, then utilizing the intentional strategy is a reasonable alternative. Dennett (1987: 23) notes that we should not adopt the intentional stance toward anything for which "we get no predictive power...that we did not antecedently have." The system in question cannot be so simple that psychological explanations are superfluous. There are two points here: First, simply because one could always adopt a physical stance toward something does not mean that intentional attributions are unwarranted. Second, we should not adopt the intentional stance toward just anything.

Further support for the latter comes from the widely held view that any intentional system must have a reasonably rich set of beliefs and goals, which acquire their content only within a web or network of belief (cf. Davidson 1984, 1985). An intentional system cannot have two beliefs and one goal. Its set of beliefs and goals must also be interconnected in various ways, e.g. inferentially interact (cf. Stich 1978). These considerations can help Dennett avoid unfair criticism. Searle (1989), for example, ignores them in casting aside a crude version of the intentional systems theory:

> ...relative to some purpose or other anything can be treated *as-if* it were mental...[even water] behaves *as-if* it had intentionality. It *tries* to get to the bottom of the hill by ingeniously *seeking* the line of least resistance, it does *information processing* in order to *calculate* the size of rocks, the angle of the slope... (Searle 1989: 198)

Thus, although Dennett is often casual in accepting an extreme "liberalism",[48] his theory clearly has the resources to avoid such a criticism.

3. Many hold that intentional states are causally efficacious, i.e. they help explain what *causes* a system to behave (Lewis 1966, Armstrong 1968, Block 1980b, and Shoemaker 1981a). All functionalists often speak of the *causal roles* beliefs play in one's behavior. The Dennett-style approach runs counter to that view (cf. Bennett 1976). Beliefs are not *identified* with causally efficacious internal structures, but rather are tools for explaining behavior. Not all explanations are causal explanations. It might turn out that most intentional systems have internal representational states which can be interpreted as beliefs and desires, but Dennett holds that this is an empirical matter and inessential to having a belief. Belief-desire attribution is surely legitimate even if we do not discover any corresponding internal representations. But, of course, there will always be *something* internal to the system which causes it

to behave as it does when it has a belief, and many of us are more inclined to *identify* it with the psychological state in question. But we need not therefore hold the very strong realist thesis that such states are literally "mental sentences" with syntactic structure.[49] Dennett (1987: 32) explains:

> It is not that we attribute (or should attribute) beliefs and desires only to things in which we find internal representations, but rather that when we discover some [system] for which the intentional strategy works, we endeavor to interpret some of its internal states or processes as internal representations.

So if such internal states can be identified, then so much the better, but that is not essential to having beliefs and goals. Dennett correctly describes the order of discovery, i.e. finding the internal representations are not what justify any initial psychological attribution. But it also seems unnecessary to hold that any attempt to interpret a system's inner states as representational is completely irrelevant. Perhaps, then, it is best to interpret beliefs and desires (or 'goal-states') as inner representational states, e.g. as distributed networks of interconnected nodes.[50]

Despite my denial of MEC11, I do think that the following is true:

> (MEC12) A system cannot have thoughts which are all nonconscious.

Thoughts, unlike beliefs and goals, are only had by systems capable of conscious thoughts. It is only reasonable to attribute thoughts to a system with a subjective point of view or a conscious perspective. There must be some conscious thinking in a system which thinks at all. There is "something it is like" to have a *conscious* thought (as is so for any conscious state), but, unlike beliefs, having any thoughts requires that the system have some conscious thoughts. However, we still need not hold (with Searle 1989) that each *individual* nonconscious thought is potentially conscious, i.e. we need not suppose that what justifies attributing a nonconscious thought is the fact that *it* could become conscious. But one can have nonconscious thoughts only to the extent that one has *some* conscious thoughts or is capable of conscious thoughts *of that kind.*

I suggest that nonconscious thoughts only *need to be attributed* to systems which are capable of conscious thoughts. If we were certain that a system did not have conscious states, then there would be no need to attribute nonconscious thoughts. Its having beliefs and goal-states can explain any behavior and its internal processes are then at best construed as "computational processes" or "information processing." It is difficult to see what lasting explanatory work thought-attributions would do if a system is not conscious.

One might object (e.g. Rey 1988) that thinking *just is* the manipulation and transformation of internal symbols or representations and offer a narrow computationalist theory of mind. But there are major problems here. First, this notion of 'thought' is very weak: thinking does not seem merely to be "...spelling (and the transformations thereof)" (Rey 1988: 9). Secondly, even if we accept such symbol manipulation as a form of thinking it is obviously not *conscious thinking*. The question remains, then, under what conditions should we treat these internal processes as nonconscious thinkings. One answer is that we should only view them as such if the system has some conscious thoughts. This echoes the earlier Searlean (1980, 1984) intuition concerning the possibility of machine thinking. A key test regarding whether a machine can think hinges on its capacity to have a conscious understanding of its own processes which involves a first-person (subjective) point of view. Machines do not think because they do not have a subjective persepctive on, or understanding of, their own states. Similarly, internal processes do not count as 'thinkings' unless the system is capable of consciously grasping them and it has a conscious perspective on the world.

Nonetheless, my view holds out limited hope for strong AI, i.e. the view that a computer or robot could actually possess a mind under appropriate conditions. Unlike Searle, I hold that *if* there were enough behavioral complexity to warrant belief-goal attribution, then a robot would literally have a mind with at least some mental states. All efforts at building such a system are not pointless from the outset (although we also know that they have run into some serious problems). However, it is much less likely that a machine could have genuine thoughts primarily because it is unlikely that it could have conscious thoughts or be conscious at all. Here I am much more sympathetic with Searle's deep skepticism regarding machine thinking and consciousness. I therefore remain cautiously supportive of weak AI (i.e. that computers are useful tools for studying the mind), although far too many researchers continue to ignore the important role of consciousness.

Much of the above also holds for the way we understand the psychological capacities of lower animals. The point at which we seriously begin to question whether a creature can think is precisely the point where we doubt that it has conscious thoughts, a subjective point of view or consciousness at all. Why don't we normally endeavor to treat the internal processes of worms, flies, and lobsters as thoughts? One answer is that we are reasonably sure that they do not have any *conscious* thoughts. It is even doubtful that they have conscious states at all. This is independent of a creature's behavioral complexity which, if mental attributions are justified at all, can be handled by beliefs and goal-states.

As I argued in section 1.4 and in connection with MEC4 above, the same goes for phenomenal states. There are nonconscious phenomenal states, but only insofar as that system is capable of conscious states of that kind. They (like thoughts) are more closely tied to consciousness than are beliefs and desires/goals. Thus, the following is still true:

> (MEC13) A system cannot have phenomenal states which are all nonconscious.

MEC13 is relatively uncontroversial since many even hold that MEC4 is true, i.e. phenomenal states are essentially conscious. However, we can allow for individual nonconscious phenomenal states, but not for systems with phenomenal states which are all nonconscious. I do not wish to stray so far from the common uses of 'phenomenal' and 'qualitative' so as to allow for completely nonconscious systems to have phenomenal states.

I conclude that all of the above interpretations are false except for the last two. Although a case has been (or can be) made for many of them, *merely* possessing mentality does not *require* consciousness. Nonetheless, the importance of consciousness to the study of mind and intentionality should not be underestimated. It is always difficult to *prove* strong entailment claims such as those I have considered, but a great deal can be learned from examining them and the fact remains that most (if not all) actual intentional systems possess some form of conscious experience. I must therefore conclude that since mentality *per se* does not entail consciousness it also does not entail self-consciousness. However, none of this should take away from our established thesis that consciousness entails self-consciousness.

CHAPTER 6

Phenomenal States

6.1 Inner and Outer Sense: Two Kinds of Phenomenal States

Perhaps the most important and widely discussed aspects of consciousness are phenomenal states and the qualitative properties of conscious experience. My aim is not to rehearse and critique the familiar arguments in the contemporary literature. It is rather to bring out some of the lesser discussed areas and show how they often support the HOT theory.

Let us first remind ourselves of some terminology and introduce a further distinction. I defined a phenomenal state as a mental state which typically has qualitative properties (cf. section 1.4). Qualia are those properties of phenomenal states which determine 'what it is like' to have them (from the first person point of view). There can be nonconscious phenomenal states if their functional-behavioral role is similar to that of its conscious counterpart. Phenomenal states do not always have their qualitative properties. I will sometimes refer to such properties as 'sensory qualities or properties.' When I speak of a 'sensory experience' or a 'qualitative state' I have in mind a phenomenal state *with* its qualitative property.

Let us also distinguish between two kinds of phenomenal state. There is an important historical connection between sensory qualities and so-called 'secondary qualities,' e.g. colors, tastes and sounds. They have long been understood as 'subjective' in some imporatant respect and very relevant to recent worries about the 'essentially subjective character of experience' (cf. Jackson 1982). The fact is, however, that many of these properties are *experienced* as belonging to *external* objects (and others are not). Red is experienced as a property of a ripe tomato, a fragrance as a property of a perfume, and a taste as a property of food despite the apparently undeniable truth that they are subjective in some sense. At the risk of being somewhat misleading, I will call these kinds of qualities 'externally experienced qualities.' They include visual and auditory qualia. On the other hand, some sensory qualities are always experienced as properties of oneself. I will call them 'internally experienced qualities,' e.g. pains, tickles, and itches.

I believe that having phenomenal states entails having at least some conscious phenomenal states. Moreover, being a conscious system entails having conscious states in the 'what it is like' sense. A conscious creature, for example, must at least have some conscious perceptual states. Being a conscious system requires having, for example, some Subj-F states (cf. section 4.4). This is not to say that Subj-C states cannot also fit this Nagelean description, but only that they are often a different kind of state given their more *cognitive* character. Cognitive states such as conscious thoughts also have qualitative properties. Thus even if it is somehow possible for there to be a conscious system without Subj-F states, it still must have some conscious (Subj-C) thoughts which do involve a 'something it is like' aspect. But the main point here is only that being a conscious system requires having phenomenal states which, in turn, require that *at least some* of them have qualitative character. If a system did not have any qualitative states, then it should not be considered conscious in the first place.

Restricting ourselves to Subj-F states, an independently interesting question arises: Why must any conscious creature have sensory states at all? The short answer is that qualia are needed for minds to differentiate regions of perceived space (in the case of externally experienced qualia) and perceived time (in the case of externally and internally experienced qualia). Borrowing Kantian terminology, we can say that having conscious experience requires a spatial manifold of *outer sense* and the temporal manifold of *inner sense*. Conscious creatures must have 'inner' and 'outer' conscious experience. Furthermore, they must be able to distinguish the objects of inner and outer sense from one another. The conscious subject must be able to differentiate the objects which comprise its train of inner and outer perceptions. This seems to be a necessary condition for having inner and outer sense. The main point here is that qualia play an essential role in these differentiating abilities.

Take 'pain' as an example of an internally experienced quale and 'visual perception' as representative of an externally experienced quale. This is not to say that every conscious creature must have visual qualia: it is just an example. It is impossible for there to be a *conscious system* which can differentiate regions of its temporal and spatial manifolds without the presence of phenomenal states, and specifically sensory qualities. Something must serve to distinguish amongst the continuous temporal manifold that is inner sense. Some kind of 'feeling' must be present in order to do so (e.g. pains). Pains are arguably a biological necessity for any enduring species, but my point here is only that *some* such state is required (e.g. emotions could also do the job). There are, perhaps, other nonconscious ways to 'track' the temporal continuity of a system. For example, it might only have a recording device that stores information about its life in temporal terms. But my claim is not that applying temporal concepts (of any kind) requires consciousness; it is rather that being a conscious system requires an 'intuition' of time. A nonconscious system would obviously not be conscious if that was its only means of 'tracking' or 'registering' time. It would not have an inner *sense* of time and that is what is necessary for being a conscious system. (This theme will be further explored in chapter nine.)

Similarly, a mind must differentiate the regions of its visual field. Once again, it is difficult to see how this could be done without something like color qualia. Radically different creatures can have very different color schemes, but the point here is only that *if* a creature has visual experiences then it must have color qualia. This view is explicitly defended by McGinn (1983) who argues that visual experience is necessarily of colored objects and, more generally, that perceptual experience requires secondary qualities. This is not the problematic Berkeleyan thesis that one cannot *conceive* of an object without it having some secondary quality. It is rather that one cannot *perceive* a world of objects without some such qualities. Once again, the fact that there could be creatures who do not have visual experience is not the issue. The claim is simply that any conscious creature must have at least some externally experienced qualities, and so the argument could be recast in terms of another modality (e.g. touch). Even a blind and deaf conscious creature would at least need to have, for example, tactile sensations if it really is to be a *conscious* creature. I am only using vision as an example, but it is interesting to note that our nervous system processes color and shape information together (Hardin 1988: 82, 111). Perhaps this is merely a fact about our neural organization, but the lure of treating it as a necessary connection is difficult to resist. After all, differentiating shapes of objects is done *via* recognizing color differences amongst their surfaces. It seems that any conscious creature must develop some color scheme to differentiate the objects in its visual field (even if they are only shades of one color). Once again, perhaps a system could differentiate portions of its spatial field in a purely nonconscious way. A robot might be programmed to acquire information about different subportions of its 'visual' field (*via* sophisticated sensors). There would be no need for qualia here, but then there is also no consciousness either. It does not really have any outer *sense* (e.g. visual *experiences*). Again, the idea is not that being able to differentiate objects within a 'visual' field (in any way) requires consciousness; it is rather that being a conscious system entails differentiating external objects with the use of qualia.

Any conscious creature must have inner and outer sense. The spatial manifold of outer sense must be differentiated into regions by some kind of property. Similarly, the temporal manifold of inner sense must be demarcated into temporal regions. The properties which are best suited for these offices are the qualitative properties which typically accompany phenomenal states.

We should note Kant's conviction that one's sense of time is more fundamental than one's spatial sense. Time is that by means of which we must apprehend inner *and* outer reality. In differentiating his position from Berkeley's Idealism, Kant (1781/1965) also argues in the "Refutation of Idealism" that there could not be a creature with only inner sense and so with only internally experienced qualia (cf. Strawson 1966: 118-52).

6.2 Phenomenal States and Self-Consciousness

I also believe that having phenomenal states entails self-consciousness. Part of the reason, of course, is that having conscious mental states (of any kind) requires self-consciousness, but I do not wish merely to rely on the results of the first four chapters here. Let us see what independent support can be found. It is worth noticing that having any particular phenomenal state does not entail self-consciousness (because of the nonconscious kind), but possession of phenomenal states *in general* does, because what makes them phenomenal states depends partly on the fact that the subject is capable of conscious states of that kind.

In any case, reference to self-consciousness seems involved in the general characterization of phenomenal (and qualitative) states. Qualia are defined, for example, as "...those intrinsic or monadic properties of our sensations discriminated in *introspection* (Churchland 1981: 121)." Others echo this sentiment by proclaiming them to be the properties by which we know and apprehend our conscious experiences (Dennett 1988: 42) and that by means of which we discriminate amongst our sensations (Rosenthal 1990: 13).

Caution is of course needed with regard to the Churchlands' use of 'introspection.' I am not sure exactly what they mean by that term, but clearly we should not use it in the very definition of qualia. It is true that *we* are *capable of* introspecting qualitative properties, but that is a more sophisticated form of self-consciousness which involves consciously focusing on one's inner states. Moreover, introspection is not necessary for merely having conscious mental states. We often have sensory states while our consciousness is directed at the world, e.g. the color qualia which accompany visual perception. There are externally experienced qualia. Thus, it would be unwise to define qualia in terms of an introspective capacity. At best, qualitative properties are *potentially* the objects of conscious thought (in some sophisticated creatures). But, of course, we can still hold that some form of meta-awareness always accompanies conscious phenomenal states.

However, it is plausible to suppose that *internally* experienced qualia entail introspection, and perhaps these are what the Churchlands' have in mind. Since they are always experienced as 'inner,' they seem to be accompanied by conscious thoughts about them. When one feels a pain, one's consciousness is directed at it and so one is introspecting it. Of course, we should not require *deliberate* introspection: dogs can have pains and emotions without having this sophisticated capacity at all. Nonetheless, the thesis that internally experienced qualia require *momentary focused* introspection is quite reasonable since they do seem to invlove a *conscious* second-order thought directed inwardly.

Moreover, the Churchlands' allow that qualitative properties are *intrinsic* properties of sensations, although they point out that the functionalist would be wise to hold that any given type of phenomenal state need not have *that* particular quale (1981: 128-9). They also urge, for example, that when I am distinguishing the 'searingness' of a pain I am just apprehending some neural property (e.g. having a spiking frequency of 60 Hz). Such a property is, of course, not distinguished *as* that neural property from the first-person point of view. But qualia are nonetheless to be understood as features of our *neural* states from, as it were, a third-person scientific perspective. This picture is compelling for a materialist. The key claim is that if one identifies sensory states or experiences with neural processes, then it is natural to identify their qualitative properties with properties of those neural states.

Presupposed seems to be the idea that there is implicit higher-order awareness of the qualitative properties in question. Crucial to the very existence of qualia *qua* experienced qualia is a higher-order apprehension of them. If one is a materialist, then one will identify phenomenal states with certain neural events. However, just having the appropriate neural event will not guarantee that the relevant quale is *experienced qua quale*. We should distinguish the existence of a quale *qua* neural property from its existence *qua* experienced quale. The former can exist without the latter and I suggest that a higher-order awareness of that neural property is what brings about its existence *qua* experienced quale. This is at least a good explanation of what goes on in brains capable of such states. Just having the relevant neural property is not enough. It must also be apprehended by the right kind of meta-awareness.

The sentiment behind this view seems implicitly held by C.L. Hardin (1988). He focuses on color qualia, and presumably much of what he says should also carry over to other kinds of qualia. He argues that if colors are to be predicated of anything, they "must be predicated of regions of the visual field" (Hardin 1988: 96). But after allaying worries that the 'visual field' is somehow nonphysical *via* a rejection of sense-data, Hardin (1988: 111) explains that:

> ...the tactic that suggests itself is to show how phenomena of the visual field are represented in the visual cortex and then to show how descriptions of the visual field may be replaced by descriptions of neural processes...

Hardin notices that we are normally in chromatic perceptual states which *are* neural states. He is eliminativist about colors *qua* properties of external objects or sense-data, but is reductivist about color *experiences*. Hardin is suggesting how certain 'phenomena or properties of the visual field' are ultimately reducible to neural properties and processes. But it seems that we are *aware of* the visual field and its objects, and the properties which differentiate them. In materialist terms, then, we are implicitly aware *of the neural properties* which are identified with qualitative properties. The higher-order awareness is required because otherwise the quale will not exist *qua* experienced quale. I think this would have to be so for any conscious creature. One type of brain process will not, by itself, yield an experienced quale because it can equally occur without the conscious experience. What is also needed is a higher-order awareness of that state.

6.3 Chase and Sanborn

In order to further explore the connection between phenomenal states and self-consciousness, it will be helpful to consider Dennett's (1989) case of two coffee tasters for Maxwell House. Mr. Chase reports that Maxwell House still tastes to him as it did when he first came to work there, but he no longer likes *that taste*. Mr. Sanborn also does not like the way it tastes to him now, but he says that it no longer tastes the same as it did to him when he first started working there. Which hypothesis is correct? Dennett argues that there is no way to know *in principle*. His goal is subversive and to deny the existence of qualia, at least insofar as they are taken to have certain defining properties, e.g. ineffability and intrinsicality.

My goal is not to examine in detail the success of his argument for eliminative materialism. Others have adequately challenged him in this direct way. For example, Hill (1991: 108-14) rejects the underlying assumption that we ought to jettison our sensory concepts whenever there is an inability to choose between hypotheses. If that were so, then "we would be obliged to dispense with concepts that stand for physical properties and relations as well. But this is wild!" (Hill 1991: 113). Flanagan (1992: 74-79) goes further and rejects the idea that we could never have good reason to prefer one hypothesis over the other given a more mature neuroscience (see also Seager's 1993 critique of Dennett).

My aim is to indicate how some of what Dennett says supports the notion that self-consciousness is involved in having phenomenal states. The key overlooked point is that it is difficult, if not impossible, to drive a wedge between a quale 'itself' and any judgment or 'reactive attitude' one has toward it. There seems to be no non-arbitrary way to decide whether the coffee-taste quale has remained constant while the reactive attitude has changed or vice versa. Is it the same taste with different tasters or a different taste with the same tasters? This is what primarily explains Dennett's skepticism about the very existence of qualia. They appear to lack clear identity conditions and so ought to be 'quined'.

Whatever one thinks about the ultimate success of Dennett's project, my point is that it does seem impossible to make sense of a given qualitative state devoid of any *reactive attitudes* at all. One is always implicitly comparing one's current sensations with past ones, and so will always (at least implicitly) have some attitude toward the phenomenal state (e.g. likes, dislikes). This is especially clear for internally experienced qualia. A creature cannot *just* feel a pain; it must have some attitude toward it. It must be aware that it is in that state. On my view, it is precisely the higher-order attitude which *renders* the state conscious. Such attitudes will also importantly figure into the FB role and the subject's subsequent behavior. If one dislikes a given quale (e.g. a serious pain), then one will take steps to relieve oneself of it. Recall also that there is a strong cognitive influence in our very feeling of pain (Melzack 1973, Nelkin 1986).

Moreover, one will always make certain implicit *comparative judgments* with respect to a present quale. For example, one must always judge whether a portion of one's visual field is lighter or darker than another. Making these judgments seems necessary for having the qualitative state at all. It is difficult to imagine a system with such states and without at least some corresponding judgments. Recall that one function of qualia is to differentiate portions of one's inner and outer sensual manifold (section 6.1). They allow the subject to make judgments about the qualitative similarity and differences within those 'fields.' This is tantamount to the claim that qualitative states must be brought under some concepts (e.g. similar, dislike, worse, brighter, etc.). Such concepts will figure into the METs (or meta-psychological judgments) directed at the states in question and which are definitive of self-consciousness.

The METs not only must accompany conscious states, but are what make them conscious. Dennett's case can be used to support this view insofar as we cannot make sense of the very *existence* of qualia in the absence of judgments and reactive attitudes. Essential to the existence of a quale is that it be accompanied by a judgment. We might, to use Dennett's phrase, treat "...such judgings as constitutive acts, in effect, bringing the quale into existence" (1988: 55). What is curious and interesting, however, is that he concludes that the qualitative property of a sensory state *cannot* be intrinsic. This may be so if we take Mr. Chase's remarks at face value: he no longer likes *that very same taste* any more. But, of course, Dennett's point is that we cannot take his remarks at face value and so it is open for us to treat the accompanying judgment as part of (and essential to) the qualitative state. We have seen that what counts as an intrinsic property of x depends upon how narrowly one individuates x (or x-types). Accordingly, we can treat qualitative states as complex states which include an intrinsic judgmental or meta-psychological component (cf. the WIV and sections 2.3 and 2.4). This is precisely the *prima facie* plausible position acknowledged by Dennett in the above quote from page 55. The judging is essential to the existence of the quale itself, but it does not follow that the judgment is extrinsic to the state of which it is predicated. If we individuate a qualitative state so as to include that element, then qualia can still be understood as intrinsic properties of some mental states. The qualitative state does not 'passively exist' independently of the judgment. This echoes the Kantian idea that one cannot have a conscious state unless it is brought under some concepts (recall sections 3.3-3.5, 4.2). It is quite natural to understand Dennett's 'judgments' and 'reactive attitudes' as instances of METs which, in turn, apply the relevant concepts and involves self-consciousness.

6.4 Unconscious Sensations, Phenomenal Information and Blindsight

We are familiar with instances of nonconscious mentality involving different sensory modalities, e.g. the long distant truck driver, awareness of objects within one's peripheral visual field, and nonconscious auditory processing. I suggest that a distinction between 'visual information' and 'visual experience' is forced on us (and likewise for the other modalities). The former is any information processed or received by a subject *via* the visual sensory apparatus, and is presumably stored in neural pathways. The latter refers to the experiential or conscious content of a visual state which carries information. But not all of the visual information is contained in a visual experience. Moreover, large amounts of visual information can be acquired without a visual experience at all. This is most dramatically seen in the well-known blindsight case where patients can sometimes accurately answer questions about objects without consciously perceiving them (Weiskrantz 1986). Let us call such information 'phenomenal information' (hereafter PI). One is almost always acquiring PI which might otherwise be consciously acquired, e.g. visual PI about the objects in one's peripheral visual field. One could acquire that same information (and much more) if one were to have a conscious visual experience directed at those objects.

Not all of the available PI will figure into the informational content of a *conscious* phenomenal state because of perceptual limitations. For example, humans cannot consciously absorb information if it is only present in their visual field for a fraction of a second. Nonetheless, such information can be acquired (and applied) during those times. We can also call such information 'visual PI' since it is still nonconsciously acquired *via* one's visual apparatus.

It might be that PI is multiply stored in different parts of the brain (as the blindsight cases seem to indicate). But it is natural to suppose that whenever one has a conscious state, it is one of those *same* neural states carrying the PI that becomes part of the conscious state. The long distance truck driver has visual PI about the road he is negotiating. It is that same information which figures into his conscious phenomenal state when he, for example, turns his head and has a conscious perceptual state directed at the road. There is a neural state containing the visual PI which *becomes conscious*, and I suggest that what best explains the change is an awareness of that state. An opposing view would have to posit two distinct neural processes in order to explain the change: one for when the PI remains nonconscious and one for when it figures into a conscious phenomenal state. It seems best to explain how a phenomenal state (and the information it carries) becomes conscious in terms of *that very information* now figuring into a conscious state rather than supposing that another state altogether has arisen. This seems to be what Hill (1991: 122) has in mind when he says that:

> It is natural to suppose that each sensation derives ultimately from a packet of information in an unconscious portion of one's mind [which] has the potential to become a sensation with a particular set of phenomenal characteristics.

Leaving aside exactly how the information becomes conscious (e.g. by introspectively 'activating it'), the idea is that the same information becomes conscious. This also seems reasonable from an evolutionary standpoint. As creatures become more and more sophisticated, they are better able to use (or access or understand) the operations of their minds. In particular, incoming information can increasingly become the object of higher-order states. In doing so, some of the information carrying states become conscious while retaining their PI. This is at least a very good general explanation of how brains develop, function, and are able to generate conscious experience.

Creatures can behaviorally and functionally display the presence of PI without having a conscious state containing it. Systems can behaviorally respond as a result of having certain PI. One might be able to discriminate features of objects and behaviorally exhibit recognition of the similarity and resemblance relations amongst them without the information being part of any conscious state. The functional-behavioral (FB) role of a phenomenal state is greatly influenced by the information it carries. For example, blindsight patients are able to discriminate shapes and detect movements on the basis of having PI while reporting no conscious experiences of the objects (Weiskrantz 1986, 1988). Similarly, prosopagnosic patients will show no conscious recognition of familiar faces, but yet exhibit noticable behavioral signs of recognition (Tranel and Damasio 1985, Ellis and Young 1988: chapter four). In these cases, visual PI is acquired but it does not figure into any conscious visual experience. However, the PI is manifested in behavior and has an FB role of its own. Some visual PI has clearly been processed and is guiding behavior without the conscious awareness or recognition that one even has it. For example, in the blindsight case, one explanation says that there are different pathways in the visual system: the primary or "geniculostriate" system and the secondary or "tectopulvinar" system. Part of the former is damaged because of the lesion to the striate cortex (area 17) which explains the corresponding blindness in the visual field. However, the secondary system bypasses the striate cortices and brings information directly to secondary areas (e.g. in the parietal and temporal lobes). This visual PI has the observed behavioral effects mentioned above without the relevant conscious awareness.

Some have suggested that these kinds of cases and other theoretical considerations justify a belief in *nonconscious qualitative states* or unfelt sensations (Nelkin 1989). Part of the idea seems to be that the very *qualitative features* of a phenomenal state make a difference in its FB role and that those qualitative features can be mapped onto certain neural properties (see also Shoemaker 1991). I think this position is ill motivated and misguided. First, it is not the qualitative properties which figure into the FB roles in such cases, but rather the PI contained in the neural pathways which causes one to behave in certain ways. There are nonconscious phenomenal states (sec. 1.4), but there is no need to stray so far from the common use of 'qualia' and 'qualitative' so as to allow for nonconscious qualitative states and properties. Even Shoemaker cannot help but call such putative nonconscious qualitative properties 'quasi-qualia' while insisting that this does not take away from his basic position. Moreover, Shoemaker (1991: 510) is forced to acknowledge the importance of self-consciousness in anything that is genuine (i.e. not 'quasi') qualia. They are 'quasi' qualia precisely because they are not introspectively accessible to the subject.

Nelkin (1989), on the other hand, insists that virtually any kind of representational state is a type of 'sensory' state. It then ultimately follows that there are unconscious or unfelt sensations. But I remain unconvinced of the need to jettison the idea that *qualitative* states are essentially conscious. To say otherwise is, at worst, to misuse the term. At best, it leads to a harmless but very dissatisfying verbal dispute. There is little reason not to reserve the term 'qualia' or 'qualitative property' for conscious states especially when other notions and distinctions can do the necessary explanatory work.

Moreover, the FB role of a conscious phenomenal state can differ from that of the nonconscious state that merely carries the PI. For example, blindsight patients will not voluntarily act toward objects in the blind field as they would if they were consciously perceiving them (Marcel 1988, Van Gulick 1989). So all of the 'qualitative' properties could not be active in the FB role when the state is nonconscious. Even if some of the properties which normally accompany qualitative states play a part in the FB role of a nonconscious state, not all of them will. The 'conscious' ones obviously cannot play such a role and so my opponent still has to make room for their effect on the FB role of the state. 'Conscious qualitative properties' would then have to be distinguished from the nonconscious kind. Perhaps this is a mere verbal matter, but I fail to see the motivation for making a 'conscious qualia with PI/nonconscious qualia with PI' distinction when 'qualitative state with PI/phenomenal state with PI' will do just as well in explaining the FB role of such states.

It may be that we will eventually discover the neural properties which subserve sensory states and even be able to "taxonomize these nonconscious states so that they resemble and differ from one another in ways isomorphic to the similarities and differences among conscious sensations" (Rosenthal 1991: 21). But, sooner or later, it must be acknowledged that some neural state or property is responsible for the *consciousness* of the qualitative or sensory state. Call the sensory state 'S-state' and the conscious making property of S-state the 'c-property.' Now, S-state will involve many neural processes of which c-property will only be one. Moreover, many of S-state's properties can occur nonconsciously and will have a significant FB role. But, of course, c-property cannot occur nonconsciously, at least insofar as it is part of S-state. If the neural process underlying c-property did occur without S-state being conscious, we would then conclude that we were mistaken about what the c-property really was. The conscious making property cannot occur without S-state becoming conscious; otherwise, it wouldn't be the c-property in the first place. I fail to see the motivation for saying that sensory states and qualitative properties can be 'nonconscious' or for accepting Rosenthal's (1991: 26) thesis that "the properties of being conscious and having sensory quality are independent of each other." An S-state need not be conscious in the sense that aspects of it carrying PI can occur nonconsciously, but this should not lead us to conclude either that an S-state *with all its properties* can be nonconscious or that the qualitative property (the c-property) can occur nonconsciously in that very same S-state. On the HOT theory, the c-property is a higher-order thought which will be identical with some neural state. But, of course, it cannot occur as part of an unconscious S-state. It is puzzling why a HOT theorist like Rosenthal wishes to divorce sensory quality from consciousness.

Perhaps Rosenthal would return to his arguments based on the intrinsic-extrinsic distinction, but they remain unsatisfactory for the reasons given earlier (in sections 2.3 and 2.4).

6.5 Access Consciousness and Phenomenal Access

In light of the last section, it will be helpful to consider briefly Owen Flanagan's (1992) criticism of Ned Block (1991) on similar matters. Though some of the issue seems merely terminological, it again is clear that deeper questions are at stake.

Block argues that we should not be so confident about the causal efficacy of consciousness, especially when it is based on evidence from blindsight cases. He distinguishes two types of consciousness: consciousness_p (PC) which is the "what it is like" or "phenomenal" kind, and consciousness_a (AC) which has to do with information flow and, for example, is available for guiding action. One can have PC without AC and it is also possible to have AC without PC. The normal person has both, but Block urges that the blindsight patient has neither. Therefore, it is possible that the lack of AC (and not PC) is responsible for the deficiency.

Flanagan (1992: 145-49) replies that we should not accept any sharp distinction between AC and PC, and we should instead adopt a superior distinction between "informational sensitivity" (IS) which involves access to information without phenomenal awareness, and "experiential sensitivity" (ES) which involves *both* phenomenal feel and access to information (cf. Flanagan 1992: 55-6). I side with Flanagan partly because his distinction is closer to mine, i.e. between nonconscious PI and qualitative state with PI. So let us make a few further observations using my terminology:

1. Unconscious PI is responsible for the FB role in the way that Flanagan describes IS. But the FB role is not quite the same when the PI is in a conscious state, and it is crucial to remember that that same PI is present in the conscious state. Block's distinction does not make this clear since he wants to separate AC from PC in a much more strict way.

It is acknowledged by all parties that the blindsight patient does not behave toward something in the blind field as he would if he were conscious of it. But then it seems clear that, to use Block's terminology, the deficits in blindsight are best explained by a lack of PC since most of the AC is still functioning and guiding behavior. Only PC is clearly lacking, and so Flanagan rightly notes that even for Block AC *is* present in the blindsight patient despite Block's claim that there is neither PC nor AC. As Flanagan (1992: 148) observes, contrary to Block's contention that we cannot tell which causes the problem, it would have to be the lack of PC which explains it. Thus, in the end, we should accept the causal efficacy of consciousness.

2. If Block still insists that the blindsighter does not even have AC, then he must redefine it in some weaker way. As it is, the blindsighter does use such information to guide behavior and it plays a role in verbal replies to questions. But if AC is weakened even further, then it becomes even more mysterious why it deserves to be called some form of 'consciousness'.

3. Like Rosenthal and Nelkin, Block unnecessarily forces the idea of calling something which is clearly nonconscious 'conscious in some sense' (in this case 'AC'). I agree with Flanagan (1992: 148) that we should treat "knowledge without awareness [= AC] as unconscious, period." This echoes the point in the previous section that there is little reason to allow for nonconscious *qualitative* states. It is again puzzling why philosophers continue to insist on using the term 'conscious' for non-"what it is like" phenomenal states. What's so wrong with the conscious-nonconscious distinction that we need instead to distinguish between such radically different kinds of conscious states? The explanatory value or additional theoretical advantage is not at all clear.

6.6 McGinn on the Hidden Structure of Consciousness

Let us examine some aspects of McGinn's (1991) view that there is a "hidden structure" to consciousness. I neither wish to summarize his argument in any detail nor to criticize it in the ordinary way that the reader may expect. Flanagan (1992: 120-28) has already done this very well in the context of rejecting the basic thesis that we could never give a satisfying naturalist account of consciousness. My aim is rather to show how some of McGinn's claims echo key elements of the HOT theory, especially in light of his discussion of blindsight.

Some stage setting is necessary: McGinn argues that there must be a "hidden structure" in order to explain several features of consciousness. One of them is the phenomenon of blindsight which shows that there is a dissociation between "surface properties, which are accessible to the subject introspectively; and deep properties, which are not so accessible" (McGinn 1991: 111). In blindsight cases, we have the deep properties without the surface ones. Flanagan objects that McGinn's argument is self-undermining mainly because he uses cases where what was once hidden is later revealed while, at the same time, he is trying to show that such features are permanently hidden and beyond the scope of our knowledge. So McGinn may be right that consciousness has a hidden structure, but wrong that it is "noumenal".

I agree that there is a hidden structure to consciousness. Indeed, one of the main purposes of this work is precisely to articulate just what that structure is. We are committed to explaining conscious mentality and revealing its hidden structure. So it is somewhat ironic that McGinn argues that such an explanation is impossible for us. Flanagan rightly criticizes him for expecting too much from a theory of consciousness and for setting an impossibly high standard of success. For all of the reasons offered in the first four chapters, I believe we have a good explanation of consciousness and remain optimistic about future investigation. While I do not wish to overstate the analogy, we might put the basic idea in McGinn's language:

A conscious mental state has a hidden structure. In the case of a first-order conscious state, a HOT is part of a complex mental state directed at the (other part of the) state which is rendered conscious. The HOT is "hidden" in the sense that one is not typically conscious of it, but it is nonetheless part of the conscious state. The HOT is the "deep" property whereas the state that we are aware of being in is the "surface" property. But what makes the surface property accessible to consciousness is the deep property accompanying it. However, there is little reason to treat the HOT (or deep property) as any more permanently hidden from us than the surface property. Moreover, the HOT is an intrinsic property of the conscious state even though, since it is nonconscious, it is not immediately revealed when one is aware of the conscious state.

Consider the following passage which echoes these sentiments:

> ...the subject is not conscious *of* the deeper layer...but it does not follow that this layer does not belong intrinsically to the conscious state itself. Just as F can be an intrinsic property of a perceptible object x without being a perceptible property of x, so conscious states can have intrinsic properties that they do not have consciously. (McGinn 1991: 98)

Thus, aside from McGinn's ill-founded skepticism, perhaps he could be a good HOT theorist in the end.

6.7 Other Psychopathological Conditions

I have said something about the blindsight phenomenon, but more needs to be said about other psychopathologies. I will offer explanations of these phenomena from the perspective of a HOT theorist.

One such deficit is known as *visual agnosia* which is the inability to recognize perceived objects, i.e. the inability to attach meaning to a sensory stimulus. Visual agnosia is only one form of agnosia, which can occur in any of the other sensory modalities. I wish to focus on the visual form, but we should keep in mind that one can have visual agnosia and yet recognize the same objects *via* other modalities. For example, a patient might be shown a whistle and have no idea what it is, but recognize it immediately when it is blown (Ellis and Young 1988: 32). But the disorder is neither due to any general intellectual deficiency nor to any basic sensory dysfunction. The visual agnosic sees things, but simply cannot recognize what they are. They often mistake one object for another; for example, thinking that a picture is a box and even mistaking one's wife for a hat (see Sacks' 1987 description of Dr. P).

How might a HOT theorist explain what has gone wrong? It is clear that we cannot blame the lower-order "sensibility" since agnosics do have sensory impressions. Visual agnosics are not blind and do not even suffer damage to the famed area 17 of the visual cortex. Moreover, we cannot suppose that no HOTs are present since the subjects do have conscious states which require at least some form of MET or HOT. Nonetheless, something is clearly wrong with the associated HOTs or, to use Kant's term, the "understanding." As

Hundert (1989: 201) remarks in a Kantian spirit:

> We might think of this...as a separation of Sensibility and Understanding: Sensibility can analyse its sensory input, but the context, the *meaning* of the information is lost without the synthetic work of Understanding.

The *meaning* is lost because the HOTs which typically accompany the "raw data" or "sensory input" do not contain the appropriate concepts, which, in turn, makes for the strange content of the conscious state from the patient's point of view. Sometimes the understanding does not function properly due to injury, and the appropriate HOTs are not triggered when one perceives an object. But again *some* HOT is present since otherwise the subject would not have the conscious state in the first place. However, the HOT contains concepts (e.g. a hat) which do not "match up" with the visual input at a given time (e.g. Dr. P's wife), or they are too specific and do not properly categorize the object. The agnosic can still have the appropriate concepts and thoughts since they are often triggered by other input or by other thoughts, but the mechanism by which they are triggered *via* that modality is clearly defective. The appropriate higher-order *cognitive judgement* is lost when a certain input is received through the visual modality.

Moreover, visual agnosics are often described as not being able to *combine* visual impressions into complete patterns which might partly explain why they cannot recognize the object in question. Sacks (1987: 10) tells us that Dr. P. would pick up "individual features...[but fail] to see the whole, seeing only details." Dr. P. would "not recognise objects 'at a glance,' but would have to seek out, and guess from, one or two features..." (1987: 22). This suggests that having the appropriate HOTs are crucial to the very *unity* of consciousness, i.e. they bring together diverse elements of experience into a unified whole. When the appropriately complex HOT or multiplicity of HOTs accompanies a visual input, the conscious state is orderly, coherent and unified in a way that is lacking otherwise. This is no doubt what Kant meant when he insisted that application of concepts to the "raw data" is necessary for the unity of consciousness. Unified consciousness involves categorization. It is also his attempt at answering the recently revisited so-called "binding problem" which asks how the brain can bring together the simultaneous awareness of many diverse features into a unified conscious state. As Searle (1992: 130) rightly notes, we do not have all the answers about how the brain achieves this unity, but Kant at least recognized the need for it and labeled the phenomenon "the transcendental unity of apperception." Hundert

(1989) does go some way toward explaining how the brain performs this amazing feat, but my point here is only that we must recognize its necessity for conscious experience and be sure to appreciate the role of HOTs in it.

Wilkerson (1980) also points to certain psychopathological phenomena which he thinks shows that consciousess does not entail self-consciousness and therefore causes trouble for Kant. Instead of addressing his arguments in section 3.4 or as objections in chapter four, it seemed best to take them on here.[51]

One of them urges that babies are not self-conscious mainly because they do not have a concept of self. I will not discuss this one here partly because it is not a psychopathological condition. Also, Wilkerson fails to recognize that there are degrees of self-concept which was used in response to the "content objection" in section 4.5. What goes for some lower animals, also goes for small infants.[52] So let us focus on the following two main cases:

1. Borrowing from Dickens' *Hard Times*, Wilkerson describes Mrs. Gradgrind who says there is a pain somewhere in the room, but isn't sure that *she* has it. She is clearly "puzzled about the ownership of the pain she feels." (Wilkerson 1980: 56) So she doesn't fulfill the Kantian conditions of self-consciousness, but is nonetheless clearly conscious. There are three problems with this.

First, we have shown the plausbility of the self-consciousness reading of Kant's "I think" in section 3.4, but Wilkerson, like Bennett and Kitcher, fail to see its virtues and opts for the "ownership" reading. But it is only under this latter reading that Mrs. Gradgrind's condition tells against Kant and the thesis that consciousness entails self-consciousness. She admittedly has some problem about the "ownership" of the pain, but can still be self-conscious in any sense that I have described. She has a higher-order thought that she is in pain. Wilkerson (1980: 56) admits as much when he notes that "[i]n context it is clear that...in some sense she is self-conscious, for she uses 'I' without hesitation. " It may not be clear which self-concept she is using, but all that we require is that she is using one of them.

Second, if Mrs. Gradgrind really does *feel* her pain, then, by the argument of the first four chapters, she must at least have a nonconscious thought to the effect that she is in pain. Nothing in the description of her case rules this out. However, what *also* seems to be happening is that she has *another* thought that the pain is not hers. This would only be further evidence for the widely held view that one can have many inconsistent beliefs or thoughts.

When one normally feels a pain, one only has a single assertoric thought that one is in pain. But in certain abnormal cases, I can apparently also have the contradictory conscious thought that the pain is not mine. This is surely strange, but not damaging to the HOT theory nor to the entailment between consciousness and self-consciousness.

Third, although Mrs. Gradgrind seems clearly to be in pain, in other similar cases a question may even arise as to whether or not the patient really is in pain. If we have someone who does not seem to be exhibiting any behavioral signs of pain at all and is merely wondering idly about the presence of some pain in the room, then we may suppose that she is not in pain and precisely because she lacks the assertoric thought that she is in pain. Recall that merely wondering or doubting that one is pain will not suffice to render one consciously in pain (section 3.1), and this may be what happens in some such cases. Indeed, Mrs. Gradgrind's sometimes uncertain tone suggests this line of reply. For example, she says that "I think there's a pain somewhere in the room" but the word 'think' in this context seems not to have assertoric force and sounds more like 'wonder' or 'believe.' And the fact that she cannot say "positively" that she has the pain suggests that she wonders if, or even doubts that, she is in pain.

2. Borrowing from a passage in William James' *Principles of Psychology*, Wilkerson discusses a man, Baldy, who was concussed by a fall and begins to refer to himself in the third person, e.g. "Who fell out?," and "Did Baldy fall...Poor Baldy!" Since Baldy has "lost all grasp of the non-observational direct consciousness of self that is central to Kantian self-consciousness" (Wilkerson 1980: 56) and yet is conscious, consciousness does not entail self-consciousness. I offer the following replies:

First, like the second reply above, it seems that Baldy has two inconsistent thoughts; one, for example, which implicitly contains "...that I am in pain," and another which says "...that Baldy [= someone else] is in pain; not me." Wilkerson acknowledges that Baldy clearly feels "certain disagreeable sensations" and that there is evidence for both kinds of thoughts.

Second, the case does not support Wilkerson's ultimate contention that Baldy lacks self-consciousness. Indeed, he (1980: 56) even notes that Baldy "refers to himself, and distinguishes himself from other people and other things." Even though Baldy refers to himself *as 'Baldy'* and not 'I,' Wilkerson does not doubt that he is still *referring to himself*. The important thing seems to be that he does *think* of himself during this time, not what *name* he uses to refer to himself. There are, of course, many different names for the same object of reference. Wilkerson (1980: 58) considers a similar reply when he notes that perhaps the "superficial grammar" does not rule out Baldy having a concept of self, but then sells short this line of reply because he is again wedded to the "ownership reading" of Kant's "I think." Since Baldy is puzzled about the ownership of the mental states, Wilkerson urges that the Kantian conditions for self-consciousness cannot be met.

Third, it is interesting that Wilkerson's interpretation of Kant has led him to acknowledge that "the behavioural evidence is systematically inconsistent" regarding which thoughts Baldy has (1980: 58). We have seen above that this may be true, but it is no reason to deny the entailment between consciousness and self-consciousness because Baldy may have both (inconsistent) thoughts. That is, we can still hold that "every conscious subject must make certain judgements [about himself]," and not simply retreat to the modified Kantian position that "self-consciousness is a necessary feature of a *coherent* experience" (Wilkerson 1980: 59).

Another bizarre condition is known as *Anton's syndrome* or *blindness denial.* These patients cannot see, but somehow persist in the belief that they can. They confabulate in order to explain their bumping into things, but there is no evidence that they are deliberately making things up merely to cover up a recognized problem. Rather, they really do not seem to be aware that they are blind. But how could you fail to know whether you are blind? One might think that such a situation is *a priori* impossible and therefore object that the case must somehow be misdescribed. Of course, it may be misdescribed especially given that such patients typically also have other serious cognitive deficits. But Patricia Churchland (1986: 229-30) is right when she says that

> I cannot agree that we can know *a priori* that it *must* be misdescribed. On my view, what is claimed to be a necessary feature of the concept of consciousness is an empirical assumption that the phenomenon of blindness denial calls into question. And only the empirical facts will determine whether the assumption stands or falls.

Empirical observation may turn out to supply evidence which calls into question a prized, and previously unchallenged, philosophical assumption about the nature of mind. Indeed, this is precisely what has happened to the once popular self-intimation and infallibility theses mentioned in section 1.4. Indeed, blindness denial is sometimes taken as further evidence for their downfall. But we should be careful about this, and also see if it causes any trouble for the HOT theory.

It is not clear that blindness denial refutes the self-intimation thesis which we should recall states that "if one is in a mental state, then one is aware that one is in it." Churchland (1986: 229) is right that it casts serious doubt on the general assumption that "if one cannot see...then one is aware...that one cannot see." However, strictly speaking, this characterization does not tell against the self-intimation thesis. For one thing, what is the *mental state* that one is *not* aware of? There doesn't seem to be a mental state that one *has*, but yet one is unaware of. On the contrary, it is the *lack* of (conscious visual) experience of which such patients are somehow unaware. The mental state cannot be the "belief that I am having conscious visual experiences," since the patient is aware of this belief (even though it is a false belief). Also, the state cannot be the "belief that I am *not* having conscious visual experiences," since there is no evidence that the patient really has this belief and is merely unaware of it. Thus, although the self-intimation thesis is false for other reasons, it doesn't seem that blindness denial makes it so.

Recall, however, the infallibility thesis which says that "if one believes or thinks something about oneself *via* introspection, then one's belief must be true." Presumably, our patient has the belief that she can have conscious visual experiences. So she has a belief about herself *via* introspection. Is the belief true? Well, it is true that she *has the belief* in question. But, of course, it is not true that she actually has conscious visual experiences, and so, in that sense, she has a false belief about herself. So it seems that blindness denial is more damaging to the infallibility thesis.

Now, it may also seem that this psychopathology causes trouble for the HOT theory. One might object: "If the blindness denial patient (hereafter BD) has a higher-order thought that he is having a conscious visual experience, but yet is really not having a (visual) conscious state, then doesn't that show that a HOT is not *sufficient* for conscious mentality?" Several replies are in order:

1. It is not clear that BD has the kind of assertoric thought about a mental state which is required for rendering the state conscious. BD may only have a *belief* that he is in that state which, given its dispositional nature, will not render the state conscious (cf. section 3.2). That is, BD is disposed to say certain things when asked and to act certain ways when walking around, but this will not suffice for conscious visual states. This is especially likely when we again note that many such patients have other higher-order cognitive deficits.

2. The content of the HOT may be something more like '...that I am picturing or imagining what is around me.' In other words, the state that is rendered conscious is (of course) not a visual state but rather one of imagination. If we close our eyes and walk around, we might have a better sense of what BD is doing and which state becomes conscious. But none of this damages the HOT theory, since we can admit that BD has these kinds of "imaginative" conscious states. Similarly, a HOT can make conscious the *belief* that he is having conscious visual experiences, but, as we saw above, it doesn't follow that it is a *true* belief.

3. There is also some question as to what (unconscious) mental state would be made conscious by the HOT in these cases. Recall that our initial question from chapter two was: what makes a mental state a conscious mental state? But, in BD's case, there doesn't seem to be any first-order mental state in the first place which could be rendered conscious by a HOT. For example, because of the extensive brain damage, there is no unconscious phenomenal state or even any phenomenal information there to be made conscious. This seems clear from the behavioral evidence since such patients continue to bump into things. Little (if any) visual PI seems to be getting through.

4. Recall also that the HOT cannot be the result of inference if it is to render a state conscious (section 4.6). It seems likely that if BD is really having the relevant HOT at all, it is mediated by inference. BD must "figure out" what is going on around him and one way to do so is to try to form thoughts about what it would be like to have a visual experience at a time. BD needs to try to figure out these things even just to get around, and the extensive confabulation is further evidence that BD is using inference and reasoning to arrive at any HOT he may have.

CHAPTER 7

The Behavior Argument

7.1 The General Strategy

The first six chapters have been mostly concerned with state consciousness. Although an examination of it will continue, I will hereafter focus more on system consciousness by exploring three arguments in chapters seven through nine for the conclusion that 'being a conscious system entails being self-conscious.' The arguments will take the following general form:

(1) Being a conscious system entails having a specific psychological capacity or ability.
(2) Having that capacity entails self-consciousness.

Therefore,

(3) Being a conscious system entails being self-conscious.

Ideally, it will be shown that 'necessarily, if S is a conscious system, then S has psychological capacity C,' and 'necessarily, if S has C, then S is self-conscious.' It follows that 'necessarily, if S is a conscious system, then S is self-conscious.' Thus, having C is a *necessary* condition for being a conscious system, and is *sufficient* for self-consciousness. Self-consciousness will thus be necessary for having C. A sound general argument can already be given based on our examination thus far:

(1') Being a conscious system entails having conscious mental states.
(2') Having conscious mental states entails self-consciousness.

Therefore,

(3) Being a conscious system entails self-consciousness.

Chapters one through four have, I hope, proven premise (2') and premise (1') is surely uncontroversial (although much of section 6.1 can be taken as support for it). Conscious systems must surely have conscious mental states, not merely 'informational states' or 'behavioral awareness.' Conscious mentality is clearly necessary for being a conscious system. Although this argument establishes the desired conclusion, it is worthwhile to look at other arguments for it. Moreover, I will not exclusively rely on the truth of premises (1') and (2') or the HOT theory in what follows, although I do take chapters seven through nine as further evidence for the plausibility of the HOT theory.

In this chapter I examine the relationship between consciousness, self-consciousness, and the ability to modify one's behavior given one's mental states. Again, the sense of 'conscious' or 'conscious mental state' that I have in mind is the same as Nagel's (1974) sense; namely, that "there is something it is like to be in that state."

In section 7.2, I present the argument and examine the first premise. In section 7.3, premise (2) is critically discussed with special attention to Robert Van Gulick's account of self-consciousness. In 7.4, I then critically examine a Dennett-style defense of premise (2) and offer a somewhat modified argument for it.

7.2 The BEHAVIOR Argument and Premise One

To argue for the main conclusion I will utilize what we can call the 'BEHAVIOR argument':

(1) Being a conscious system entails having the ability to modify one's own behavior on the basis of internal mental states.
(2) Having the ability to modify one's own behavior on the basis of such mental states entails self-consciousness.

Therefore,

(3) Being a conscious system entails being self-conscious.

We must first clarify the content of premise (1) and the expressions "modify one's own behavior" and "internal mental states" in order to judge its truth.[53] The reason for 'internal *mental* states' rather than merely 'internal states' should be clear. Premise (1) would be trivial and uninteresting if it were weakened to read:

(1*) Being a conscious system presupposes being able to modify one's own behavior on the basis of various *internal states*.

Using (1*) as our first premise would at best provide a trivial necessary condition for consciousness. Some primitive instruments or machines might be able to modify their behavior on the basis of clearly nonmental internal states (e.g. informational states). Thermostats might even be thought of as doing certain things on the basis of such states, i.e. as having behavioral outputs based on some (nonmental) internal states. Learning that a system satisfies such a weak necessary condition would not help in deciding whether it is a serious candidate for consciousness. In short, consciousness requires having at least some mentality in the first place (e.g. thoughts and desires). Also, such a weak condition could not be sufficient for self-consciousness as would be required for premise (2).

Second, the term 'modify' in "modify one's own behavior..." cannot mean '*consciously* modify...' if that is taken as 'modifying one's own behavior always as a result of being consciously aware of one's own mental states.' A system can be conscious without always consciously modifying its own behavior in such a way. One need not have conscious awareness of one's mental states in order to modify behavior on the basis of them. Cats are clearly conscious but do not seem to introspect their mental states in any consciously reflective way. However, a cat could still modify its own behavior to that of running after a mouse on the basis of a desire to kill and eat it. The cat need not have conscious thoughts about the desire. Requiring that a system be able to introspect in order to behave in the relevant ways would rule out clear cases of conscious systems. Indeed, in order to explain the behavior of a system in terms of its beliefs and desires, we need not assume that it has any conscious access to them. A conscious system need only be able to 'nonconsciously modify' its own behavior on the basis of its mental states, i.e. alter its behavior as a result of (nonconsciously) detecting the presence of certain mental states.

Third, although premise (1) refers to 'behavior' in its necessary condition, clarification will show that it does not fall prey to standard 'paralytic' counter-examples, i.e. cases where one is conscious or thinking though unable to exhibit behavior at all. Premise (1) does not require that conscious beings exhibit any *actual* behavior, but rather counterfactual behavior or dispositions to behave in certain ways under certain conditions. There is a perfectly good sense in which even the paralytic is able to modify his own behavior. It is not always obvious how best to understand 'ability' claims, but surely one way to view the paralytic is in terms of counterfactuals such as 'if he had a normally functioning nervous system, then he would do such-and-such on the basis of his mental states,' or 'in the nearest possible world where he is not physically disabled, he would behave in certain ways given his mental states.' The paralytic can meet the necessary condition, and so is not in danger of being rendered a nonconscious system. He is able to modify his own behavior given his mental states. He has the ability, but just cannot exercise it given his actual condition.

It is also worth noting that perhaps "one's own behavior" need not even refer to *bodily movements* at all. Alston (1981, 1985) has convincingly argued that there is room within a general functionalist framework for predicating 'actions' and 'behavior' to incorporeal beings such as God. One need not have a body in order to behave and act toward the world. 'Behavior' need not mean 'bodily behavior.' This is related to the more metaphysical issue of whether materialism is necessarily true. That is, even if all of our mental states are physical and essentially related to bodily input and output, must any mind function in such a way? Is there a possible world where non-physical minds exist? I am inclined to allow for such a possibility, and so perhaps all that is necessary for a mind to 'behave' is that it *seems to the agent* that it has a body which acts toward the world regardless of whether it *really* does. After all, anyone who takes seriously the metaphysics of idealists such as Leibniz and Berkeley is already open to this possibility even if one rejects their actual truth.

In any event, the emphasis is meant to be on 'modify', not on 'behavior.' Premise (1) should *not* be read as 'being a conscious system entails actually bodily behaving in certain ways *and* being able to modify it on the basis of internal mental states.' Rather, it should be taken as '*given* that a system is capable of some kind of behavior and has some mental states, it must be able to *modify* its behavior on the basis of those states if it is to be conscious.' The issue is not whether all conscious systems must behave in certain ways, but rather whether all conscious behaving systems must be able to alter their behavior as a result of their mental states.

Is premise (1) true? I think so. It embodies the generally plausible idea that consciousness must be linked with behavior *in some way*. If there were a conscious system which lacked the ability to modify its own behavior on the basis of its mental states, then it would continue to behave in the same way regardless of internal and environmental changes. Its internal states would not lead it to actively change its own behavior, which should lead us to question whether it really has mental states in the first place since they would play no role in the modification of behavior.

I do not wish to defend any form of behaviorism but, even on many functionalist views, part of what makes a state a *mental* state is the causal role it plays in the *adaptive* behavior of the system (cf. Van Gulick 1980). At the least, mental states acquire their content partly in virtue of their (actual and possible) relations to input and output or behavior. Many functionalists want to connect mentality (especially intentionality) with behavioral outputs in some way. Such a view seems quite reasonable. If a system has states which are utterly incapable of having effects on its own (actual or counterfactual) behavior, then it should lead us to doubt whether it has mental states at all. We might say that if a system is utterly unable to *learn*, then it could not be a conscious system. That is, at least some ability to learn is necessary for being a conscious system.[54] Moreover, if a system does not have at least some intentional states, then it is difficult to see why it should be treated as a candidate for consciousness. If a system is conscious, it surely must have at least some conscious thoughts, desires, or perceptual states which are themselves intentional.

7.3 Premise Two and Van Gulick's View

Robert Van Gulick has offered a view of self-consciousness which would render premise (2) true. He presents his position thus:

> The basic proposal is to identify self-consciousness with the possession of reflexive meta-psychological information. An organism is self-conscious in the relevant sense in so far as it understands or is informed about the nature, properties, and operations of its own mind. (Van Gulick 1988a: 163)

It should be clear that premise (2) is true on Van Gulick's view. If a system is able to modify its own behavior in virtue of its mental states, then some higher-order states of the system must be able to acquire and apply information about its lower-order states. Let us take a perceptual state as an example. If a system is to modify or alter its behavior in virtue of occurrent visual stimuli, then the system must use or apply the relevant information. The lower-order states are accessed and used by higher-order states. Some meta-psychological informational state must be directed at the first-order mental state in order for the system to modify its behavior. Some state of the system possesses information about another. Premise (2) is true, on this view, because any system which has the ability to modify its own behavior *on the basis of its own mental states* must thereby possess (at least) higher-order informational states directed at them. Being self-conscious (in Van Gulick's sense) is necessary for modifying one's own behavior on the basis of internal mental states. The problem is that Van Gulick's notion of self-consciousness is very weak and so makes premise (2) trivially true. Let us see clearly why.[55]

1. Imagine a system — Robo — to which we have found reason to attribute beliefs and desires (or just goals). We find them indispensable in explaining and predicting its behavior (Dennett 1987). Suppose further that Robo was found on a crashed UFO and that it overtly resembled a very sophisticated machine. It might be a futuristic version of the kind we now send into space. We can leave open whether it has any conscious states — perhaps it need not. Robo has various sensors which apparently have causal effects on its internal states. Its behavior is very complex, e.g. it displays a rather complex range of behavior even when presented with the same input at different times. It turns out that Robo was sent here by aliens precisely for the purpose of finding out about the Earth and its inhabitants. We can even further suppose (for simplicity) that, upon studying the internal constitution of Robo, it is reasonable to interpret some of its internal states as *representing* its beliefs and goals. Robo moves around in a complex pattern of behavior driven by those mental states.

Let us also imagine that on Robo's home planet, Info, the inhabitant organisms monitor Robo's mental states in such a way that they come to possess information about about the contents of its mind. Various recording devices secure information about its psychological states. For example, one device might register a '1' (rather than a '0') if Robo believes that Earthlings are intelligent creatures or if it desires to bring some Earth fragments back to its ship. It is obvious that the mere possession of this meta-psychological information is not sufficient for *Robo's* being self-conscious. So far Van Gulick can agree for two reasons. One is that:

a. the meta-psychological information is merely passively received, and the information must be possessed in the active sense:

> An organism can be informed about its own structure and about its own functional and psychological organization...To be informed about one's

> own organization is to be able to interact with it in ways that are specifically adapted to its nature. (Van Gulick 1988a: 158)

Thus the meta-psychological information must also play a causal role in altering the psychological subsystems it regulates. The information must actively modify the behavior of the system on the basis of the psychological states it is directed at. The higher-order state must make some difference to the present and future behavior of the system. It cannot merely be a passive storing or recording of information as in the cases of a "fossil contain[ing] information about the Cretaceous inhabitants of the lake bed, and the pattern of light falling on the astronomer's photographic plate..." (Van Gulick 1988a: 153). The rings of a tree are also examples of such 'passive information possession' which is not the (active) kind Van Gulick has in mind and does not indicate the presence of mentality at all. Let us call this the 'activity condition.'[56]

b. The second reason that Robo is not self-conscious in Van Gulick's view is presumably that the meta-psychological information is not 'in' Robo. The information, in short, is not possessed *by Robo*. In no sense is Robo informed about the operations of its own states. Only the inhabitants of Info have the information. I will call this the 'internal condition.'

We can alter my story to meet the above conditions. Let us make the devices on Info play an active role in the alteration and production of Robo's behavior. They no longer merely passively receive or record the states in question and so the activity condition is met. There is an active interaction between the meta-psychological states and Robo's first-order intentional states. For example, whenever '0' is registered, Robo adjusts its behavior in virtue of having that information. If registering '0' involves believing that Earthlings are intelligent creatures, then Robo would subsequently be led to behave differently in the presence of humans. Robo might come to form other beliefs and desires which, in turn, have their behavioral effects, and so on.

Secondly, we can meet the internal condition by imagining that the recording devices in question are implanted in Robo. This additional condition provides Robo with a new found self-sufficiency. It can now modify its own behavior *via* the possession of active meta-psychological information. Given that the activity condition is also met, Robo might now be able to answer questions or reveal information about its own states when examined. Our key question is: Why should satisfying these conditions render Robo self-conscious? Van Gulick would now have to treat our modified Robo as self-conscious, but I do not see how this information possession can result in self-consciousness. The information is still what Van Gulick calls 'opaque', i.e. the system has a very restricted understanding of the information it has and its mental processes. Indeed, this is stretching the use of the term 'understanding' in the first place. Imagine the activity condition met, but the recording apparatus still on Info. Robo is clearly not self-conscious. It is not clear how moving the apparatus inside Robo should suddenly have any further effect on our intuitions here. Van Gulick's notion of self-consciousness is much too weak. What are needed are meta-psychological *thoughts*.

2. Dissatisfaction with Van Gulick's proposal can also be motivated by noting that a system can be self-conscious in his sense and yet not be conscious (in the Nagelian sense that most of us are concerned with). But, surely, being self-conscious entails being conscious. More specifically, if M is the content of a self-conscious state, then M must be conscious. But it is clear that Van Gulick's meta-psychological *information* cannot render their objects conscious.[57]

If a system can have intentional states which are all nonconscious (recall MEC11 in section 5.3), then it could satisfy Van Gulick's definition of self-consciousness without being conscious at all. If a system can have intentional states without consciousness, then Van Gulick's view cannot ensure that a self-conscious system (in his sense) is conscious in the Nagelian sense. I find this absurd. But even if intentionality entails consciousness, a system might still possess meta-psychological *information* and not be conscious at all. It is an odd theory which implies that a system can be self-conscious but not conscious. Perhaps Robo would be just such a system.

I am sympathetic with Van Gulick's overall project of bringing self-consciousness back into the heart of a theory of mind, but he has gone too far. Self-consciousness must at least require consciousness, and premise (2) of BEHAVIOR should not be defended by using such a weak notion. Van Gulick would no doubt reply that he is not trying to provide us with a view which accords with many of our 'common-sense' intuitions on self-consciousness. As he has told me in conversation, his main objective is more a matter of proposing a theory that may be helpful in thinking about psychological organization. Nonetheless, I prefer not to stray so far from common-sense and common usage. Van Gulick's proposal does render premise (2) true, but the cost is too high. It makes self-consciousness exceedingly weak and almost trivial.

In general, the weaker one's view of self-consciousness, the easier it is to prove a premise like premise (2) in BEHAVIOR. And the weaker the condition, the more likely that it is necessary for being a conscious system. Similarly, the stronger one's conception of 'being a conscious system,' the more likely that it is sufficient for having a certain capacity. *But* we should be careful not to let these facts, by themselves, lead us to adopt an uneccessarily weak form of self-consciousness or an even stronger conception of consciousness.

7.4 Another Attempt at Premise Two

It might be that premise (2) of the BEHAVIOR argument is not true as it stands. Perhaps we cannot *demonstrate* the strong logical entailment required. Self-consciousness does not seem *required* for merely being able to modify one's behavior on the basis of first-order intentional states. Robo could have that ability without having meta-psychological *thoughts*, which is definitive of self-consciousness. Robo might only even have Van Gulick's meta-psychological information. Thus, self-consciousness is perhaps not a *necessary* condition for the ability in question. Having complex learning mechanisms also do not *guarantee* the presence of self-consciousness (or even consciousness).

But all is not lost. In light of this, we might revise premise (2) to read:

> (2*) Having the ability to modify one's own behavior on the basis of one's mental states *in a controlled, swift, intelligent, and efficient manner is best accomplished by* a self-conscious system.

(2*) is weaker than (2) and is at least a highly plausible empirical hypothesis. It expresses an inductive claim rather than the stronger deductive entailment found in premise (2). Let us examine its *prima facie* plausibility.

Some systems are capable of a higher degree of swift and controlled manipulations of their internal states (e.g. mental representations or symbols) than others. A system, A, might be able to more quickly process its own mental representations than another system B. One reason could be that B has limited higher-order understanding of its states. Its understanding of its own processes is, to use Van Gulick's term, 'opaque'.[58] One explanation for why

A can more swiftly process its internal states would be that it has some higher-order thought-awareness of those states. A will more likely display clearer signs of intentional and intelligent activity than B. Human beings and many other organisms are examples of an A-type system whereas present day robots are examples of a B-type system. A-type systems are better equipped to react and modify their behavior in so-called 'real time.' In his "Fast Thinking," Dennett (1987: 326) puts it thus:

> Speed...is 'of the essence' for intelligence. If you can't figure out the relevant portions of the changing environment fast enough to fend for yourself, you are not *practically* intelligent...

Similarly, the faster one can modify one's own behavior in light of one's changing internal states, the more practically intelligent one will be. A-type systems are better able to swiftly process their internal states than B-type systems. We are, of course, oversimplifying the matter in speaking of two types of systems. More accurately, we ought to say that there is a continuum with A-types on one end and B-types on the other, along which varying degrees of the ability to swiftly and intelligently manipulate and grasp one's internal symbols can be located.

Dennett offers one explanation for why a system might be closer to the A-end of the continuum. In the context of discussing the possibility of machine consciousness, he (1987: 324) endorses the following empirical claim:

> (D) There is no way an electronic digital computer could be programmed so that it could produce what an organic human brain, with its particular causal powers, demonstrably can produce: control of the swift, intelligent, intentional activity exhibited by normal human beings.

Dennett puts forth (D) as a reasonable empirical hypothesis. He argues that it might be true for the simple reason that, as a matter of fact, human-like brains have a virtue that no computer could have, i.e. a tremendously high speed of operation. He explains that neurophysiology is probably so important that if he ever saw a system getting around in the world with "real-time cleverness," he would be willing to bet that it is "controlled — locally or remotely — by an organic brain. Nothing else (I bet) can control such clever behavior in real time" (Dennett 1987: 334).

Although I probably would bet with Dennett, we will see that two controversial assumptions lie at the heart of his reasoning. As I have said,

Dennett provides us with *one* explanation of how a system could be better equipped to get around in the world with 'real-time cleverness.' It has to do with a physical property of organic brains; namely, the ability to swifty process and operate on its mental representations.

One problem here is that the reliance on the actual physical properties of brains can lead to a conflict with the multiple realizability of mental states. Dennett's explanation of how a system is able to swiftly process its mental representations relies on a brain property which may not be had by other systems with that capacity. Dennett (1987: 327-9) recognizes this problem and realizes it is unclear that the processing *rates* or transmission *speeds* of a brain could not be matched in electronic massive parallel processors. He then speculates further in order to support his neurophysiological explanation. For example, he hypothesizes: "suppose...that the information processing prowess of any single neuron (its relevant input-output function) depends on features or activities in subcellular organic molecules" (Dennett 1987: 328). He admits that these types of suppositions are quite speculative.

Another related problem is that Dennett relies too heavily on the *speed* of the processing in question. We should be careful not to so closely associate consciousness, intelligence, or intentionality with an ability to very swiftly process or manipulate internal symbols. We are capable of making tremendously fast connections in a nonconscious manner, and computers or calculators (lacking self-consciousness) can manipulate their internal states even faster than we can. In short, self-consciousness does not explain how a system is able to so *swiftly* modify its own behavior on the basis of its inner states. Nonconscious processing of (mental or nonmental) states can be just as fast; indeed, sometimes consciousness hampers the speed of such processing.

I suggest a better explanation for why some systems are closer to the A-end of the continuum is that they are capable of meta-psychological thoughts (i.e. self-consciousness) which, as I have urged throughout, involve an immediate awareness of their objects. Even if having such thoughts do not better enable a system to more *swiftly* process its internal symbols, there are other related advantages. The system has a higher-order awareness of the processes of its own mind very far from an 'opaque' access. Such immediate awareness will embody what Van Gulick calls a 'semantic transparency' between the higher and lower-order state. It is at the opposite end of the continuum from 'opaque understanding' (see also Van Gulick 1988b). A system blessed with such semantic transparency has, or at least very likely has, conscious mental states, and so will be better suited to produce the efficient, controlled, intelligent activity described in (2*). Self-consciousness allows a system to grasp more lower-order states at once; it enables it to better understand those states and to recombine them in a very selective way. Systems without consciousness may be just as fast in such processing, but they are 'rigid' and merely perform 'routinized' procedures. They will likely not have the higher-order flexibility that comes with self-consciousness, which allows a system to operate on its own states in a more selective way. Being self-conscious helps one to accomplish modifying one's own behavior on the basis of such states in the most efficient way. Being able to selectively survey and recombine one's inner mental representations allows one to act in a more intelligent, controlled, and efficient manner. Self-consciousness *best explains* why some systems are better able to modify their own behavior on the basis of their internal mental states, and this is all that (2*) claims. The best explanation for the efficient excercise of such a capacity is the presence of self-consciousness. We know, in fact, that it does the job very well and it seems to be the best explanation for why other systems are able to modify their behavior in swift and intelligent ways. The more 'transparent' the awareness of one's mental states, the better one will be able to efficiently and selectively produce intelligent activity and modify one's behavior on the basis of one's inner states.

Notice that my explanation is *a priori* as opposed to Dennett's neurophysiological story. But this is precisely what gives it the explanatory power that his lacks. First, it does not rely so heavily on the mere speed of the physical processing in question. It explains how self-consciousness enables a system to produce the relevant behavior, even if other systems can just as quickly process its own states. Second, it does not flirt with the problematic denial of multiple realizability. It leaves open which kinds of physical systems could have METs. The point here is not merely to leave open the possibility of machine consciousness (or machine 'thinking'), but also to allow for self-consciousness in physiologically different creatures. It is unclear how far Dennett is willing to go in his bet. *How different from us* must a system be before he would think about making his wager?

Where exactly to 'draw the line' in attributing consciousness to other kinds of creatures is a genuine difficulty for all of us, but the key point here is that my explanation in terms of METs also helps to show (2*) true. A system with METs is better suited to modify its own behavior on the basis of its mental states in the manner described. This is largely because it will have greater immediate awareness and higher-order understanding of those states, and will be better able to selectively recombine them. Self-consciousness best explains the ability to modify one's own behavior on the basis of one's mental states *in a controlled, swift, intelligent, and efficient manner*. Perhaps it is also true that

> (T) Only organic brains are capable of producing meta-psychological thoughts and, so, conscious mental states.

I am somewhat sympathetic to T, but it seems wiser not to rely on it in supporting (2*). Conscious thinkers, first and foremost, need meta-psychological thoughts. *If* T is *also* true, then they also need organic brains (perhaps very much like ours). But the truth of T is a further matter and independent of the plausibility of premise (2*).

I believe our discussion of premise (2) can help shed some light on the well-known "frame problem" encountered in cognitive science and artificial intelligence (see e.g. Fodor 1990, Tienson 1990 and Dennett 1990a). The problem is basically how to represent information in a system in such a way that it can adjust to a changing environment over time and recognize which bits of information are *relevant* to a given situation. It is an enormous problem which somehow humans are naturally able to solve, but it is a key obstacle to advancement in artificial intelligence. Most seem to view it as an epistemological problem of "common sense" or one primarily to do with a problem of "inference;" namely, how to build a system that has all the information but also "knows" when to ignore irrelevant inferences and to make only the relevant inferences. Examples of the problem abound in the literature and I do not wish to discuss many in detail, but we should illustrate with one:

Consider Dennett's (1990a) robot which was designed to find an energy supply in a locked room with a bomb inside set to go off soon. There was a wagon in the room and the battery was on the wagon, and so the robot did "figure out" that it could remove the battery by removing the wagon. The wagon was removed before the bomb went off, but the bomb was also on the wagon! So changes were made to ensure that the robot would "realize" the obvious implication of its planned act, and resulted in a second robot which would make many more of these "deductions" but, then, by the time that it finished making numerous (irrelevant) inferences, the bomb exploded. And so on with every adjustment made.

Again, how do we make a system which pays attention to the relevant information and implications while ignoring the irrelevant ones? After all, as we saw earlier, speed is often "of the essence" for intelligence. A truly intelligent system must not only be able to figure things out, but do so at a pace that will ensure practical survival. "[S]tored information that is not reliably accessible for use in the short real-time spans typically available to agents in the world is of no use at all" (Dennett 1990a: 155).

My aim is not to offer any detailed help for cognitive scientists concerning robot architecture, but rather to point out an interesting connection in this context. The fact remains that any fairly intelligent rational creature on earth does not have the frame problem, and we should wonder why. Moreover, if we knew why, then that may help explain what is missing in robots, which, after all, are supposed to be designed to duplicate our intelligent activity.

I suggest the best way to think of the frame problem is that a robot cannot currently be constructed with an ability to behave (and modify its behavior) on the basis of its "inner states" in a swift and efficient manner. In particular, such systems are incapable of selectively surveying their inner states in the flexible way that we so easily can. All this should be familiar by now from our discussion of premise (2*). The reason for the difficulty, we may suppose, has to do with the system's lack of self-consciousness and, therefore, the inability of the system to act in the same swift, intelligent, and efficient way that we would in similar situations. This is one reason that robots are at the B-end of the continuum regarding the higher-order understanding of their inner states. As Van Gulick would say, they have a very 'opaque' (not semantically 'transparent') higher-order awareness. We can leave open here whether such a system could be conscious or whether T is true, but the frame problem may well persist as one clear manifestation of a lack of self-consciousness. That is, the lack of self-consciousness may well *explain* the difficulty and even the very presence of the frame problem. We may or may not be able to build a robot so as to solve the frame problem, but if we can it seems likely that it will thereby have self-consciousness (and so conscious mental states). If not, then this seems to be further evidence that we cannot build a conscious and truly 'intelligent' robot. Consider the following sample of quotes which reflect these claims in somewhat different ways:

> ...we must have internal ways of updating our beliefs that will fill in the gaps and keep our internal model, the totality of our beliefs, roughly faithful to the world. (Dennett 1990b: 262)

> Cognition...requires both being able to see that certain information is relevant, and being able to find relevant information from the whole data base that consists of all of one's knowledge. Easy for us, hard for them. (Tienson 1990: 384)

> Intelligence is (at least partly) a matter of using well what you know. (Dennett 1990a: 150)

> The information manipulation may be unconscious and swift, and it need not (it *better* not) consist of hundreds or thousands of...testing procedures, but it must occur somehow, and its benefits must appear in time to help me as I commit myself to action. (Dennett 1990a: 157)

These statements seem in the spirit of premise (2*), though none of the authors are willing to make the further rather obvious claim that some form of consciousness is precisely what is responsible for the difference in ability. At the least, self-consciousness is a very good explanation for why we can do the sorts of things mentioned while robots cannot. Unfortunately, many cognitive scientists shy away from invoking consciousness to explain the problem, and some want to do away with it all together. One philosopher who does neither and recognizes the importance of consciousness in an adequate theory of mind is John Searle. He rightly acknowledges the place of consciousness when he notes that:

> ...conscious behavior has a degree of flexibility and creativity that is absent from [unconscious mechanisms]...Consciousness adds powers of discrimination and flexibility even to memorized routine activities. (Searle 1992: 108)

This seemingly obvious fact is not only ignored by those struggling with the frame problem, but it can also help us to re-focus the issue in the manner described above. Moreover, we should remind ourselves (as Searle does in his context) that there are very good *evolutionary* reasons which support his claim and premise (2*). Naturally, the better a creature is able to do the sorts of things mentioned above, the more likely it will survive. Indeed, consciousness presumably evolved for this very reason. Moreover, on my view, some degree of self-consciousness always accompanies consciousness and this is specifically what better enables organisms to modify their own behavior in a swift, intelligent and efficient manner.

Two final points. One might again wonder what third-person or 'behavioral' evidence there could be for attributing METs and conscious mental states to a system. I have not become unnecessarily involved in this way of thinking about consciousness (but recall some of the animal experiments noted in section 4.5). It is not obvious that there *must always* be clear and determinate behavioral signs of consciousness. I am not convinced that necessary and sufficient conditions for the presence of consciousness can be attained, or that deductive inferences can be made from behavior to consciousness. However, the discussion in this section suggests that having METs will have a generally noticeable effect on the behavior of systems, i.e. they will be better suited to exhibit a wide range of swift and intelligent intentional action.

Second, the modification of premise (2) in BEHAVIOR damages its formal validity. Substituting (2*) for (2) no longer leaves BEHAVIOR as an instance of a hypothetical syllogism. We have not established the strong deductive or logical entailment reflected in the original premise (2). Perhaps this is the best that can be done with the argument, but it should not take much away from the value of our inquiry. Interesting sound deductive arguments should be desired and are nice to have, but are often difficult to find.

CHAPTER 8

The *De Se* Argument

8.1 The *De Se* Argument

In this chapter I wish to explore another connection between consciousness and self-consciousness, i.e. concerning so-called *de se* attitudes (hereafter DSAs). DSAs have been described in many ways depending upon the intentional attitude in question.[59] It is not clear that there is complete agreement on what they are supposed to be, but it is fair to say that a DSA is an attitude (desire, belief, thought, etc.) directed toward oneself. For any intentional state, I, there is a potential DSA involving I. A system S might *believe* that *he himself* (or 'he*' to use Castaneda's terminology) has some property F. S might *think* that he* has F. S can *want* herself to have F; and so on. In general: 'S I's that he* has F.' Given any intentional attitude, one potentially has a DSA for that same attitude.

It is at least *prima facie* plausible to think of DSAs in terms of self-consciousness. Philosophers also talk about 'indexical thoughts' (McGinn, Perry) and the 'self-ascription of properties' (Lewis). McGinn (1983: 19) speaks of DSAs in terms of "thinking of objects as standing in a relation to yourself" and it seems natural to suppose that some form of self-consciousness is involved. Perry (1979) argues that unless I have indexical thoughts I will not act in the appropriate way in certain contexts. Unless I 'realize' that *I* am the object of my belief or thought, I will not act appropriately. DSAs are not reducible to *de dicto* or *de re* attitudes, and so are "essential" indexicals. Perry uses the example of a shopper who is making a mess in the supermarket and suddenly realizes that he* is making the mess. Lewis and Chisholm's use of 'self-ascription,' 'self-location,' and 'self-attribution' also seem to carry connotations of self-consciousness.[60]

One might also suppose that being a conscious system requires having at least some primitive intentional attitudes. If so and if having intentional states entails having DSAs (as Lewis and Chisholm believe), then having some intentional states entails self-consciousness. There are many ways to present a formal argument utilizing DSAs, but I will primarily explore the following which I call '*De Se*':

(1) Being a conscious system entails having some intentional attitudes.
(2) Having intentional attitudes entails having DSAs.
(3) Having DSAs entails self-consciousness.

Therefore,

(4) Being a conscious system entails self-consciousness.

I will first address premise (1) in section 8.2. Sections 8.3 and 8.4 are devoted to a critical exposition of Lewis' argument for premise (2). In 8.5 I provide some independent support for premise (2). Section 8.6 explores an inconsistent triad involving the relation between intentionality, DSAs and consciousness. A somewhat modified version of *De Se* is also briefly presented. Lastly, in 8.7, I consider the plausibility of premise (3) while re-examining self-consciousness.

8.2 Premise One

Premise one reads: Being a conscious system entails having some intentional attitudes or states. Examples are believing, hoping, intending, thinking, conceiving, and desiring. When one has an intentional attitude, one is related in some way to its content. On a standard account, believing or desiring that p involves standing in some relation to a proposition (Perry 1979, Stalnaker 1987). We can take the basic form of a *de dicto* belief to be:

> 'P believes *that* a is F' where 'P' is some system, 'a' names some object, and 'F' expresses a property.

Similarly, we can say that *de re* beliefs involve a relation between a subject and the object of the belief. I will take the typical form of a *de re* belief to be:

> P believes *of* a that it is or *has* F.

Of course, one often has a *de dicto* belief in virtue of having a *de re* belief. It is also common to translate one type of belief into the other (cf. Perry 1979: 90-1), but that is not my concern here.[61]

Of course, being a conscious system does not even *prima facie* require having a very broad range of intentional attitudes. There are conscious creatures who are not capable of having many *kinds* of intentional states. Some states involve a sophisticated introspective capacity not possessed by every conscious creature. Fish and chicken cannot 'consider' or 'hope.' Very few kinds of intentional attitudes are presupposed by conscious systems, but premise (1) only says that some are. Consciousness seems to go far down on the evolutionary scale while many intentional attributions end much earlier. It is plausible, however, to think that beliefs, goal-states, and certain primitive perceptual states are some exceptions. They are more fundamental than other intentional attitudes and are often attributed to lower animals. So it is not clear that consciousness outruns intentionality. Indeed, being a conscious system entails that there are some counterfactual truths about its behavior which cannot be explained in some simple mechanistic manner. Any conscious creature will likely display enough complex patterns of behavior which warrant attributions of at least some primitive beliefs and desires (or goals). This may be somewhat controversial, but even those who deny that dogs can have certain kinds of beliefs usually do not deny that they can have *any* intentional states. At the least, any conscious creature will have some conscious *sensory* experiences (e.g. visual experiences) which have an intentional aspect.

Thus, we should restrict the intentional attitudes in question to a select few (e.g. beliefs, thoughts and desires) in order to maintain the initial plausibility of premise (1). But just as it is unreasonable to presume that any conscious system must have all kinds of intentional states so it is unwise to suppose that they must be able to have *all kinds of beliefs, thoughts and desires*. There are, for example, good reasons not to require that every conscious system have beliefs about the distant past, beliefs containing universal quantification, or desires directed at the distant future. They might still, however, possess *present tense* intentional attitudes directed at *particulars* in the world (cf. Bennett 1964 and 1976). A dog may not have beliefs about what happened three weeks ago or believe that all bones are white, but that does not show it has no beliefs or desires at all. Dogs, and many other conscious creatures, might only be capable of having certain kinds of beliefs and desires.

Moreover, some are more hesitant to attribute *de dicto* attitudes (hereafter DD attitudes) to brutes than *de re* attitudes (DR attitudes). Some link the capacity to have DD states more closely with linguistic ability or to having a fairly rich conceptual scheme so that sense can be made of referentially opaque attributions. The viability of these claims is not clear partly because of difficulties with the distinction itself (Bach 1982: 129ff). My only point here is that to the extent that DR states are had by more primitive conscious systems, premise (1) ought to be restricted to them. DR attitudes seem more primitive in that they apparently only involve a relation between a subject and an external object. On the surface, they do not commit one to talk of relations to propositions, which are perhaps more at home when 'that-clauses' are used. On the other hand, it is difficult to imagine cases where a DR attribution is justified without the corresponding DD attitude. If a creature can have the requisite concepts for a DR attitude, then why shouldn't it also have the relevant DD attitude which involves standing in relation to a proposition? But if sense can be made of brutes having DR states without DD attitudes, then we should mainly restrict ourselves to DR states. The idea would be to weaken the necessary condition as much as possible so that premise (1) can retain its plausibility. Thus, premise (1) *at minimum* should be read as:

(1) Being a conscious system entails having at least some particular, present tense *de re* beliefs and desires.

Premise (1) is plausible but one might object that I have unjustly ruled out the possibility of a system with only (non-intentional) phenomenal states. Haven't I unfairly restricted my claim to familiar kinds of creatures? I do not think so. It is difficult to imagine a system simply having phenomenal states without, for example, having some beliefs, desires, or preferences with respect to those states. Mustn't the system also have beliefs or thoughts about what phenomenal state it is in at a particular time? Mustn't it have beliefs about the relative similarity between its various states? Mustn't it have some kind of *perceptual* states (which have an intentional aspect)? I am inclined to think so. It is difficult to make sense of a 'purely passive' consciousness which does not at least have some intentional attitudes toward the objects of its psychological (phenomenal) states.

Of course, *on the HOT theory*, consciousness entails intentionality because having a conscious state entails the presence of an intentional attitude (i.e. a thought) directed at it. Indeed, the HOT is what makes the mental state conscious. But premise (1) links consciousness and intentionality in an independently plausible manner.

8.3 Premise Two and Lewis' View

David Lewis (1979) is the best known supporter of premise (2) (along with Chisholm 1981). DSAs are the fundamental psychological attitudes which "subsume the *de dicto*, but not vice versa" (Lewis 1979: 139). Lewis (1979: 156) explains that his analysis of belief *de re* is also "a reduction of *de re* generally to *de se*." Lewis is motivated by a desire to provide a uniform theory of intentional objects in terms of relations between subjects and *properties* (as opposed to 'propositions'). Only properties will suffice as the uniform objects of intentional states. For theoretical simplicity, if nothing else, we ought to desire a theory which always takes the same kind of thing as those objects. I will call this type of view the 'property theory.'

(I ask the reader to forgive me for the rather lengthy summary in the remainder of this section, but it is necessary to include for those who are not very familiar with Lewis' work and because much of it will be presupposed throughout the remainder of this chapter. Moreover, any briefer treatment would not have provided enough background for my specific critical purposes in sections 8.4 and 8.6.)

Lewis (1979: 135) understands a 'property' to be "a set: the set of exactly those possible beings, actual or not, that have the property in question." I am not particularly concerned with Lewis' terminology or the idiosyncracies of his metaphysics. We could treat a property as a universal which is, or can be, instantiated in various individuals while preserving the basic idea of the property theory. At any rate, Lewis' announced intention is to show that "sometimes property objects will do and propositional objects won't" (1979: 136) while properties will do whenever propositional objects will. He distinguishes DD attititudes from DR attitudes, and ultimately wants to show that both are parasitic upon DSAs. Let us look at Lewis' analysis of each to gain an overall picture.

Why does Lewis think that the *de se* subsumes the *de dicto*, but not vice versa? Precisely because properties, and not propositions, are best suited to be the objects of intentional attitudes. The standard view of belief content involves a relation between a subject and a proposition. Lewis tries to show that propositional objects will not do in cases where properties will. By a 'proposition' he (1979: 134) means "a set of possible worlds, a region of logical space" and so:

> ...to believe a proposition is to self-ascribe the corresponding property. The property that corresponds to a proposition is a locational property: it is the property that belongs to all and only the inhabitants of a certain region of logical space...To believe a proposition is to identify oneself as a member of a subpopulation comprising the inhabitants of the region of logical space where the proposition holds. (Lewis 1979: 137)

So to believe that snow is white is to self-ascribe the property 'being in or inhabiting a world where snow is white.' One thereby has a belief *about oneself*; namely, that one is inhabiting a world included in the set which just is the proposition that snow is white. The self-ascribed property corresponds to the proposition, and so property objects can always do the job that propositions have traditionally done.

Lewis then tries to establish that self-ascription of properties, and so DSAs are fundamental by showing that sometimes propositional objects cannot do the job where property objects can:

a. Lewis borrows Perry's (1977) tale of amnesic Rudolf Lingens lost in a library and who reads a biography of himself. He also reads a detailed account of the library in which he is lost. Lewis explains that this 'book learning' will only help Lingens locate himself in *logical* space, i.e. the more propositions he will come to believe and the more he will find out about the world he lives in. But:

> ...none of this, by itself, can guarantee that he knows where *in the world* he is. He needs to locate himself not only in logical space but also in ordinary space. (Lewis 1979: 138)

The idea is that locating oneself in logical space (i.e. in terms of propositions) is not fine-grained enough because it does not establish that Lingens knows who he is and where he is in the world. Lingens also needs to self-ascribe a property such as 'being in the fifth aisle on the sixth floor of the Main Library in Stanford' and this is one of the properties that does not correspond to a propositon.

This is somewhat similar to Perry's (1979) conclusion that the traditional doctrine of propositions is inadequate because it cannot accommodate essential indexicals (e.g. 'I am the one making the mess in the supermarket'). Sentences which contain them cannot identify or pick out a unique proposition because they do not have absolute truth-values. It is also always possible for a subject not to know that he* is the described subject if the description contains no indexical elements. Perry takes this to show that there is a "conceptual ingredient" which cannot be captured in the traditional doctrine of propositions. What is needed is a more 'fine-grained' way of individuating propositions *via* the missing conceptual ingredient. Perry's 'conceptual ingredient' is very much like a Fregean 'mode of presentation,' i.e. he becomes concerned with *the way* something is believed and not merely the object of belief. He speaks of "belief states" as opposed to "the believed object." Lewis, unlike Perry, takes such cases to establish that propositions are not the objects of intentional attitudes at all.

b. Lewis also uses the case of the two gods who are in the same world and know every true proposition at it. They are omniscient with respect to propositional knowledge. But still Lewis contends:

> I can imagine them to suffer ignorance: neither one knows which of the two he is. They are not exactly alike...But if it is possible to lack knowledge and not lack propositional knowledge, then the lacked knowledge must not be propositional. (1979: 139)

There is more to know for the gods, e.g. exactly which mountain they live on. But this is not propositional knowledge. We have a case of belief or knowledge that is irreducibly *de se* and it consists in the self-ascription of properties. Thus: if corresponding to each proposition there is some property *and* if propositional objects won't do where properties will, then we ought to treat properties as the uniform objects of intentional attitudes (and so treat DSAs as the fundamental intentional attitude). More specifically,

> ...all belief is 'self-locating' belief. Belief *de dicto* is locating belief with respect to logical space; belief irreducibly *de se* is self-locating belief at least partly with respect to ordinary time and space, or with respect to the population. (Lewis 1979: 140)

How does Lewis characterize *de re* attitudes (e.g. DR beliefs) given that he wants to treat all beliefs as involving a self-ascriptive relation between subjects and properties? The details of his treatment need not detain us. For our purposes, the key idea is that to assert 'X believes of a that it has F' is at least to assert that there is a state of affairs such that:

(a) X has a particular *de se* belief and so self-ascribes the property of bearing some relation R to something which has F; and
(b) X bears R uniquely to a.[62]

R is understood as a relation of acquaintance, under some description, that X bears to a. Lewis' final proposal includes a causal restriction on R, i.e. R involves some causal link between X and a. He explains that "I and the one of whom I have beliefs *de re* are so related that there is an extensive causal dependence of my states upon [the properties of the objects of my belief.]" (Lewis 1979: 155). DR attitudes involve a DSA plus a causal relation.

So Lewis thinks that DSAs are essential to DR attitudes. This is perhaps a more modest way of phrasing his position since he sometimes speaks of *reducing* the latter to the former. It might be true that:

> ...other-ascription of properties are not further beliefs alongside the self-ascription, but rather are states of affairs that obtain partly in virtue of the subject's self-ascriptions and partly in virtue of facts not about his attitudes. (Lewis 1979: 156)

But I am not sure this warrants Lewis' (1979: 157) later claim that "beliefs *de re* are not really beliefs." In any case, we can understand DR beliefs as a *de se* belief and a causal relation. The main point in terms of premise (2) is that *if* Lewis is right, then having any intentional attitude entails having the relevant DSA as well.

One reason that Lewis holds this view is that self-ascription is not the same as *de re* ascription to oneself (*pace* Boer/Lycan 1980). He contends that "belief *de re* about oneself turns out to cover more than self-ascription of properties." (1979: 156) Suppose I watch myself in a mirror unaware that I am watching myself. Watching is a relation of acquaintance. I may *ascribe to myself* the property of 'wearing pants that are on fire' under the description 'the one that I am watching' without *self-ascribing* that property. I have a DR belief about someone (who is in fact myself) under one description but who I do not realize is myself. I believe *de re* of the one I am watching that his pants are on fire. But I have that belief in virtue of self-ascribing the property of wearing pants under the description 'the one I am watching' and *not* under the description 'person identical with me' or 'myself.' So it seems that some cases of DR belief about oneself (i.e. when a=X) do not involve the special 'identity' relation of acquaintance that a subject can bear to himself.

Let us briefly look at Lewis' account of desires as well.[63] He (1979: 145) thinks that "desire *de se* subsumes desire *de dicto*, but not vice versa." I will not summarize Lewis' parallel arguments here. Suffice it to say that a DD desire can be understood as a relation between a subject and a property that one desires to have. Having a desire that cyanoacrylate dissolves in acetone is desiring to have the property of 'inhabiting a world where cyanoacrylate dissolves in acetone.' The subject presumably desires to be in a world which is a member of the set of worlds, which, in turn, is the proposition in question. However, many desires cannot be adequately explained merely in terms of wants to inhabit *some world or other* satisfying a given condition. Some involve, in a more fine-grained way, the more specific want to have a property which *only some of the inhabitants of a world possess.*

How does, for example, Lewis handle DR desires directed at particular and present objects? Presumably we can construe the typical form of a DR desire to be:

X wants or desires of a that it have F.

The analysis would then include X self-ascribing the property of bearing R to something which has F. A person might want his dog to stop making a noise. This at least involves him self-ascribing the property 'being related to a dog who is *not* making noise.' The person wants *himself* to be related to a particular submember of a set in a given world population with the property 'not making noise.' For Lewis, the set just is that property. (R presumably also has some kind of causal restriction placed on it.)

What about the case where a=X? What about cases where the subject wants himself to have some property? Suppose a cat wants to eat some food. Presumably Lewis would say that the cat self-ascribes the property 'being a member of the set of (actual or possible) creatures that are currently eating some food.' This is what it is for the cat to desire to eat some food. The cat, in effect, wants itself to be a member of the 'food eating' set. This certainly sounds odd as an account of what having such desires amounts to, but this is where Lewis' analysis leads us.

Lewis contends that similar analyses can be done for the other intentional attitudes, i.e. whenever one has a particular DR or DD attitude one must have the corresponding *de se* attitude. The key idea is that when one has an intentional state about something one will also have a state of that kind directed at oneself. For example, having a thought about a tree entails having a thought about oneself being related to that tree. In section 8.5 I will offer independent support for this view, but first we need to critique Lewis' notion of 'self-ascription'.

8.4 Three Kinds of Self-Ascription

Lewis' view is implausible as a *psychological theory* about what it is to have various intentional attitudes (i.e. as what is going on in one's mind). Some philosophers seem to recognize this, but my aim is to show more clearly why it is so and why Lewis does not gain any significant advantage over his opponents.

One kind of self-ascription is a conscious one. But, of course, this could not be required for self-ascription in general or for the property theory. When one self-ascribes a property one need not do so consciously.[64] I now have a belief that my computer is grey. On Lewis' account, this at least involves self-ascribing the property 'being in a world which has a grey computer' and having a unique causal relation to my particular one. There is no reason to suppose that I have this belief only when I am consciously aware of such self-ascription. (This goes for both DD and DR attitudes.) One can have intentional attitudes prior to a conscious grasp of them or of any self-ascription of properties. Surely I do not consciously self-ascribe properties whenever I have an intentional state. Otherwise we would also unjustly rule out the possibility of many lower animals having intentional states. Some creatures are clearly incapable of any sophisticated conscious self-ascribing while capable of having intentional states. It is interesting how Lewis' arguments always center around human (and even 'divine') examples of believing, knowing, and desiring. Moreover, if a system can have some intentional states without consciousness at all (i.e. if MEC11 in section 5.3 is false), then intentionality cannot essentially involve conscious self-ascription. As a HOT theorist we might say: A system can have first-order intentional states (conscious or not) without introspecting them, i.e. without having conscious second-order thoughts about them.

If this point is missed, then one is led astray as to even the initial plausibility of the property theory. Markie (1983) does not properly distinguish conscious from nonconscious self-ascription. He criticizes the property theory precisely on the grounds that "surely we can adopt *de dicto* attitudes without being actively aware of ourselves" (1983: 234). Presumably, by 'being actively aware of oneself' he means the kind of conscious self-awareness which could *not* be required by the theory. He seems to have in mind higher-order conscious thoughts, i.e. introspective awareness. If he realized that the property theory did not require conscious self-ascription, then he could not criticize it on the grounds that we do not always have such awareness while 'believing' or 'considering' some p. Markie is primarily addressing Chisholm's views, but surely no property theorist should require conscious self-ascription.

What then *is* involved in the self-ascription of properties? The natural alternative is that it is *nonconscious*. But there is a problem here as well. When we attribute nonconscious states to a system we often presuppose that it can grasp the concepts which figure into them. For example, it is unreasonable to attribute to a five-year-old child the nonconscious thought that her toys are made up of electrons and other subatomic particles. The child does not possess the relevant concepts. Perhaps what best explains our unwillingness to do so is her inability to have the corresponding *conscious* thought (cf. MEC12 in chapter five). In any case, the same should hold for Lewis' self-ascribed properties especially given the rather sophisticated concepts involved. Does the child merely *nonconsciously* self-ascribe 'being in a world where she is related to a toy which is F' (for *any* 'F')? It is not clear that this is what the child even nonconsciously does in the way, for example, that she might nonconsciously resent her mother for not letting her stay up late. For one thing, she may not have many of the F-concepts that figure into the self-ascribed property. Secondly, she certainly does not have the concept of a possible (or even actual) world in the philosopher's sense. Very few of us do. So why suppose that she nonconsciously self-ascribes properties which contain reference to concepts well beyond her cognitive grasp? I see no reason. Moreover, if various lower animals have intentional attitudes, then they also cannot nonconsciously self-ascribe such sophisticated properties. It is difficult to make sense of the idea that a cat has nonconscious attitudes involving properties like 'being a member of the set of (actual or possible) creatures that are currently eating some food.'

One might object that more standard accounts suffer from a similar difficulty and so Lewis is not really worse off. But that is not quite right. Consider the more common view that intentional states involve a relation between a subject and a proposition (see e.g. Stalnaker 1987). While this 'propositional theory,' as I will call it, does have its own problems, it does not face the above worry because it does not require the subject to have the sophisticated concepts involved in the Lewisian self-ascription of properties (e.g. concepts of 'worlds' and 'actual or possible creatures'). The subject is only required *to stand in the appropriate relation* to the proposition, which can be achieved without having the concept of a possible world or the concept of a possible object. For example, one might ascribe intentional attitudes to a system on the basis of its (non-verbal and/or verbal) behavior and its interaction with objects in its environment. One might come to stand in relation to a proposition in virtue of one's dispositions to behave in certain ways in the presence of varied stimuli.

In any case, the propositional theory does not require that the intentional system have such sophisticated concepts. It only requires that one have the concepts involved in the content of the intentional attitude. One can be related to something without having all of the concepts that might be associated with it upon philosophical reflection. The five-year-old can have beliefs without (consciously or unconsciously) having the concept of a possible object or world. However, the same does not hold on Lewis' account because *self-ascribing* a property seems to require that the subject be able to grasp the concepts mentioned in the property name. Ascribing a property to myself requires having the concepts involved in the ascription. Of course, many propositional theorists also further characterize propositions in terms of possible worlds (e.g. as functions from possible worlds to truth-values), but it does not follow that anyone who has an intentional state directed at a proposition must also grasp the concepts involved in the analysis. In contrast, Lewis' account does imply that any intentional system grasp the concepts it self-ascribes.

Recall also that Lewis understands propositions simply to be sets of possible worlds. Of course, the propositional theorist need not even adopt this characterization of a possible world, but, even if she did, she would still not be forced to hold that one has the concept of a possible world simply in virtue of standing in relation to a proposition. Furthermore, it is worth mentioning that some hold a sharply contrasting view: rather than understanding propositions as sets of possible worlds (as Lewis does); possible worlds are construed as (maximal) sets of propositions. Possible worlds are understood in terms of propositions, not vice versa (see e.g. Adams 1979 and Lycan 1979).

At minimum, the problem is that talk of 'self-ascribing' is very misleading. At worst, Lewis gains no advantage over his opponent in using such a locution in his strategy. The connotation is that the system *does something* or has some further cognitive state when self-ascribing properties. This, in turn, requires that the subject have the concepts involved in such properties. This seems mistaken and helps to explain one's almost natural initial dissatisfaction with Lewis' analysis. There is really no *self*-ascribing of Lewisian properties when one has an intentional attitude. Lewis might reply that he is not concerned with offering a theory that accommodates the psychological facts. He is not doing psychology here, but rather is providing a theory which has the advantage of theoretical uniformity regarding intentional objects. At this point, we should seriously question whether such simplicity is not gained at the expense of greater complexities and difficulties elsewhere (especially given Lewis' rather idiosyncratic ontological views). It is surely more important to have a theory of intentionality that answers to the psychological facts, even if it does not result in uniform objects of intentional attitudes.

Perhaps Lewis can jettison all talk of 'self-ascription' while preserving his main thesis that propositions are not the objects of intentional attitudes. We might even acknowledge that Lewisian properties are *true of* intentional systems. Certain complex properties might be true of intentional systems from, as it were, a third-person and philosophically sensitive point of view. *We* can analyze what it is for another to have intentional states in terms of Lewis' properties and possible worlds, but there is really no *self*-ascribing going on at all. The cat and the child only come *to have* these properties, but not in virtue of any 'ascribing' on their part. Perhaps we can call it 'implicit' self-ascription, but for the reasons given it is not appropriate to think of it as 'self-ascription' at all. When one has an intentional attitude, one will implicitly come to have other related properties (e.g. 'being in a world such that ...'), but Lewis has built so much into the relevant properties that speaking of 'self-ascribing' them belies the proper use of that term. We cannot require that intentional systems consciously or nonconsciously self-ascribe such properties. Lewis then needs to explain, like the propositional theorist, how intentional states acquire their content and in virtue of what the cat and child *do* come to have such properties. His answer ultimately echoes the one offered by most propositional theorists; namely, that in order to individuate most intentional states and propositions in a sufficiently fine-grained way, we must make some reference to the subject's inner mode of presentation (e.g. Perry's 'belief states'). Nothing useful is gained by Lewis' somewhat dramatic and eccentric notion of 'self-ascription.'

Where does that leave us? It shows that mere Lewisian considerations will not help us prove the soundness of *De Se*. For one thing, premise (3) looks to be in serious danger because 'self-ascribing,' by itself, cannot carry with it connotations of self-consciousness. However, a key Kantian idea can still be preserved (and seems to be a consequence of Lewis' view); namely, that when one has an intentional state one will thereby have the corresponding DSA. Intentionality might, in the end, presuppose DSAs. This is the crux of premise (2) and can still be maintained without adopting the entire Lewisian account involving 'self-ascribing' sophisticated properties.

8.5 More on Premise Two

What other support might one adduce for premise (2)? As we saw in section 4.5, the general idea has important historical roots in Kant who argued that the conscious self is implicitly represented in the structure of experience. When one has conscious thoughts about external objects one must also implicitly have thoughts of the form 'that object seems to *me* to be such-and-such.' One cannot just think about a tree without thinking of oneself as related to that tree. At minimum, conscious experience involves being able to differentiate oneself from the outer world. The key point is that a conscious being must have implicit thoughts about himself if he is to take his experience to be of an objective world. Such *de se* thoughts are therefore presupposed in conscious experience itself and implied by having conscious perceptual states.

A similar claim ought to be true of at least beliefs and desires. Does having them entail having the corresponding DSA? Let us suppose that a squirrel has certain primitive DR beliefs and desires. For example, it might believe of the tree in front of it that it has nuts. Mustn't the squirrel then also have the corresponding *de se* belief, i.e. believe of itself that it is related to a tree with nuts? It seems reasonable to suppose that it must at least be able to locate itself with respect to the tree, and so also have that belief about itself. The squirrel not only believes that 'there is a tree here now with nuts' but also that 'there is a tree here now with nuts *in front of me* which *I* am now perceiving.' At minimum, the squirrel must believe that it* stands in a unique spatial relation to the tree. This *de se* belief must be one of the squirrel's psychological states because it helps explain its behavior and motivation in certain contexts (cf. Perry 1979). Some of its dispositions to behave are best explained *via* the attribution of these *de se* attitudes. Furthermore, consider again the so-called 'belief-desire-behavior' triangle and its role in psychological explanation. If our squirrel has the above belief, then it will also have desires (e.g. some directed at the tree). But it also seems that having other-directed desires will ultimately involve having implicit *de se* desires as well. The squirrel does not merely want some nuts from the tree to eat, but it wants *itself* to have and eat those nuts. In Lewisian terms, it wants itself to have a property which it presently lacks. This much seems right even if we do not accept other aspects of Lewis' account. We therefore should remain quite sympathetic to the idea that having intentional attitudes presupposes having the corresponding DSA.

8.6 *De Se* Attitudes and Consciousness

In this section I wish to explore an inconsistent triad. Each claim seems to be held by supporters of the property theory. The focus will be on the centrality of consciousness in the *de se* literature. On the one hand, there seems to be ineliminable reference to "missing conceptual ingredients," "belief states," "cognitive significance," and Fregean "modes of presentation." On the other hand, it is unclear whether those same philosophers believe that merely having intentional attitudes requires consciousness. Thus, let us explore the following inconsistent triad:

(A) Having beliefs and desires need not require consciousness.
(B) Possession of beliefs and desires requires possession of DSAs.
(C) Having DSAs ultimately involves reference to consciousness.

We have already seen some support for all of these claims, especially A and B. Chapter five was devoted to the question of whether mentality requires consciousness. We saw that A is plausible and there is little reason to think that Lewis would deny it. We have also seen reason to accept B (especially in sections 8.3 and 8.5). I have hinted at C throughout, but it is time to make its plausibility more explicit. I will then explore various ways to escape the inconsistency.

Lewis and Perry often refer to consciousness in giving an account of irreducible DSAs. In his 'two gods' case, Lewis acknowledges the Nagel-like claim that all of the objective propositional knowledge does not exhaust one's entire body of knowledge. We seem to have Nagelian 'subjective facts' entering the picture. As McMullen (1985) argues, there is also an interesting similarity between the Nagel-Jackson worries and Perry's 'shopper case,' i.e. they both involve essential reference to indexicals and demonstratives. Moreover, the 'burning pants/mirror' case involves reference to 'belief states' and 'missing conceptual ingredients.' It is natural to construe such cognitive states as involving some conscious mental abilities. Similarly, crucial to Lewis' analysis of DR attitudes is that the relation R must be taken *under some suitable description* (e.g. 'the one I am watching'). This theme is so prominent in the property theory that Davidson (1985: 397) has understandably suggested that:

> ...statements of the form 'X believes of a that it has [F]' are elliptical: when fully stated they read 'X believes of a under description, D, that it has [F].'

This much seems right, and therefore *de se* beliefs will be "those beliefs a person holds, of themselves, under a particular relation, namely identity." (Davidson 1985: 398) Irreducibly *de se* beliefs are those beliefs about oneself which involve the special 'identity' relation of acquaintance that a subject may bear to himself. X believes something of himself under the description 'person identical with me.'

This theme is closely related to the issue of referential opacity. It is commonly thought that beliefs and DSAs cannot be individuated in a referentially transparent way, i.e. sameness of reference will not guarantee sameness of intentional content and truth-value. On the *de se* side, the idea is that the following are not equivalent:

(a) X believes of X that he has F.
(b) X believes of he* that he has F.

They are not equivalent because the truth of (a) does not guarantee the truth of (b). The knowledge or belief in question can come under different descriptions, e.g. in the mirror or amnesic cases. Perry argues that they are inequivalent on the grounds that they differ in explanatory power. *De se* beliefs are not equivalent to DR beliefs about oneself because the former can fill a role in explaining behavior that the latter cannot.[65] My point here is simply to echo Davidson (1985: 398) that we do not "have *de re* beliefs of individuals *simpliciter*, but of individuals under certain descriptions." He rightly incorporates the 'described as' or 'under some description' clause into his formal characterization of DR belief. In chapter five, we acknowledged that intentionality generally requires opacity. But then it may be objected that one way to distinguish *de re* from *de dicto* beliefs is precisely that the former can be specified or attributed in a referentially transparent way, i.e. in a way that makes no commitment as to how the believer conceptualizes the object of belief. On this account, *de re* belief does not require opacity. There may be good pragmatic reasons for such a method in certain contexts. However, even though it may be possible to attribute DR beliefs in such a way, it is still not possible for the believer to *have a belief* about an object x without conceptualizing x in some way or other, i.e. without taking it 'under some description'.[66]

A natural way to cash out the 'described as' clause is in terms of conscious cognitive capacities, e.g. in the way that one who holds having beliefs requires consciousness might urge. It can be filled in with belief states or missing conceptual ingredients (Perry) or with Nagel-like subjective facts (Lewis). Noticing the connection between essential indexicals and 'knowing what it's like,' McMullen (1985: 230) suggests that such clauses represent the "*cognitive significance* of a referring expression" which "consists in the ideas which the speaker associates with the expression. Ideas can be descriptions, various kinds of perceptual images, memories, etc." This clearly suggests Fregean "modes of presentation" and "conceptual points of view." Systems must take the objects of their intentional attitudes in a certain way. They must *seem* some way *to the subject*, i.e. *qua* something or other.[67]

This should suffice as *prima facie* support for C, and the inconsistency involved in A-C should be clear. If DSAs require reference to consciousness and having any intentional attitude entails having DSAs, then A must be false. Attributions of beliefs and desires would then ultimately involve reference to consciousness. If B and C are true, then A is false. On the other hand, if A is true, then one must deny either B or C (or both). One cannot hold both that mentality does not require consciousness and that DSAs do require consciousness (provided that one accepts the link between intentional attitudes and DSAs). How might one escape this inconsistency?

First option: One could give up A and continue to hold B and C. That is, perhaps mentality *does* require consciousness and, in particular, having any intentional state involves a conceptual point of view which incorporates varying modes of presentation. The subject of a belief must be able to think about the objects referred to in its content under different aspects (cf. Searle 1989). But I have argued at length in chapter five that this is not the most promising option, i.e. all of the 'belief interpretations' in 5.2 of 'mentality requires consciousness' are false. Intentionality need not require consciousness or a subjective point of view. Thus, let us consider a second option.

Second option: One could continue to maintain A and B, and give up C. Those who are at all sympathetic with the tone of chapter five might find this position attractive. It would not be true that a proper analysis of DSAs *must* ultimately involve reference to consciousness. For example, *de se* beliefs (DSBs) are one kind of DSA and, for the reasons given in chapter five, it is not clear that they require consciousness even if other kinds of DSAs do. So even if having *de se thoughts* (DSTs) require consciousness (see MEC12), that is not enough to render C true because other DSAs do not. Just as having first-order beliefs do not require consciousness, so having DSBs do not. A system might have beliefs about itself and not even be conscious at all (e.g. Robo from chapter seven, or Rey's imagined system).

Unfortunately, Davidson and McMullen do not explain the strength of their claims. They do not indicate, for example, whether *any* belief must be a belief under some description involving consciousness or just many of the one's *we* have. I suspect that they are caught up in simply analyzing *human* intentionality and are not concerned with the modal question of whether consciousness is necessary for mentality. Similarly, Lewis and Perry only use sophisticated conscious creatures in their arguments. But we should wonder what must be involved in the so-called 'described as' clause. We can agree that DSAs (and *de re* attitudes) must include some such clause, but deny that they *must always* involve reference to consciousness (e.g. McMullen's perceptual images and memories). Consciousness is not always required to fill in the 'described-as' clause. 'Under different descriptions' need not always mean 'under different modes of presentation.' Robo might, for example, have DSBs under different descriptions without supposing that each involves a different way that he consciously thinks of, or 'subjectively views,' himself. They might include 'the one from Info,' 'the one who came to this planet,' 'the one being examined by the scientist' and even 'the one identical with me.' Its behavior might be such that its beliefs about itself are best interpreted as incorporating any of these different descriptions. Thus, we can deny C and even still hold that DSTs can only be had by creatures capable of conscious thoughts and a subjective point of view.

The *third option* would be simply to give up B. It leaves room for the idea that even if all DSAs require consciousness, they are still not necessary for having intentional attitudes directed at other things. That is, one might hold that DSAs require consciousness while intentional attitudes do not by denying the key link between them. This would be to take issue with the Lewisian arguments presented in 8.3, the discussion of section 8.5 and some of the Kantian views put forth. This option directly denies premise (2) of the *De Se* argument. I do not wish to defend further that premise at this point. I think it is true for reasons already given, and my aim in this chapter is primarily to show how *if* Lewis is right then there is another important connection between consciousness and self-consciousness. Moreover, if one already holds that DSAs require consciousness (i.e. C is true), then one will likely believe that DR attitudes also do since the former are often treated as a special case of the latter.

I think that the second option is the most promising. We ought to give up the strong claim in C, i.e. consciousness is necessary for having *any* DSA. But our discussion has therefore been damaging to premise (3) of the *De Se* argument. Not just any DSA will entail self-consciousness, e.g. merely having DSBs will not. Meta-psychological *thoughts* are required, and so premise (3) looks false as it stands. What is needed is to restrict premise (3) to *de se* thoughts (DSTs). But doing so causes a ripple effect back through the first two premises. Consider the following alternative argument which we can call *De Se**:

(1*) Being a conscious system entails having conscious thoughts.
(2*) Having conscious thoughts entails having DSTs.
(3*) Having DSTs entails self-consciousness.

Therefore,

(4) Being a conscious system entails self-consciousness.

*De Se** has the advantage of a more plausible third premise. It also has a second premise which better captures the Kantian spirit on the issue. Premise (1*) is just as plausible as the first premise of *De Se*. However, there have been three good dialectical reasons for initially using the *De Se* formulation.

First, many interesting aspects of the property theory would no longer apply if I ignored the 'non-thought' intentional attitudes. Lewis, for example, focuses on beliefs and desires. Questions about the relations *amongst* the different attitudes are lost in *De Se**.

Second, if consciousness is built right into the first two premises, then (on my view) self-consciousness immediately emerges and the need for premise (3) is all but eliminated. It is far more interesting (at this point) to ask whether having certain intentional attitudes requires consciousness *via* a continuing discussion of whether 'mentality requires consciousness.' Premise (1) in *De Se* brings the issue below the level of consciousness and then the task is to see whether it can be brought back up to self-consciousness. In doing so, we were able to explore the inconsistent triad in this section.

Third, the most interesting aspect of *De Se** still remains from the original *De Se* argument; namely, whether having one type of DSA (DSTs) requires self-consciousness. While (3*) is *prima facie* more plausible than premise (3) in *De Se*, it is still perhaps not obviously true and needs further clarification. (3*) is a restricted version of premise (3) and is the focus of the next section.

8.7 *De Se* Thoughts and Self-Consciousness

Recall my view that self-consciousness consists in having meta-psychological thoughts. Two conditions need to be met: (a) the state must be *meta-psychological* (see section 2.2), and (b) it must be a *thought* of the right kind as described in chapters three and four. Merely having a DSA does not entail having a DST and so we have moved to the more specific premise (3*). Let us grant that condition (b) is met. Two key questions still remain: (1) Why does (a) need to be met? That is, why must the thought be meta-psychological to count as self-consciousness? (2) Does even having DSTs entail meta-psychological thoughts?

1. Throughout this chapter I have spoken of 'thoughts about oneself.' But perhaps this involves nothing more than thoughts *about one's body or bodily states*. For example, the Kantian style of defending premise (2) seemed only to stress being able to 'differentiate oneself from other things.' Perhaps this can be accomplished by simply having thoughts about one's physical body in contrast to other physical objects in the environment. Moreover, I have allowed 'I *qua* this body or physical thing' to be a degenerate kind of self-concept (see section 4.5). So one question is: why isn't such a 'thought about body' good enough for self-consciousness? Why must it be meta-*psychological*? I now offer two reasons: the first is ontological and the second is epistemological.

a. The first touches on the problem of personal identity. Importantly related questions are: What is the self? What does identity over time consist in? How can we re-identify the self over time? It is not my aim here to review the literature, nor is it to explore in detail the options on this vexed topic.[68] My point here is that it seems reasonable to most philosophers to tie personal identity in with some complex entity involving *mental states* and their relations to each other (as opposed to some kind of 'bodily continuity'). I cannot argue for my preference here though I will say that continuity, and various other relations, amongst mental states seem better to approximate our intuitions about the nature of the self (if anything does). Thus, if the self is closely tied to mentality in any significant way, then *self*-consciousness must be meta-psychological. It must involve some kind of awareness of oneself *qua* owner of mental states. If self-consciousness is awareness *of oneself* or of some feature of oneself, then it at least must involve a meta-psychological or higher-order aspect. Some philosophers even urge that some kind of brain continuity is necessary and sufficient for personal identity (Wiggins 1967, Mackie 1976 and Nagel 1986). This may be so and is a somewhat different view of personal identity. Indeed, I am sympathetic with this position, but if mental states are brain states, then the above point holds provided that the meta-psychological states are within, and directed at events in, the same persisting brain.

b. I do not think that we (or any creature) are infallible with respect to self-knowledge. However, there is still a significant difference between the epistemic access to our mental states and bodily knowledge. This is widely acknowledged and various examples in the *de se* literature even serve to illustrate it (e.g. the 'mirror case'). It is difficult to make sense of parallel cases with respect to knowledge of our own mental states. One may not have infallibility with respect to the *contents* of one's own mind, but when one has a mental state one thereby knows that it *is* one's own mental state. Perhaps one just *presupposes* that it is one's own, but this is further evidence for the epistemic immediacy enjoyed with respect to one's own mental states. We can say with Shoemaker (1968: 8) that there is a use of 'I' which is "...immune to error through misidentification." Nothing could apparently count as evidence that a given experienced mental state is not one's own. When we speak of self-consciousness we have in mind this kind of epistemic priority or immediacy, which can be lacking in having 'thoughts about body' (see "The Man Who Fell out of Bed" in Sacks 1987).

One might object that in abnormal cases (e.g. split personality) one can even have a thought about a mental state, and yet not take it as one's own.

Moreover, it seems possible for there to be creatures which regularly have meta-psychological thoughts *about another's mental states*. Such creatures might have developed a sophisticated system of telepathic communication. The problem would then be that one could have meta-psychological thoughts which do *not* entail *self*-consciousness. I am not convinced that such cases spell trouble for premise (3*). For one thing, if such thoughts are not 'about oneself' to begin with, then they are not properly *de se* attitudes at all. Premise (3*) only says that having DSTs entails self-consciousness, not that having any meta-psychological thought does. We need not hold that every meta-psychological thought is a *de se* thought. Moreover, it would seem that if a subject could have such thoughts about another's mental states, then he also must have some directed at his own mental states. It is difficult to make coherent the idea of a creature with intimate meta-psychological thoughts directed *only* at another's mental states. There must be something about those states which indicates to the subject that they are not one's own as opposed to when they are. Something must serve to differentiate those mental states from one's own, i.e. one must take some of the mental states to be one's own if one is to know that some are not one's own. At the least, some genuine thoughts about oneself seem presupposed in having meta-psychological thoughts at all.

2. Let us turn to the second question: Does having DSTs entail having meta-psychological thoughts? Could the DSTs just be about one's own body? If so, then they do not entail self-consciousness. Recall that DSTs do not require that the constitutive concepts be very sophisticated. One might again urge that they need only differentiate one's body from other things. A pigeon might only be capable of this kind of self-concept. DSTs are 'indexical' but perhaps they need not contain reference to mental states at all.

We might (with Davis 1989) use Strawson's (1959) notions of 'M' and 'P' predicates to describe different types of self-concepts which can figure into DSTs. M-predicates pick out material characteristics. They are those predicates that apply to material bodies to which we would not ascribe states of consciousness. P-predicates pick out psychological characteristics and are those which ascribe states of consciouness, or which "...imply the possession of consciousness on the part of that to which they are ascribed" (Strawson 1959: 105). As we saw in section 4.5, some of the experiments designed to test an animal's ability to recognize itself in a mirror leave open whether they are capable of anything more than the application of M-concepts (see also Gallup 1975, Premack and Woodruff 1978, Epstein et al. 1980, Bennett 1988 and especially Davis 1989). This suggests the possibility that some creatures have DSTs which contain no P-concepts and, if this is so, then merely having DSTs would not imply self-consciousness. Meta-psychological capacities do not seem *to follow* from merely having DSTs. If so, then even premise (3*) of *De Se** is false because having DSTs does not imply self-consciousness. Perhaps we cannot *prove* (3*) to be true, but a good deal can be said in an attempt to save it.

First of all, Davis (1989: 255) rightly notes that only grasping M-characteristics "..does not entail being *un*aware of one's own thinking and other psychological states." But it also does not seem that having M-concepts entails having P-concepts. For example, the pigeon will not think of its mental states *qua* its own. But if it is able to think of (or be aware of) its own mental states at all, then it must be capable of having *some kinds of P-concepts*. It need not have concepts of *types* of mental states, but it would still have at least some rudimentary P-concepts. The real issue is whether there could be a creature with DSTs who is utterly incapable of possessing P-concepts. Perhaps awareness of one's own mental states does not deductively follow from a creature having DSTs, but it is difficult to imagine one capable of 'thoughts about other things' and 'thoughts about its body' without meta-psychological awareness at all. It is, for example, not obvious that very many M-concepts are somehow easier to grasp or acquire than every P-concept. Moreover, it is difficult to imagine a scenario in which both types of concepts are not used in tandem in the development of a species.

Second, there is the Kantian reason to hold that any creature capable of thoughts *about external objects* must also be able to have at least some primitive thoughts *about its mental states*, i.e. having thoughts about oneself involves more than just 'thoughts about body.' In order to have thoughts about external objects one must be able to differentiate them from oneself, but 'oneself' must also include one's *mental states*. Having objective concepts presupposes an implicit grasp of the objective/subjective contrast. Part of grasping this contrast is realizing that the objects in question are to be distinguished from one's fleeting subjective (i.e. mental) states. Having objective experience presupposes grasping that the objects 'seem,' 'appear,' or 'look' to me to be a certain way. This shows that applying M-predicates to the external world implies applying P-predicates and so a higher-order understanding of mental states. Having concepts such as 'appearing' and 'seeming' surely imply having some P-concepts. The pigeon (and any creature capable of conscious experience) must not only distinguish its body from external objects, but also its mental states from the objects they represent. If it did not, then it would treat the enduring objects of experience as merely momentary subjective mental states which, in turn, would make objective experience impossible.[69] It seems, then, that having DSTs will ultimately involve the application of P-concepts and therefore self-consciousness. A conscious system cannot just apply M-concepts to external objects and its own body. Premise (3*) does then seem true and so *De Se** is sound.

CHAPTER 9

The Memory Argument

9.1 The Argument and Varieties of Memory

My aim in this chapter is to argue that consciousness entails self-consciousness *via* an examination of episodic memory. In establishing this thesis I am concerned with the following questions: (1) Does consciousness require episodic memory? and (2) Does episodic memory require self-consciousness? To answer them I will draw both on recent developments in memory research and some familiar Kantian theses. To argue for the main thesis I utilize the 'MEMORY argument,' as I will call it, which incorporates answers to the above questions:

(1) Being a conscious system entails having episodic memory.
(2) Having episodic memory entails being self-conscious.

Therefore,

(3) Being a conscious system entails being self-conscious.

It is hardly necessary to mention that the MEMORY argument is valid since it is merely an instance of a hypothetical syllogism. What is at issue can only be the truth of the premises. This section includes a glimpse of the empirical literature on memory and distinguishes episodic memory from other types of memory. Section 9.2 argues for the truth of premise (1). In section 9.3, I demonstrate the plausibility of premise (2).

Memory is often divided into two types: procedural and declarative (Tulving 1983, Squire 1987 and Roediger *et. al.* 1989). This roughly coincides with the classic distinction between *knowing how*, i.e. interacting with the environment in ways difficult to verbalize or put in terms of explicit rules, and *knowing that*, i.e. having some kind of propositional knowledge (see Ryle 1949: chapter two). Declarative memory subdivides further into episodic memory and semantic memory. *Semantic memory* involves knowing that a given fact is true, knowing what a particular object is and does, knowing what the capital of France is, etc. *Episodic memory* is a more personal type of remembering and at least involves awareness of a particular past event in one's life. It is sometimes called 'autobiographical memory'.

Many different types of procedural memory have also been distinguished. Among them are memory of skills and priming. One can know how to play the piano or use a computer and thus have memory of various learned *skills*. Furthermore, one's existing response predispositions can be systematically biased on the basis of previous experiences (which need not themselves be consciously available to the subject). This is *repetition priming* which involves the facilitation in the processing of a stimulus as a result of a recent encounter with it. The tests most often used in priming research are lexical decision, word identification, and fragment completion.

One motivation for distinguishing types of memory in this way results from the plethora of dissociations discovered among many of them (Ellis and Young 1988: chapter ten; Weiskrantz 1988; Roediger and Craik 1989). For example, various amnesic patients do quite well in some procedural tasks (e.g. mirror-writing and maze learning) despite performing very poorly on declarative tests such as recall or recognition. They know *how* to do something *via* repeated exposure to a task without remembering *that* they have learned it. There are also cases of retaining an ability for skill *acquisition* in the absence of episodic memory. Many investigators have inferred from this that multiple memory storage systems exist in humans, although others have grave reservations about the validity of such inferences (Ellis and Young 1988, Kinsbourne 1989 and Neely 1989). Procedural memory and especially priming are typically construed as a kind of 'implicit' memory. (See Schacter 1987 and 1989 for excellent summaries on implicit memory. The implicit-explicit distinction seems roughly to coincide with the procedural-episodic division.)

My emphasis is on episodic memory because it is the type of memory which could make premise (2) true. Procedural memory, for example, is not a candidate for the MEMORY argument because it would render premise (2) false. A premise that reads 'procedural memory entails self-consciousness' is not even *prima facie* plausible. Procedural memory can occur with high efficiency without consciousness at all (not to mention self-consciousness). Thus, no form of procedural memory could be sufficient for self-consciousness.

Episodic memory has been defined and described in various ways. For example, Tulving (1983) held that autobiographical memories are recollections of specific personal experiences and requires that the subject consciously recollect the temporal-spatial context in which he or she previously experienced an event. The idea is that in having an episodic memory one thereby knows where and when the episode initially occurred. No doubt this occurs in some cases, but it is a much too strong criterion. One clearly need not remember the precise temporal-spatial context of an event in order to have an episodic memory. For example, I might episodically remember seeing an old friend without remembering exactly when or where it was. I might recall having a smell sensation without knowing where or when I experienced it. These kinds of examples abound and so it is unnecessary to build such a stringent spatial and temporal restriction into the very definition of episodic memory. We often have episodic memories without being able to date or locate them. We must acknowledge this if we are even to explore the possibility that various animals can have episodic memories. Placing Tulving's strong condition on them unnecessarily biases the case against animals since they are less able to grasp sophisticated spatial and temporal concepts.

However, we still need a modest type of temporal restriction; namely, that the event or episode is simply remembered as occurring in the past. If a conscious mental state is to be an episodic memory, then the subject must (at least nonconsciously) take it as representing something in the past. One must apply the concept of 'pastness' to that state, since one does not take it as representing some present or future state of affairs. In order to have an episodic memory one must take that episode as representing something in the past. This can be shown by the following cases:

1. Consider a person, Jane, who has just fallen asleep (or is even just daydreaming). Her husband wakes her up when he returns from work and she explains to him that she had a very strange dream. It involved having visual images of many different smiling faces. She did not recognize any of them and thought that the dream was very strange. Jane is later looking through a family album and it turns out that one of the smiling faces in her dream very closely resembled her Aunt Mildred whom she had met only once as a small child. It would be odd suddenly to treat the visual image *as it occurred during her dream* as a case of 'remembering Aunt Mildred.' Jane had a series of fleeting visual images which were not cases of remembering. If one of the other faces turned out to resemble a woman who baby sat her as a child,

should we say that that image too was a case of episodically remembering? I think not. Having a present image of a past event is not sufficient for having an episodic memory. One must view oneself as temporally related to that event. What is missing in Jane's case is her taking the visual image to represent some past state of affairs. She did not take herself to be in a state which represented a past experience.

2. Consider Mary who thinks of herself as a clairvoyant or at least as having some psychic powers. Mary is often used by the police to help them solve crimes even though her talents are not acknowledged by everyone. She often has visions which tell her that something horrible is happening elsewhere or will happen in the future. One day she has a vision of a lady being brutally stabbed by a man wearing a stocking over his face. Mary calls the police to warn them because she thinks that such a crime is about to take place. No crime of that kind is reported for days. A police officer then recalls that Mary's mother had been killed in the way that she describes in her vision. Mary was very young at the time and no one knew to what extent she may have witnessed the crime. Of course, nobody wanted to relay the ugly details to her. Mary had never shown any indication that she had seen the killing: she has succesfully repressed the event. This further fact provided by the officer does not thereby make her initial visual image an episodic memory of her mother's murder. She did not even take that image to represent a past event. As a matter of fact, she thought it might represent some future state of affairs. The event did not *seem to her* to be something in her past. What is required is that she take the conscious state to represent some past experience or state of affairs. There is nothing intrinsic to the conscious state which labels it 'past' or 'previously occurring,' but if the subject does not take it in such a way then it is not an episodic memory. Having the appropriate causal relation to the past event is a necessary, but not sufficient, condition for episodic memory. (Similar cases can easily be constructed for the other sensory modalities.)

The above considerations show that having episodic memories requires having a sense of time and, in particular, a concept of the past. It is not enough to have a present awareness of what is in fact a past event. Time, as Kant (1781/1965) taught us, is the form of inner sense and is that by means of which we must apprehend inner reality. Moreover, having a sense of time (of the kind required for episodic memory) requires placing oneself along a temporal continuum. It involves viewing oneself as temporally related to the remembered event. One cannot place an event in time without relating it to one's own temporal place, i.e. without temporally relating it *to oneself.* This, in turn, requires having thoughts about oneself. Having an episodic memory ultimately involves having thoughts about oneself *qua* temporally related to the item thought about. So a creature C has an episodic memory (hereafter EM) if and only if:

a. *either* C has a conscious thought about itself experiencing doing something *or* C has a conscious thought about experiencing something happening to C; *and*
b. C takes that conscious thought as representing some past state of affairs or experience.

A potential ambiguity should be guarded against. One may remember *that* one has met a person without remembering meeting that person, or remember *that* a certain episode has occurred without remembering the episode. I am concerned with remembering the event, not merely with remembering (or knowing) *that* the event occurred. This needs to be reflected in clause (a) which has the potentially ambiguous expression 'conscious thought about...' There is a sense in which I can have a conscious thought about myself meeting someone without recalling the episode. The object of my conscious thought would still be 'my experience of meeting that person.' If this is so, then I would not have provided a sufficient condition for having EMs. But I am concerned with EMs as a kind of 'reexperiencing' the remembered event, not merely remembering (or knowing) that some event happened to me or was done by me. The 'conscious thought about...' expressions in clause (a) are to be understood in this stronger sense and as precluding the weak 'remembering that' reading. Thus, 'C has a conscious thought about C's experiencing something...' must be taken as 'C has a conscious thought about C *as* experiencing something.' The weaker 'knowing that' or 'remembering that' sense should be excluded for the same reason that I am not concerned with procedural memory, i.e. it could not be sufficient for self-consciousness. This semantic kind of declarative memory will not make premise (2) true. C's conscious mental state must be directed at the episode *as experienced* by C. A similar point is made by Tulving *et. al.* (1988: 15) when they note that the "episodic/semantic distinction also applies to a person's autobiographical knowledge." Knowing certain *facts* about personal events (e.g. by someone else telling you) must be distinguished from knowing them by virtue of consciously remembered episodes. I am concerned with the latter.

9.2 Does Consciousness Require Episodic Memory?

Let us first examine premise (1) of the MEMORY argument. One general way to determine whether A is a necessary condition for B is to imagine a case of B without A and then expose the difficulties or incoherencies that arise. Accordingly, I will try to imagine a case of consciousness without EM. My strategy, in part, will be to describe an actual human case of amnesia and then to examine the hypothetical limiting case of that syndrome.

Oliver Sacks describes his relationship with a patient Jimmie G. who suffers from a severe form of amnesia called Korsakoff's syndrome, which is brought on by chronic alcoholism and causes degeneration of the mammillary bodies, thalamus, and hippocampus (see "The Lost Mariner" in Sacks 1987). Jimmie is a forty-nine year old who shows excellent ability in intelligence testing and in arithmetical calculations as long as they could be done quickly. He has severe retrograde amnesia, i.e. the inability to remember events that occurred prior to its onset. His autobiographical memories just seem to end at age nineteen during his navy years (about 1945) even though his heavy drinking did not climax until about 1970. Jimmie knows his name, birth date, where he was born, and his school days. He vividly remembers his early years and his older brother, but interestingly uses the present tense to describe his navy days. He thinks that it is still 1945, and is shocked and becomes frantic when he looks in the mirror. Jimmie also shows no sign of recognition when Sacks re-enters the room after only a few minutes. When his brother visited him, Jimmie not only failed to recognize him but thought it was a joke and insisted that his brother is a young man in accounting school.[70]

Jimmie was asked to keep a diary, but the result was that he "could not recognize his earlier entries...He does recognize his own writing and style [but] is always astounded to find that he wrote something the day before" (Sacks 1987: 35). He could not do anything that required any significant length of time, e.g. solve puzzles, watch a television show, etc. He was, however, able to recover some of his procedural skill memory (e.g. typing). Sacks occassionally interjects provocative quasi-philosophical descriptions and conclusions regarding Jimmie's condition. For example, Jimmie is described as "isolated in a single moment of being" and as "a man without a past (or future), stuck in a constantly changing, meaningless moment." (Sacks 1987: 29) Sacks (1987: 30) invites us to agree that Jimmie in some sense:

> ...had been reduced to a 'Humean' being...a genuine reduction of a man to a mere disconnected, incoherent flux and change.

Jimmie seems reduced to a mere succession of unrelated or unconnected impressions. He is later described as "having settled into a state of permanent lostness" (1987: 110). Sacks is no doubt exaggerating the extent of Jimmie's condition, but Jimmie has clearly lost some ability to form an integrated self-concept or sense of who he is (this effect of amnesia is stressed in Marcel 1988 and Van Gulick 1989). A substantial loss in the capacity to form or recall EMs results in severe deficiencies in one's conscious life and one's concept of oneself. However, that is not enough to show that EM is a necessary condition for being a conscious system. Let us try to imagine the limiting case of amnesia and then ask: In *that* case, is the hypothetical subject conscious?

Recall that Jimmie does have EMs of his early years. He is also able to remember events which take place in the very recent past — within the last few minutes. In the limiting case (a) there would be *no* EMs of events in one's life; and (b) memory for recent episodes would also be eliminated. Thus let us imagine a system S who meets both conditions. Tulving et al. (1988: 13) describe an actual patient, KC, who seems to meet the first condition, i.e. "his amnesia for personal happenings is total and complete." But KC does not meet condition (b) because his short-term memory "is essentially normal...he can hold a long question in mind for at least up to a minute," (1988: 8) and can play a hand of cards without handicap. S, however, would also not be able to recall events which occur even just a split-second into the past. We need to imagine that the 'single moment of being' into which S is isolated is as brief as possible. S's conscious mind is perpetually confronting the world for the first time. We can imagine one snapping one's fingers as fast as possible and at each moment S's EMs are wiped away or prevented from forming. It is difficult to grasp what such an existence would be like 'from the inside.' There would be no conscious links to the past and no thoughts of the future. S would have no sense of temporal continuity and would not be able to hold a conversation. S would be the epitomy of 'lostness' and there is little reason to suppose that he could engage in any prolonged rational activity. But would S be conscious?

'Being a conscious system' presumably requires not only having some individual conscious mental states but also having a 'stream of related and continuous conscious mental states.' One must have a *stream of conscious-*

ness and be capable of living in a 'specious present' which involves connecting one's present experiences with at least some past experiences. Premise (1) is to be understood as 'having EM is necessary for having a stream of consciousness.' The idea is that conscious systems have a series of related (i.e. temporally and in content) conscious mental states. This is a reasonable understanding of what conscious systems are and one that can be used to support premise (1). Moreover, it is plausible to suppose that having a stream of consciousness requires experiencing the world and its objects as temporally extended or enduring. Strawson (1966: 97) echoes this Kantian sentiment when he says that "...for a series of diverse experiences to belong to a single consciousness it is necessary that they should be so connected as to constitute a temporally extended experience of a unified objective world." Uniting diverse experiences into a single consciousness requires temporally extended experiences of objects. The idea is that we take the objects of our experience as persisting through time rather than fleeting subjective momentary states of consciousness, *and* this is precisely what *gives unity to a consciousness*. Furthermore, experiencing the world as temporally enduring requires EM. EMs are needed to 'tie together' one's experiences of the world before one's mind and into a stream of consciousness. Living in a specious present requires having EMs because EMs are needed to experience the world as temporally extended. Jimmie *is* able to live in a specious present: he can hold a short conversation, write a few related and continuous sentences, solve short problems, etc. He does have a stream of consciousness or at least many unrelated stream*s*, even though his 'streams' do not cover the same temporal stretch as ours normally do. But our hypothetical system S is not as fortunate. S has no EMs and so cannot experience the world and its objects as temporally extended. Therefore, S cannot have a stream of consciousness and so is not a conscious system. We can put this more formally as follows (call it the TEMPORAL argument):

(T1) Being a conscious system requires experiencing the external world and its objects as having temporal duration.

(T2) Experiencing the world and its objects as temporally enduring requires having EMs.

Therefore,

(T3) Being a conscious system requires having EMs.

The conclusion of the TEMPORAL argument is identical with premise (1) of the MEMORY argument. One may seek even more support for its premises. Is there any independent reason to hold (T1)? I think there is. A necessary condition for being a conscious system is being able to apply concepts to objects within one's experience. It is natural to view concepts as playing a Kantian role, i.e. they make experience possible. Being a conscious system implies having, and being able to apply, concepts. Moreover, having a concept of an external object involves thinking of it as persisting through time. Part of what it is to have the concept 'lion' is to understand that it is a temporally enduring thing. So having and applying concepts of objects entails having temporal concepts (e.g. past, enduring, future, etc.). Of course, one might allow that temporal concepts can be applied in the absence of conscious experience, e.g. a system might be able to 'register' or 'track' the passage of time without having EMs or being conscious at all. Although I am not inclined to understand 'temporal concepts' in such a way, I can still allow such a construal. It might not be that applying temporal concepts *of any kind* entails consciousness, but surely in order to apply temporal concepts *within conscious experience* one must *experience* the world and its objects as temporally extended, i.e. have a sense of the past and one's place in time. Having and applying objective concepts would thus require having EMs since EMs are required for experiencing the world as temporally enduring. The claim is only that *conscious* systems must experience the world as temporally enduring, which, in turn, requires having EMs (and ultimately self-consciousness).

Let us try to imagine S walking around the zoo. He is not even able to remember anything in his immediate past. Suppose that he is staring at a mountain lion for a period of time. Normally we might say 'he seems fascinated by the lion,' 'perhaps the lion reminds him of one that he had seen long ago,' 'he thinks that this exhibit is better than the last one,' etc. But such attributions are unjustified in S's case. Even if S still has some procedural or semantic memory of lions, it is difficult to make sense of him applying the concept 'lion' within experience. In short, it is not clear that S recognizes what a lion is.

Moreover, he could not even answer questions about lions because (unlike Jimmie and KC) he could not hold them in mind long enough. It takes time to grasp the instructions which could show that S has some implicit memory or understanding of lions. There would at least be the very difficult *practical* problem of getting S to manifest any implicit memory he might have (assuming that such behavioral evidence is sufficient for concept possession in the first place). If one's conscious mind is perpetually confronting a 'new' world at every instant, then how can one *apply* a concept it has? It is no longer obvious that S even *has* the concept on the principle that having a concept requires being able to apply it.

In any case, we can support (T1) in the TEMPORAL argument with the following (call it the CONCEPT argument):

(C1) Being a conscious system requires being able (within experience) to apply concepts to the external world and its objects.
(C2) Being able (within experience) to apply concepts to the external world and its objects requires having temporal concepts.
(C3) Having temporal concepts (of the kind that can be applied within experience) requires experiencing the world and its objects as temporally enduring.

Therefore,

(T1) Being a conscious system requires experiencing the world and its objects as temporally enduring.

One might object that further support is also needed for (T2) in the TEMPORAL argument, i.e. experiencing the world and its objects as temporally enduring requires having EMs. The objection might be put thus: (T2) is not true as it stands because EMs, as your definition states, requires not only having thoughts directed at the external world but also thoughts 'of oneself....' To ensure that EMs are necessary for having experiences of a temporally enduring world of objects you must give some reason to think that having such experiences requires having 'thoughts about oneself as experiencing that world.' Why couldn't there be a purely 'other directed' consciousness?

We have already seen one way that 'thoughts about oneself' are involved in having EMs; namely, in that the subject must view himself along a temporal continuum. But another familiar Kantian thesis can help to answer this type of objection more directly and is worth repeating in this context. Kant, as Van Gulick (1989: 226) notes, argued at length that "the notions of subject and object are interdependent correlatives within the structure of experience." The idea is that when one has conscious thoughts about (or experiences of) what one takes as external objects one must also implicitly have thoughts of the form 'that object seems to *me* to be such-and-such.' One cannot just think about an external object without implicitly thinking of oneself as related to that object. At minimum, one must be able to differentiate oneself from the outer world. Experience of an 'objective realm' of objects involves distinguishing them from oneself and one's mental states. Presupposed in one's experience of external objects is thinking of those objects as distinct from oneself. In taking the objects represented in a mental state to be 'objective' one implicitly takes them to be distinct objects of which one is aware. This involves having thoughts about oneself. The 'there is some x which is F' thought must be such as to provide room for the 'x seems to me to be F' thought. One way to put this point is: to have concepts that apply to the objective world (i.e. objective concepts) one must be able to distinguish how things *are* from the way they *appear* to oneself. Otherwise, one should only take those objects of conscious states to be fleeting subjective states which do not leave much room for the appearance-reality distinction. This is not to say that we are always consciously differentiating appearance from reality or that we do not often take things to be as they appear, but rather that one is always implicitly distinguishing oneself (and one's mental states) from the outer world.

Another way that self-concepts are involved in having outer experiences comes from concerns regarding psychological explanation. In trying to explain the behavior of a cat avoiding a dog which previously chased it, it is not enough to attribute to it thoughts (or beliefs) such as 'it thinks that the dog chased *some* creature in the past.' Such mental attributions do not seem sufficient to explain the highly motivated behavior which the cat displays in running away or trying to remain carefully hidden from the dog. The cat must also have an indexical thought to the effect that 'it was *me* that that dog chased...' This is not to say that the cat infers what it ought to do now *via* reasoning about its past; only that the content of the cat's thought must make some reference to itself in order to explain its behavior. As we have seen, this rather Kantian idea has been revived recently in a new guise in the literature on *de se* attitudes (cf. Lewis 1979 and Perry 1979).

Having experiences of objects implies experiencing oneself as distinct from them. The key point for us is that since one takes those objects as temporally extended, then one must *also* take the subject of those experiences to be temporally enduring. If one treats the objects of one's experiences as persisting through time, then one must view oneself as a persisting subject which experiences the same objects at different points in time. One experiences oneself as a subject with a past, i.e. as a temporally enduring thing. But, of course, EMs are necessary for being able to think of oneself as a temporally enduring subject. Experiencing oneself as a subject with a past requires having EMs. They are needed to 'tie together' one's experiences before one's mind. One's experience of time is what Kant calls an 'intuition,' i.e. a kind of sensory state such that there is 'something it is like to have temporal experiences.' One's experience of time is more like a sensory state than a mere intellectual idea. One literally has a *sense* of time and one's place in it. (It must again be emphasized here that mere 'thinking-that' or 'remembering-that' is not the operative notion involved in having EMs.)

We therefore have good reason to endorse the following KANTIAN argument in support of (T2):

(K1) Experiencing the world and its objects as temporally enduring requires experiencing (or thinking of) oneself as a temporally enduring subject with a past.

(K2) Experiencing (or thinking of) oneself as a temporally enduring subject with a past requires having EMs.

Therefore,

(T2) Experiencing the world and its objects as temporally enduring requires having EMs.

I take the above to show that S could not be a conscious system, i.e. could not have a stream of consciousness. S has no EMs and so cannot experience himself as a temporally enduring subject. S therefore cannot take the objects of his experiences to be temporally extended. He would have to think of them as purely momentary and fleeting states of consciousness. Thus, S fails to live up to premise (T1) in the TEMPORAL argument which says that experiencing the world and its objects as temporally extended is necessary for being a conscious system. Moreover, S is incapable of having temporal concepts, or at least is unable to apply them to external objects (within experience). S, then, also fails to meet (C1) in the CONCEPT argument which requires that a conscious system be able to apply objective concepts.

There is another Kantian line of thought worth mentioning. When discussing the 'imagination,' Kant emphasizes the so-called 'threefold synthesis' found in all knowledge. The imagination is one of the "...three original sources...of the possibility of all experience..." (A94). The threefold synthesis 'performed by' the imagination consists in:

> ...the *apprehension* of representation as modifications of the mind in intuition, their *reproduction* in imagination, and their *recognition* in a concept. (A97)

Kant explains that the 'apprehension' has to do with having experience over some temporal stretch. The 'reproduction' involves the recollection of one's past states in light of one's current states. The 'recognition' includes knowing that one is correctly associating one's present states with one's past states. This leads commentators such as Bennett (1966: 136) to say that:

> Imagination, then, is closely connected — if not identical — with intellectually disciplined memory; and Kant is here expounding his view that the rational grasp of one's present experience requires the relating of it with remembered past experience.

The relevance of this is (a) if the 'imagination' is required for experience (as it seems to be) and EM is involved in the imagination, then experience requires EM; and (b) one cannot rationally grasp one's present states (i.e. apply concepts) without EMs. The first point serves as a very brief statement of the TEMPORAL argument. The second echoes the spirit behind the CONCEPT argument.

I wish to go a step further. It seems that S still has conscious sensations, thoughts, and perceptual states even though he is not capable of a 'stream' of them. Similarly, some lower animals might be thought to have some rudimentary conscious states without having EMs or a stream of consciousness.

There is a good reason to think that even this natural position is misguided. It arises from considerations relevant to the CONCEPT argument and Kant's threefold synthesis. *If* S (or some lower animal) is lacking in *any* ability to apply concepts because he is so isolated to the present, then it is no longer clear that he has conscious states at all. We can adopt the more general thesis that having any experience whatsoever must involve a conceptual component (recall chapters three and four). With an inability to apply concepts comes the corresponding inability to have experiences under some *mode or modes of presentation.* A being with such deficiencies would not even have conscious mental states because it could not have experiences which are thought under *some* mode of presentation. S lacks a 'conceptual point of view' on the world *and on his own mental states* and one cannot have conscious states without such a point of view. What makes a mental state a conscious one is that it is thought under some mode (or medium) of presentation, and this is an ability which S lacks. S literally lives in a series of 'meaningless moments.' They are 'meaningless' because there is nothing it is like *for him* to be in those states. What could be more meaningless than not even being able to conceptualize one's own inner states?

Creatures such as worms and frogs are likely to have similar conceptual deficiencies. If they cannot experience a specious present with EMs, then they cannot bring their experiences under some conceptual point of view. And if they do not have any such conceptual capacity, then they are not capable of having conscious states at all. I do not know exactly where the cut-off is on the evolutionary scale, but that need not be decided in order to acknowledge the above conditional claims. These creatures (like S) are still able to respond to stimuli in some rudimentary way and can even have some procedural or implicit memory, but that is not sufficient for conscious mentality. It is not clear that there is room for conscious mental states at all in the limiting case of amnesia. Even though Jimmie has some conscious states, it is far from obvious that our hypothetical subject S would. S would likely have such a degenerate sense of who or what he is that he literally would not have conscious mental states. He would not be able to relate any present 'states' with even the most recent ones because he has no such temporal concepts. This presumably would *not* be the case for many lower animals (e.g. cats and lions) who might live in the more 'moment-to-moment' way that Jimmie does. Such creatures are still conscious because they can still have streams of consciousness even though they will involve much less than ours. Their 'specious present' may just cover less time than ours.

9.3 Episodic Memory and Self-Consciousness

In the previous section, I argued for the truth of premise (1) in the MEMORY argument. Let us now turn to premise (2); namely, that having EMs entails being self-conscious. We have already seen some support for it, but we should first set aside one important strategy that is *not* available. An episodic memory can be retrieved, or arise, in two ways. One could intentionally think back and recall a past experience or episode. In this case the retrieval process is initiated *via* a deliberate act on the part of the subject. Examples would be trying to recall the facial image of an old school friend upon questioning, trying to recall an answer to a test question by thinking back to studying experiences, etc. Humans are capable of this rather sophisticated type of retrieval. In these 'internally triggered episodes,' as I will call them, the subject himself is the proximate cause of the memory retrieval. On the other hand, external events might cause the occurrence of an episodic memory without any deliberate attempt to bring it about on the part of the subject. For example, episodically remembering a friend because of seeing someone who looks like him, being reminded of the death of a parent by a similar event in a movie, etc. Let us call these 'externally triggered episodes.' Presumably, many animals are only capable of this kind of initiated retrieval (to the extent that they have episodic memories at all). As Schacter (1989) points out, we should distinguish the manner in which retrieval is *initiated* from the conscious mental state which is the *product* of the retrieval process. The expression 'conscious remembering' is ambiguous between the two and I have been mainly concerned with the latter; that is, the conscious mental state which is the resulting episodic memory itself. Being able to *internally trigger* an EM is sufficient for self-consciousness, but internal triggering is clearly *not* necessary for merely having EMs. Internally triggering an EM involves a sophisticated form of self-consciousness (i.e. deliberate introspection) which need not be present in many actual, or possible, creatures capable of EMs. Most of our EMs are probably also externally triggered. Thus, we cannot argue for premise (2) on the grounds that having EMs requires one to consciously initiate the recollection of past events.

But we have already seen good reasons to hold premise (2). My aim in this section is simply to make them more explicit. There are two broad ways in which self-consciousness must be involved in having EMs: (a) it is involved in having 'thoughts about oneself...' or in the ability to have some kind of self-concept; and (b) it is required in order to apply temporal concepts to one's present mental states. These are reflected in our definition of EM: the former in clause (a) and the latter in clause (b).

In discussing the KANTIAN argument we noted the implicit concepts and thoughts of oneself present in having experience of an 'objective realm.' Moreover, conscious systems must think of themselves as temporally enduring subjects of experiences. We also saw that taking EMs to be of oneself is essential for explaining the behavior and motivation of organisms. One does not just remember *someone* experiencing *something*. Rather one remembers *oneself* having certain experiences. Similarly, the cat does not merely remember *some* cat being chased by the dog, but rather *itself* being chased by the dog and what it felt at the time (i.e. fear). If the cat did not take the EM to be of itself, then it would be difficult to explain its highly motivated behavior in avoiding the dog (cf. again Perry 1979). It is difficult to see how EMs could motivate in the way they do if they are not intentionally represented as one's own. There are, of course, various degrees of 'self-concept.' Human beings are capable of more sophisticated self-concepts than cats, but both involve self-consciousness nonetheless.

We saw *via* Kant's 'threefold synthesis' that in order to have an experience one must be able to compare and associate it with other (past) states. It is natural to construe this as relating present experiences to (at least very recent) past ones given the discussion of the TEMPORAL and CONCEPT arguments. This is precisely one role that we should expect self-consciousness to play. Having conscious experiences requires being able to have higher-order capacities (e.g. associating, comparing, etc.) with respect to those states.

This is closely related to the idea that having EMs requires locating oneself along a temporal continuum. One takes oneself and one's experiences as present to oneself in a continuous temporal manifold. One has a sense (intuition) of time and one's place in it. When one has an EM one takes it to represent a past event and so one views oneself as temporally related to that event. This requires having a higher-order capacity; namely, thinking about one's mental state as previously occurring and so taking it to represent a past state of affairs. A higher-order application of the concept of 'pastness' must accompany an EM because otherwise nothing would explain why the subject does not take the mental state to be of some present or future state of affairs (as in the clairvoyant case). There is nothing intrinsic to a conscious state which labels it 'past' or 'previously occurring.' Jimmie loses the ability to apply the appropriate temporal concept to his present conscious states when he speaks of his navy days in the present tense. In any event, if one is to take a conscious mental state *as an EM*, then one must at least have an implicit meta-psychological thought to the effect that 'I am now in a state which is very much like one that I was in in the past.' That is, one must be aware (at least implicitly) that one is in a mental state that represents something in the past. Thus, there is an awareness of a feature of one's own mental state.

Lastly, I would be remiss if I did not show the relevance of this to the related notion of the 'future.' Sacks notes that Jimmie has 'no future.' In cases of amnesia the subject's sense of the future is equally deficient. Living in the present carries with it an inability to form plans of action and exercise organizational skills. Jimmie lost his sense of the future as the amnesia took control. Lower animals, we suppose, are not merely deficient in their grasp of the past, but are correspondingly limited in their sense of the future. Tulving et al. (1988: 13-4) also conclude that KC "possesses no consciously apprehensible past or, for that matter, future: He seems to live in a 'permanent present'." With the loss of a sense of past comes a loss in one's grasp of the future, which is manifested in the inability to plan, organize, and form a coherent self-concept. Interestingly, it has been argued (by Marcel 1988 and Van Gulick 1989) that these abilities require higher-order psychological capacities. This is obviously an idea to which I am sympathetic. Having EMs as well as being able to plan and organize require a higher-order understanding of one's states of mind. It is worth mentioning that those who suffer frontal lobe damage which results in impaired organizational and planning skills also show a variety of amnesic symptoms. It seems that deficiencies in grasping the past result in a lack of a sense of future, and difficulties in performing tasks involving 'future concepts' result in signs of amnesia. Senses of the past and future are two sides of the same coin. One must locate oneself along a temporal continuum which not only looks back but also ahead.

Thus, there are good reasons to think that the MEMORY argument is sound. In section 9.2, I provided support for premise (1) with the aid of a series of arguments and some Kantian considerations. Various conceptual difficulties regarding the possibility of a consciousness without EMs were also exposed *via* an examination of hypothetical subject S. It also became clear throughout section 9.2 that self-consciousness is necessary for having EMs. In section 9.3, I made explicit those reasons in support of premise (2).

9.4 Conclusion

I believe I have shown that having conscious mental states entails self-consciousness partly *via* a defense of the HOT theory. When we understand the nature of mental states, we see that higher-order mentality is built right into the structure of conscious mentality. A careful defense of the HOT theory lends support for the idea that conscious mental states are complex states with a meta-psychological component. When we are careful about distinguishing various forms of self-consciousness, we are able to answer the objection that some primitive conscious creatures do not seem to be self-conscious. We have also seen the value of Kant's theory of mind in developing and supporting the HOT theory. My hope is that I have shown the relevance of Kant in this contemporary debate about consciousness while also shedding historical light on his theory of mind and some of his central claims. In doing so, we arrive at a better understanding of conscious mentality and of the structure of conscious minds in general. Conscious minds use a combination of the understanding (with thoughts and concepts) and sensibility to produce conscious experience. Higher-order mentality is essential to this process and helps us to learn how conscious experience is possible.

However, it is important to remember that mentality *per se* does not entail self-consciousness because having some mental states (e.g. beliefs) does not require consciousness at all. So we must leave room for the possibility of an utterly nonconscious system with some form of genuine mentality (e.g. beliefs and goals).

Finally, when we shifted to system consciousness, we saw that there are three distinct and ultimately successful ways to argue for the conclusion that 'being a conscious system entails self-consciousness.' We saw that conscious systems must have episodic memory, *de se* thoughts, and an ability to modify their own behavior. All of these psychological capacities, in turn, entail some form of self-consciousness. So again we better understand how a conscious mind is structured in such a way that its abilities presuppose higher-order cognitive states. I leave it to the reader to determine just how successful I have been.[71]

Notes

1. We can of course agree that pains are often *representational* in some sense, e.g. that my brain state represents something in my back or foot. However, this type of representation falls short of the kind of propositional attitude mentioned. Moreover, the well-known phantom limb phenomenon provides good reason to believe that pains are "in the brain" and are not 'about' one's limbs in a way which presupposes their existence. See Melzack 1992 for more on this phenomenon.

2. For related concerns about the ability of a materialist theory to successfully explain conscious mentality, see Jackson 1982, Levine 1983 and McGinn 1989. For a sample of the literature on the other side of the debate, see Horgan 1984a, Van Gulick 1985, Churchland 1985, Hardin 1985, Loar 1990, Lycan 1990, Flanagan 1992 and Van Gulick 1993.

3. For excellent critical summaries of the alternatives, see McGinn 1982: chapter two; and Churchland 1988: chapter two.

4. For interesting and more direct arguments against Kripke's position, see Horgan 1984b and Tye 1986.

5. This theme in particular and the nature of phenomenal states in general will be further discussed in chapter six. I have purposely restricted my discussion here to only one kind of phenomenal state (i.e. pain) for that reason.

6. I will often use the expression 'meta-psychological thought' (MET) instead of 'higher-order thought' (HOT) because, on my view, the conscious rendering state is part of the first-order conscious state and so is technically not 'higher-order.' However, I may sometimes use the 'HOT' abbreviation *à la* Rosenthal.

7. For the notion of 'reference fixing' see Kripke 1972 and Putnam 1975. The basic idea is that what fixes the extension of a term need not coincide with what is essential to the objects in the extension.

8. As far as I can see, Rosenthal continues to make several of the same methodological errors in his more recent reply (1993b) to Natsoulas' (1993) concerns about what he calls the 'appendage theory of consciousness.' For example, Rosenthal (1993b: 159-60) still insists that "[w]hat motivates the [WIV] is the idea that being conscious and being mental are the same," which again is simply not true. See also Rosenthal (1993b: 157, 163-4) regarding analyzability, intrinsicality and relationality.

9. See e.g. Chisholm 1957; Sellars 1968, 1975; and Tye 1975, 1989. For one opposed to the adverbial theory, see Jackson 1975 and 1976.

10. I ignore proprioception here as a distinct type of conscious state only for lack of immediate relevance.

11. For some explanation of how a functionalist might handle meta-psychological beliefs, see Van Gulick 1980, 1982.

12. But much more is said on this issue in chapter five, including discussion of Searle's arguments.

13. The problem of just how sophisticated the METs must be given the apparent primitiveness of some conscious states is addressed in section 4.5.

14. I will not enter into this debate here but for an excellent discussion, see McGinn 1982: chapter four.

15. This theme is further explored in chapter five.

16. For an illuminating discussion of the difficulties faced by one who treats the sensory on a continuum with the intellectual, see Bennett 1966: 53-56; and especially Bennett 1974: 9-19.

17. See e.g. A97 where Kant says that the threefold synthesis "performed by" the imagination consists in "...the *apprehension* of representations as modifications of the mind in intuition, their *reproduction* in imagination, and their *recognition* in a concept."

18. Nonetheless, the idea that possessing concepts is a simple, primitive or unanalyzable capacity of minds has been recognized as a viable alternative in the absence of any better account. See e.g. Wittgenstein 1958 and McGinn 1984: 154ff.

19. Witness Armstrong's (1973) attempt at analyzing concept possession in terms of the ability to have 'ideas.'

20. But for some insights into Kant's theory, see Warnock 1948; Walsh 1957; Bennett 1966: chapter ten; and Chipman 1972.

21. In this section, however, it will sometimes be necessary to use the terms 'thought' and 'belief' interchangeably because Davidson does this so often and much of what follows will be devoted to addressing his arguments.

22. My treatment of Davidson will somewhat follow Heil (1992: 184-225), but see also Bishop 1980 and Ward 1988.

23. For a particularly inexcusable example of this type of error, see Carruthers 1989 and then my reply in Gennaro 1993.

24. I owe the inspiration behind this division to Robert Van Gulick.

25. Again, I do not take this or what follows as decisive against the *ontology* of materialism. See note 2 for the relevant literature.

26. For an excellent critical discussion of Nagel and Jackson, see Flanagan 1992: chapter five. For an interesting analysis of the problems with Nagel's notion of a 'point of view,' see Francescotti 1993.

27. Again, see my more direct reply to Carruthers in Gennaro 1993 (especially sections I and II).

28. See Gennaro 1992 which is virtually reprinted in chapter nine.

29. See e.g. Premack and Woodruff 1978; and Seyfarth and Cheney 1992. But also see Bennett 1988: 205-6.

30. See e.g. Castaneda 1966, 1967, 1968, and 1987; Shoemaker 1968; Perry 1977, 1979; and Chisholm 1981. See chapter eight for more on its relevance to my main thesis.

31. This theme will be further explored in section 4.10.

32. I am grateful to Robert Francescotti for several helpful discussions on what I have called the 'straight denial objection.'

33. For more on experimental cases revealing the cognitive influence on feeling pains, see Melzack 1973.

34. See e.g. Armstrong 1984: 108-37; but also see Shoemaker (1986, 1994) for an opponent of the perceptual model. I do not wish to adjudicate their dispute here. As will become clear, many of their points are not relevant here since my primary purpose is to discuss the two models *within the context* of the HOT theory. However, I hope that my discussion sheds some light on this rather traditional problem.

35. See Natsoulas 1992b: 393-5 and Rosenthal 1993b: 157-60 for more on this issue.

36. I thank Daniel Howard-Snyder for helping me to see more clearly this way of phrasing the objection.

37. Indeed, the distinction itself has come under serious attack and just how to characterize the difference remains somewhat obscure, so I am not sure that it can help us here. See, for example, Bach 1982 and Dennett 1982: 60-90. The relevance of this distinction for my purposes will be shown more clearly in chapter eight in the context of discussing *de se* attitudes.

38. This was apparently held by Locke. Consider his claim that "consciousness...is inseparable from thinking, and...essential to it" and "consciousness always accompanies thinking" (Locke's 1689 *Essay* Bk. II, chapter 27; chapter 9).

39. This was arguably held by Descartes. He said that "no thought can exist in us of which we are not conscious at the very moment it exists in us." (Fourth Replies) He also remarked that "the word 'thought' applies to all that exists in us in such a way that we are immediately conscious of it." (Second Replies) Adherence to MEC3 was perhaps not Descartes' considered opinion, but I will not pursue this point of exegesis here.

40. See e.g. Kripke 1972 who holds that having a pain (or being in pain) is the same as *feeling* a pain.

41. See Nelkin 1986, 1989; Rosenthal 1986, 1991; and Shoemaker 1991. Although I agree with these authors that MEC4 is false, it should become clear the extent to which I disagree with them as well.

42. Once again, keep in mind that I do not construe beliefs in the same way as thoughts even though the term 'thought' is sometimes used in the generic sense covering all types of mental states. I understand beliefs primarily to be dispositions to behave (verbally or non-verbally) in certain ways under certain conditions, whereas thoughts are inner, occurrent, momentary episodic mental events.

43. But see Bennett 1976 and Dennett 1987 for sustained attempts. In the next section, I further explore the relevance and importance of Dennett's position (especially in examining MEC11).

44. In his unpublished paper entitled "Does Mentality Require Consciousness?" which partly inspired me to work on this chapter.

45. I thank Robert Van Gulick for permission to use this direct quote from his unpublished paper "Does Mentality Require Consciousness?" For another criticism of Searle's position, see Armstrong 1991.

46. For more direct and detailed criticisms of Davidson's position, see Bishop 1980 and Ward 1988. For an excellent recent critical review of Davidson's arguments, see Heil 1992: 184-225. Recall also the critical discussion in section 3.6.

47. Dennett (1991) has more recently addressed this realism/anti-realism issue partly in an attempt to defend himself against the charge that (on his view) there really are no beliefs.

48. See Dennett (1987: 68fn.) when he says that his view "embraces the broadest liberalism, gladly paying the price of a few recalcitrant intuitions for the generality gained."

49. Cf. Fodor (1975, 1981) and the so-called "language of thought" hypothesis. Fodor holds that mental processes involve a medium of mental representation which has the key features of a language. For an excellent recent critical summary of representational theories of mind, see Sterelny 1990.

50. This is the so-called "connectionist model" which is often contrasted with the language of thought hypothesis and other representational theories. See Sterelny 1990: chapter eight.

51. For related (but not identical) pathologies to the two main upcoming cases, see "The Disembodied Lady" and "The Man Who Fell out of Bed" in Sacks 1987.

52. See again my 1993 critique of Carruthers (1989) who argues that infants do not have conscious pains partly because they cannot introspect their pains.

53. Although it can be controversial, I will for the sake of argument often treat such internal mental states as real causally efficacious structures. There is some debate over whether some intentional states (especially beliefs) ought to be treated this way (cf. section 5.3). However, for our purposes here, it is harmless to assume that at least *some version* of the representational theory of mind is true. For a nice summary of the alternatives, see Sterelny 1990.

54. An interesting possible exception or perhaps even a problem for theism would be the idea of an all-knowing God. Presumably such a Being could not learn anything since it already knows everything. So God is either an unusual exception to the idea that learning is necessary for being a conscious system, or the existence of a conscious all-knowing Being must be called into question on these grounds.

55. What follows can be viewed as a more elaborate way of criticizing Dennett's objection to the HOT theory from section 4.7. We can think of Robo as a more sophisticated version of zimbo and, while my main goal here is to show why Van Gulick's notion of self-consciousness is too weak, much of it also applies to Dennett's contention that an unconscious system with various higher-order states spells doom for the HOT theory.

56. For elaboration on the manner in which a system can meet this condition, see Van Gulick 1980 and 1982.

57. Actually, it is not always clear how Van Gulick's "active meta-psychological possession" differs from "meta-psychological beliefs" given the way he emphasizes the adaptive causal role in the production of behavior (in which case the argument of section 3.2 can also be used here). Presumably, the former can be mere subdoxastic states and so are more primitive.

58. Of course, many of us are not likely to use the term 'understanding' the more opaque the higher-order access becomes. I agree with Van Gulick that there are degrees of understanding, but not about where to draw the line at the lower end.

59. See Castaneda 1966, 1967, 1968, 1987; Lewis 1979; Perry 1979; Chisholm 1981; McGinn 1983; Davidson 1985; and McKay 1988 for a sample of the relevant literature.

60. I am grateful to John O'Leary-Hawthorne for first pointing out to me the *prima facie* connection between DSAs and self-consciousness, and its relevance to this project.

61. I distinguish *de re* from *de dicto* attitudes here mainly because of its importance in Lewis' treatment of DSAs. However, there are serious problems with the distinction itself, e.g. that perhaps they are not really two different types of beliefs but instead only two types of belief attribution (Dennett 1982: 60-90). This is not the place to address in detail all of the problems, though I will raise some when relevant to my specific treatment of the DE SE argument. It seems, however, at least important to distinguish between the two *sentence forms* which are typically associated with them. But, again, even this practice is questionable as a way of differentiating them in any important way (Bach 1982: 129ff).

62. Here I follow Davidson's (1985) treatment to a great extent.

63. Lewis, of course, holds that his analysis applies *mutatis mutandis* to all of the other well-understood intentional attitudes.

64. This should be relatively obvious, but, as we shall see, it has been overlooked by some commentators (Markie 1983).

65. However, Boer and Lycan (1980) argue that Perry's point does not show that *de se* beliefs are not just special cases of *de re* beliefs. They argue that the same difficulties can be found for *de re* beliefs in general.

66. And, once again, we should note Bach's (1982: 129ff) contention that this is not an adequate way to distinguish *de re* from *de dicto* attitudes.

67. It is worth noting that many who argue *against* the Nagel/Jackson worries about a materialist explanation of conscious experience use the notion of fine-grained individuation of knowledge in terms of differing modes of presentation (see e.g. Tye 1986 and Lycan 1990). The idea is that one can come to know the same fact in different ways, i.e. stand in different cognitive relations to the same object of knowledge. One might wonder whether the Nagel/Jackson line of argument can be recast in terms of the modes of presentation themselves. However, once again, I remain unconvinced that such worries present an unanswerable threat to the *ontology* of materialism.

68. But see McGinn (1982: chapter six) for a nice summary. See also Vesey 1974, Perry 1974 and Rorty 1976. I do not mean to imply in what follows that my preferred view is without its own significant problems.

69. This theme will be much further developed in the next chapter (especially in section 9.2).

70. For more on Korsakoff's syndrome, see Sanders and Warrington 1971, Oscar-Berman 1980, Squire 1982, Butters 1984, and Butters and Cermak 1986. I use Sacks' discussion of Jimmie G. mainly because it best lends itself to philosophical commentary.

71. Some readers familiar with the work of Jean-Paul Sartre, Edmund Husserl and Martin Heidegger may be disappointed with the lack of reference to these central figures since they had a great deal to say on the general topic of consciousness. I can only say that I am aware of their importance but made a conscious choice not to discuss their work *in this book* for various reasons. I hope, however, to take them on in some of my future research on conscious experience, time, and higher-order mentality. For those readers not very familiar with these philosophers, please do not take my lack of reference to them as implying that they are unimportant or irrelevant to my overall thesis.

References

Adams, R. 1979. Theories of actuality. In *The Possible and the Actual*, M. Loux (ed), 190-209. Ithaca: Cornell.

Alston, W. 1981. Can we speak literally of God? In *Is God GOD?*, A. Steuer and J. McClendon, Jr. (eds). Nashville: Abingdon Press.

Alston, W. 1985. Functionalism and theological language. *American Philosophical Quarterly* 22, 221-230.

Armstrong, D.M. 1968. *A Materialist Theory of the Mind*. New York: Humanities.

Armstrong, D.M. 1973. *Belief, Truth, and Knowledge*. Cambridge, MA: Cambridge.

Armstrong, D.M. 1980. What is consciousness? In *The Nature of Mind and Other Essays*. Ithaca: Cornell.

Armstrong, D.M. and Malcolm, N. 1984. *Consciousness and Causality*. Oxford: Basil Blackwell.

Armstrong, D.M. 1991. Searle's neo-Cartesian theory of consciousness. In *Consciousness*, E. Villanueva (ed), 67-71. Atascadero, CA: Ridgeview Publishing Company.

Bach, K. 1982. *De Re* belief and methodological solipsism. In *Thought and Object*, A. Woodfield (ed), 121-151. Oxford: Clarendon.

Bennett, J. 1964. *Rationality*. London: Routledge and Kegan Paul.

Bennett, J. 1966. *Kant's Analytic*. Cambridge, MA: Cambridge.

Bennett, J. 1974. *Kant's Dialectic*. Cambridge, MA: Cambridge.

Bennett, J. 1976. *Linguistic Behaviour*. Cambridge, MA: Cambridge.

Bennett, J. 1988. Thoughtful brutes. *Proceedings and Addresses of the American Philosophical Association* 62, 197-210.

Bennett, J. 1990. Why is belief involuntary? *Analysis* 50, 87-107.

Bishop, J. 1980. More thought on thought and talk. *Mind* 89, 1-16.

Block, N. 1980. Are absent qualia impossible? *Philosophical Review* 89, 257-272.

Block, N. (ed). 1980. *Readings in the Philosophy of Psychology, Vol. I*. Cambridge, MA: Harvard.

Block, N. 1991. What does neuropsychology tell us about a function of consciousness? (unpublished manuscript)

Boden, M. (ed). 1990. *The Philosophy of Artificial Intelligence*. New York: Oxford.

Boer, S. and Lycan, W. 1980. Who, me? *Philosophical Review* 89, 427-466.

Brentano, F. 1874/1973. *Psychology From an Empirical Standpoint*. New York: Humanities.

Bullock, T.H. *et. al.* 1977. *Introduction to Nervous Systems*. San Francisco: W.H. Freeman.

Burge, T. 1979. Individualism and the mental. In *Midwest Studies in Philosophy, IV*, P.A. French, T.E. Uehling and H.K. Wettstein (eds), 73-121. Minneapolis: University of Minnesota Press.

Burge, T. 1982. Other bodies. In *Thought and Object*, A. Woodfield (ed), 97-120. Oxford: Clarendon.

Burge, T. 1986. Individualism and psychology. *The Philosophical Review* 95, 3-45.

Butters, N. 1984. Alcoholic Korsakoff's syndrome: An update. *Seminars in Neurology* 4, 226-244.

Butters, N. and Cermak, L. 1986. A case study of the forgetting of autobiographical knowledge: Implications for the study of retrograde amnesia. In *Autobiographical Memory*, D.C. Rubin (ed), 253-272. Cambridge, MA: Cambridge.

Carruthers, P. 1989. Brute experience. *Journal of Philosophy* 86, 258-269.

Castaneda, H. 1966. 'He:' A study in the logic of self-consciousness. *Ratio* 8, 130-157.

Castaneda, H. 1967. Indicators and quasi-indicators. *American Philosophical Quarterly* 4, 85-100.

Castaneda, H. 1968. On the logic of attributions of self knowledge to others. *The Journal of Philosophy* 65, 439-456.

Castaneda, H. 1987. Self-consciousness, demonstrative reference, and the self-ascription view of believing. In *Philosophical Perspectives, 1*, J. Tomberlin (ed), 405-454. Atascadero, CA: Ridgeview Publishing Company.

Chipman, L. 1972. Kant's categories and their schematism. *Kant-Studien* 63, 36-50. Reprinted in 1982 *Kant on Pure Reason: Oxford Readings in Philosophy*, R. Walker (ed), 100-116. New York: Oxford.

Chisholm, R. 1957. *Perceiving*. Ithaca: Cornell.

Chisholm, R. 1981. *The First Person*. Minneapolis: University of Minnesota Press.

Churchland, P.M. and Churchland, P.S. 1981. Functionalism, qualia, and intentionality. *Philosophical Topics* 12, 121-145.

Churchland, P.M. 1984. *Matter and Consciousness*. Cambridge, MA: MIT/Bradford.

Churchland, P.M. 1985. Reduction, qualia, and the direct introspection of brain states. *Journal of Philosophy* 82, 2-28.

Churchland, P.S. 1986. *Neurophilosophy*. Cambridge, MA: MIT/Bradford.

Crick, F. and Koch, C. 1990. Towards a neurobiological theory of consciousness. *Seminars in the Neurosciences* 2, 263-75.

Davidson, D. 1984. Thought and talk. In *Inquiries into Truth and Interpretation*. New York: Oxford/Clarendon.

Davidson, D. 1985. Rational animals. In *Actions and Events*, E. LePore and B. McLaughlin (eds). Cambridge, MA: Oxford/Basil Blackwell.

Davidson, B.L. 1985. Belief *De Re* and *De Se*. *Australasian Journal of Philosophy* 63, 389-406.

Davies, M. and Humphreys, G. (eds). 1993. *Consciousness*. Cambridge, MA: Blackwell.

Davis, L. 1989. Self-consciousness in chimps and pigeons. *Philosophical Psychology* 2, 249-259.

Dennett, D.C. 1969. *Content and Consciousness*. London: Routledge and Kegan Paul.

Dennett, D.C. 1978. *Brainstorms*. Cambridge, MA: MIT/Bradford.

Dennett, D.C. 1982. Beyond belief. In *Thought and Object*, A. Woodfield (ed), 1-95. Oxford: Clarendon.

Dennett, D.C. 1987. *The Intentional Stance*. Cambridge, MA: MIT/Bradford.

Dennett, D.C. 1988. Quining qualia. In *Consciousness in Contemporary Science*, A. Marcel and E. Bisiach (eds), 42-77. New York: Oxford/Clarendon.

Dennett, D.C. 1990a. Cognitive wheels: The frame problem of AI. In *The Philosophy of Artificial Intelligence*, M. Boden (ed), 147-170. New York: Oxford. Originally published in 1984 *Minds, Machines, and Evolution: Philosophical Studies*, C. Hookway (ed), 129-151. Cambridge, MA: Cambridge.

Dennett, D.C. 1990b. Artificial intelligence as philosophy and as psychology. In *Foundations of Cognitive Science*, J. Garfield (ed), 247-264. New York: Paragon. Originally published in D.C. Dennett 1978, 109-128.

Dennett, D.C. 1991. *Consciousness Explained*. Boston: Little, Brown and Company.

Descartes, R. 1984. *The Philosophical Writings of Descartes, Vol. 2*, trans. by J. Cottingham, R. Stoothoff, and D. Murdoch. Cambridge, MA: Cambridge.

Dretske, F. 1993a. Conscious experience. *Mind* 102, 263-283.

Dretske, F. 1993b. The nature of thought. *Philosophical Studies* 70, 185-199.

Ebbesson, S. (ed). 1980. *Comparative Neurology of the Telencephalon*. New York and London: Plenum Press.

Ellis, A. and Young, A. 1988. *Human Cognitive Neuropsychology*. Hillsdale, NJ: Lawrence Erlbaum.

Epstein, R. *et. al.* 1980. Self-awareness in the pigeon. *Science* 212, 695-696.

Flanagan, O. 1992. *Consciousness Reconsidered*. Cambridge, MA: MIT/Bradford.

Fodor, J.A. 1975. *The Language of Thought*. New York: Crowell.

Fodor, J.A. 1981. *Representations*. Cambridge, MA: MIT/Bradford.

Fodor, J.A. 1983. *Modularity of Mind*. Cambridge, MA: MIT/Bradford.

Fodor, J.A. 1987. *Psychosemantics*. Cambridge, MA: MIT/Bradford.

Fodor, J.A. 1990. Modules, frames, fridgeons, sleeping dogs, and the music of the spheres. In *Foundations of Cognitive Science*, J. Garfield (ed), 235-246. New York: Paragon.

Francescotti, R. 1993. Subjective experience and points of view. *Journal of Philosophical Research* 18, 25-36.

Franks, B. 1992. Realism and folk psychology in the ascription of concepts. *Philosophical Psychology* 5, 369-390.

Gallup, Jr., G.G. 1975. Towards an operational definition of self-awareness. In *Socioecology and Psychology of Primates*, R. Tuttle (ed). The Hague: Mouton.

Garfield, J. (ed). 1990. *Foundations of Cognitive Science*. New York: Paragon.

Gazzaniga, M. 1988. Brain modularity: Towards a philosophy of conscious experience. In *Consciousness in Contemporary Science*, A. Marcel and E. Bisiach (eds), 218-238. New York: Oxford/Clarendon.

Geach, P. 1957. *Mental Acts*. London: Routledge and Kegan Paul.

Gennaro, R. 1992. Consciousness, self-consciousness, and episodic memory. *Philosophical Psychology* 5, 333-347.

Gennaro, R. 1993. Brute experience and the higher-order thought theory of consciousness. *Philosophical Papers* 22, 51-69.

Gennaro, R. 1994. Does mentality entail consciousness? *Philosophia* 24.

Grice, H.P. 1941. Personal identity. *Mind* 50, 330-350. Reprinted in J. Perry 1975.

Griffin, D. 1992. *Animal Minds*. Chicago: University of Chicago Press.

Hardin, C.L. 1987. Qualia and materialism: Closing the explanatory gap. *Philosophy and Phenomenological Research* 48, 281-298.

Hardin, C.L. 1988. *Color for Philosophers*. Indianapolis: Hackett.

Harrison, P. 1991. Do animals feel pain? *Philosophy* 66, 25-40.

Heil, J. 1992. *The Nature of True Minds*. Cambridge, MA: Cambridge.

Hill, C. 1991. *Sensations: A Defense of Type Materialism*. Cambridge, MA: Cambridge.

Horgan, T. 1984a. Jackson on physical information and qualia. *The Philosophical Quarterly* 34, 147-152.

Horgan, T. 1984b. Functionalism, qualia, and the inverted spectrum. *Philosophy and Phenomenological Research* 44, 453-469.

Hundert, E. 1989. *Philosophy, Psychiatry and Neuroscience: Three Approaches to the Mind*. Oxford: Clarendon.

Jackson, F. 1975. On the adverbial analysis of visual experience. *Metaphilosophy* 6, 127-135.

Jackson, F. 1976. The existence of mental objects. *American Philosophical Quarterly* 13, 23-40.

Jackson, F. 1982. Epiphenomenal qualia. *The Philosophical Quarterly* 32, 127-136.

Kant, I. 1781/1965. *Critique of Pure Reason*, translated by Norman Kemp Smith. New York: St. Martin's.

Kaye, L. 1993. Are most of our concepts innate? *Synthese* 95, 187-217.

Kinsbourne, M. 1989. The boundaries of episodic remembering. In *Varieties of Memory and Consciousness*, H. Roediger and F. Craik (eds), 179-191. Hillsdale, NJ: Lawrence Erlbaum.

Kitcher, P. 1990a. Apperception and epistemic responsibility. In *Central Themes in Early Modern Philosophy*, J.A. Cover and M. Kulstad (eds), 273-304. Indianapolis: Hackett.

Kitcher, P. 1990b. *Kant's Transcendental Psychology*. New York: Oxford.

Kripke, S. 1971. Identity and necessity. In *Identity and Individuation*, M. Munitz (ed), 135-164. New York: New York University Press.

Kripke, S. 1972. *Naming and Necessity*. Cambridge, MA: Harvard.

Kripke, S. 1982. *Wittgenstein on Rules and Private Language*. Cambridge, MA: Harvard University Press.

Leibniz, G. 1989. *Philosophical Essays*, translated by R. Ariew and D. Garber. Indianapolis: Hackett.

LePore, E. and McLaughlin, B. (eds). 1985. *Actions and Events*. Cambridge, MA: Oxford/Basil Blackwell.

Levine, J. 1983. Materialism and qualia: The explanatory gap. *Pacific Philosophical Quarterly* 64, 354-361.

Lewis, D. 1966. An argument for the identity theory. *Journal of Philosophy* 63, 17-25. Reprinted in Lewis 1983.

Lewis, D. 1979. Attitudes *De Dicto* and *De Se*. *The Philosophical Review* 88, 513-543. Reprinted in Lewis 1983.

Lewis, D. 1983. *Philosophical Papers, Vol. I*. New York: Oxford.

Loar, B. 1990. Phenomenal states. In *Philosophical Perspectives, 4*, J. Tomberlin (ed), 81-108. Atascadero, CA: Ridgeview Publishing Company.

Locke, J. 1689/1975. *An Essay Concerning Human Understanding*. P. Nidditch (ed). Oxford: Clarendon.

Loux, M. (ed). 1979. *The Possible and the Actual*. Ithaca: Cornell.

Lycan, W. 1979. The trouble with possible worlds. In *The Possible and the Actual*, M. Loux (ed), 274-316. Ithaca: Cornell.

Lycan, W. 1987. *Consciousness*. Cambridge, MA: MIT/Bradford.

Lycan, W. 1990. What is the "subjectivity" of the mental? In *Philosophical Perspectives, 4*, J. Tomberlin (ed), 109-130. Atascadero, CA: Ridgeview Publishing Company.

Mackie, J.L. 1976. *Problems from Locke*. Oxford: Clarendon.

Mandelker, S. 1991. An argument against the externalist account of psychological content. *Philosophical Psychology* 4, 375-382.

Marcel, A. 1988. Phenomenal experience and functionalism. In *Consciousness in Contemporary Science*, A. Marcel and E. Bisiach (eds), 121-158. New York: Oxford/Clarendon.

Marcel, A. and Bisiach, E. (eds). 1988. *Consciousness in Contemporary Science*. New York: Oxford/Clarendon.

Markie, P. 1984. *De Dicto* and *De Se*. *Philosophical Studies* 45, 231-237.

Martin, C.B. 1987. Proto-language. *Australasian Journal of Philosophy* 65, 277-289.

McGinn, C. 1982. *The Character of Mind*. New York: Oxford.

McGinn, C. 1983. *The Subjective View*. Oxford: Clarendon.

McGinn, C. 1984. *Wittgenstein on Meaning*. Oxford: Basil Blackwell.

McGinn, C. 1989. Can we solve the mind-body problem? *Mind* 98, 349-366.

McGinn, C. 1991. *The Problem of Consciousness*. Oxford: Blackwell.

McKay, T. 1988. *De Re* and *De Se* belief. In *Philosophical Analysis*, D.F. Austin (ed), 207-217. Berlin: Kluwer Academic Publishers.

McMullen, C. 1985. 'Knowing what it's like' and the essential indexical. *Philosophical Studies* 48, 211-233.

Melzack, R. 1973. *The Puzzle of Pain*. New York: Basic Books.

Melzack, R. 1992. Phantom limbs. *Scientific American* (April), 120-126.

Nagel, E. 1977. Teleology revisited. *Journal of Philosophy* 74, 261-301.

Nagel, T. 1974. What is it like to be a bat? *Philosophical Review* 83, 435-450.

Nagel, T. 1986. *The View From Nowhere*. New York: Oxford.

Natsoulas, T. 1978. Consciousness. *American Psychologist* 33, 906-914.

Natsoulas, T. 1983. Concepts of consciousness. *The Journal of Mind and Behavior* 4, 13-59.

Natsoulas, T. 1985. An introduction to the perceptual kind of conception of direct (reflective) consciousness. *The Journal of Mind and Behavior* 6, 333-356.

Natsoulas, T. 1989. An examination of four objections to self-intimating states of consciousness. *The Journal of Mind and Behavior* 10, 63-116.

Natsoulas, T. 1991a. The concept of consciousness$_1$: The interpersonal meaning. *Journal for the Theory of Social Behavior* 21, 63-89.

Natsoulas, T. 1991b. The concept of consciousness$_2$: The personal meaning. *Journal for the Theory of Social Behavior* 21, 339-367

Natsoulas, T. 1992a. The concept of consciousness$_3$: The awareness meaning. *Journal for the Theory of Social Behavior* 22, 199-225.

Natsoulas, T. 1992b. Appendage theory — pro and con. *The Journal of Mind and Behavior* 13, 371-396.

Natsoulas, T. 1993. What is wrong with appendage theory of consciousness. *Philosophical Psychology* 6, 137-154.

Neely, J. 1989. Experimental dissociations and the episodic/semantic memory distinction. In *Varieties of Memory and Consciousness*, H. Roediger and F. Craik (eds), 229-270. Hillsdale, NJ: Lawrence Erlbaum.

Nelkin, N. 1986. Pains and pain sensations. *Journal of Philosophy* 83, 129-148.

Nelkin, N. 1989. Unconscious sensations. *Philosophical Psychology* 2, 129-141.

Oscar-Berman, M. 1980. Neuropsychological consequences of long-term chronic alcoholism. *American Scientist* 68, 410-419.

Paterson, D. 1980. Is your brain really necessary? *World Medicine* 3, 21-24.

Peacocke, C. 1983. *Sense and Content*. Oxford: Clarendon.

Peacocke, C. 1992. *A Study of Concepts*. Cambridge, MA: MIT Press/Bradford.

Perry, J. (ed). 1975. *Personal Identity*. Los Angeles, CA: University of California Press.

Perry, J. 1977. Frege on demonstratives. *Philosophical Review* 86, 474-497.

Perry, J. 1979. The problem of the essential indexical. *Nous* 13, 3-21.

Pettit, P. and McDowell, J. (eds). 1986. *Subject, Thought, and Context*. Oxford: Clarendon.

Pippin, R. 1987. Kant on the spontaneity of mind. *Canadian Journal of Philosophy* 17, 449-475.

Premack, D. and Woodruff, G. 1978. Does the chimpanzee have a theory of mind? *The Behavioral and Brain Sciences* 1, 515-526.

Putnam, H. 1975. The meaning of 'meaning.' In *Mind, Language, and Reality: Philosophical Papers Vol. 2*. Cambridge: Cambridge University Press.

Quine, W.V.O. 1960. *Word and Object*. Cambridge, MA: MIT Press.

Quinton, A. 1962. The soul. *The Journal of Philosophy* 59, 393-409. Reprinted in J. Perry 1975.

Rey, G. 1988. A question about consciousness. In *Perspectives on Mind*, H.R. Otto and J.A. Tuedio (eds), 5-24. D. Reidel Publishing Company.

Rock, I. 1983. *The Logic of Perception*. Cambridge, MA: MIT/Bradford.

Roediger, H. and Craik, F. (eds). 1989. *Varieties of Memory and Consciousness*. Hillsdale, NJ: Lawrence Erlbaum.

Roediger, H. *et. al.* 1989. Explaining dissociations between implicit and explicit measures of retention: A processing account. In *Varieties of Memory and Consciousness*, H. Roediger and F. Craik (eds), 3-41. Hillsdale, NJ: Lawrence Erlbaum.

Rorty, A. (ed). 1976. *The Identities of Persons*. Los Angeles, CA: University of California Press.

Rosenthal, D. 1986. Two concepts of consciousness. *Philosophical Studies* 49, 329-359.

Rosenthal, D. 1990. A theory of consciousness. Report No. 40/1990 on MIND and BRAIN. Perspectives in Theoretical Psychology and the Philosophy of Mind (ZiF). University of Bielefeld.

Rosenthal, D. 1991. The independence of consciousness and sensory quality. In *Consciousness*, E. Villanueva (ed), 15-36. Atascadero, CA: Ridgeview Publishing Company.

Rosenthal, D. 1993a. Thinking that one thinks. In *Consciousness*, M. Davies and G. Humphreys (eds), 197-223. Cambridge, MA: Blackwell.

Rosenthal, D. 1993b. Higher-order thoughts and the appendage theory of consciousness. *Philosophical Psychology* 6, 155-166.

Ryle, G. 1949. *The Concept of Mind*. London: Hutchinsen and Company.

Sacks, O. 1987. *The Man Who Mistook His Wife for a Hat and Other Clinical Tales*. New York: Harper and Row.

Samet, J. 1986. Troubles with Fodor's nativism. In *Midwest Studies in Philosophy, X*, P.A. French, T.E. Uehling and H.K. Wettstein (eds), 575-594. Minneapolis: University of Minnesota Press.

Sanders, H. and Warrington, E. 1971. Memory for remote events in amnesic patients. *Brain* 94, 661-668.

Sarnat, H. and Netsky, M. 1974. *Evolution of the Nervous System*. New York: Oxford.

Schacter, D. 1987. Implicit memory: History and current status. *Journal of Experimental Psychology: Learning, Memory, and Cognition* 13, 501-518.

Schacter, D. 1989. On the relation between memory and consciousness: Dissociable interactions and conscious experience. In *Varieties of Memory and Consciousness*, H. Roediger and F. Craik (eds), 355-389. Hillsdale, NJ: Lawrence Erlbaum.

Seager, W. 1993. The elimination of experience. *Philosophy and Phenomenological Research* 53, 345-365.

Searle, J. 1980. Minds, brains, and programs. *The Behavioral and Brain Sciences* 3, 417-424.

Searle, J. 1984. *Minds, Brains, and Science*. Cambridge, MA: Harvard.

Searle, J. 1987. Indeterminacy, empiricism and the first person. *Journal of Philosophy* 84, 123-146.

Searle, J. 1989. Consciousness, unconsciousness, and intentionality. *Philosophical Topics* 17, 193-209.

Searle, J. 1992. *The Rediscovery of the Mind*. Cambridge, MA: MIT/Bradford.

Sellars, W. 1968. *Science and Metaphysics*. London: Routledge and Kegan Paul.

Sellars, W. 1975. The adverbial theory of the objects of sensation. *Metaphilosophy* 6, 144-160.

Seyfarth, R. and Cheney, D. 1992. Inside the mind of a monkey. *New Scientist* 133, 25-29.

Shoemaker, S. 1968. Self-reference and self-awareness. *The Journal of Philosophy* 65, 555-567. Reprinted in Shoemaker 1984.

Shoemaker, S. 1975. Functionalism and qualia. *Philosophical Studies* 27, 291-315. Reprinted in Shoemaker 1984.

Shoemaker, S. 1981a. Some varieties of functionalism. *Philosophical Topics* 12, 83-118. Reprinted in Shoemaker 1984.

Shoemaker, S. 1981b. Absent qualia are impossible — a reply to Block. *The Philosophical Review* 90, 581-599. Reprinted in Shoemaker 1984.

Shoemaker, S. 1984. *Identity, Cause, and Mind*. Cambridge, MA: Cambridge.

Shoemaker, S. 1986. Introspection and the self. In *Midwest Studies in Philosophy, X*, P.A. French, T.E. Uehling and H.K. Wettstein (eds), 101-120. Minneapolis: University of Minnesota Press.

Shoemaker, S. 1991. Qualia and consciousness. *Mind* 100, 507-524.

Shoemaker, S. 1994. Self-knowledge and "inner sense." *Philosophy and Phenomenological Research* 54, 249-314.

Singer, P. 1980. Animals and the value of life. In *Matters of Life and Death*, T. Regan (ed), 338-380. New York: Random House.

Smith, D.W. 1986. The structure of (self-)consciousness. *Topoi* 5, 149-156.

Squire, L.R. 1982. The neuropsychology of human memory. *Annual Review of Neuroscience* 5, 241-273.

Squire, L.R. 1987. *Memory and Brain*. New York: Oxford.

Stalnaker, R. 1987. *Inquiry*. Cambridge, MA: MIT/Bradford.

Sterelny, K. 1989. Fodor's nativism. *Philosophical Studies* 55, 119-141.

Sterelny, K. 1990. *The Representational Theory of Mind*. Cambridge, MA: Oxford/Basil Blackwell.

Stich, S. 1978. Beliefs and subdoxastic states. *Philosophy of Science* 45, 499-518.

Strawson, P.F. 1959. *Individuals*. London: Methuen.

Strawson, P.F. 1966. *The Bounds of Sense*. New York and London: Methuen.

Tienson, J. 1990. An introduction to connectionism. In *Foundations of Cognitive Science*, J. Garfield (ed), 381-397. New York: Paragon. Originally published in 1987 *The Southern Journal of Philosophy, Supplement* 26, 1-16.

Tranel, D. and Damasio, A.R. 1985. Knowledge without awareness: An autonomic index of facial recognition by prosopagnosics. *Science* 228, 1453-1454.

Tulving, E. 1983. *Elements of Episodic Memory*. Oxford: Clarendon.

Tye, M. 1975. The adverbial theory: A defence of Sellars against Jackson. *Metaphilosophy* 6, 136-143.

Tye, M. 1986. The subjective qualities of experience. *Mind* 95, 1-17.

Tye, M. 1989. *The Metaphysics of Mind: Cambridge Studies in Philosophy*. Cambridge, MA: Cambridge.

Van Gulick, R. 1980. Functionalism, information, and content. *Nature and System* 2, 139-162.

Van Gulick, R. 1982. Mental representation — a functionalist view. *Pacific Philosophical Quarterly* 63, 3-20.

Van Gulick, R. 1985. Physicalism and the subjectivity of the mental. *Philosophical Topics* 13, 51-70.

Van Gulick, R. 1988a. A functionalist plea for self-consciousness. *The Philosophical Review* 97, 149-181.

Van Gulick, R. 1988b. Consciousness, intrinsic intentionality, and self-understanding machines. In *Consciousness in Contemporary Science*, A. Marcel and E. Bisiach (eds), 78-100. New York: Oxford/Clarendon.

Van Gulick, R. 1989. What difference does consciousness make? *Philosophical Topics* 17, 211-230.

Van Gulick, R. 1993. Understanding the phenomenal mind: Are we all just armadillos? In *Consciousness*, M. Davies and G. Humphreys (eds), 137-154. Cambridge, MA: Blackwell.

Van Gulick, R. Does mentality require consciousness? (unpublished manuscript)

Vesey, G. 1974. *Personal Identity*. Ithaca: Cornell.

Villanueva, E. (ed). 1991. *Consciousness*. Atascadero, CA: Ridgeview Publishing Company.

Walsh, W. 1957. Schematism. *Kant-Studien* 49, 95-106.

Ward, A. 1988. Davidson on attributions of beliefs to animals. *Philosophia* 18, 97-106.

Warnock, G. L. 1948. Concepts and schematism. *Analysis* 9, 77-82.

Weiskrantz, L. 1986. *Blindsight*. Oxford: Clarendon.

Weiskrantz, L. 1988. Some contributions of neuropsychology of vision and memory to the problem of consciousness. In *Consciousness in Contemporary Science*, A. Marcel and E. Bisiach (eds), 183-199. New York: Oxford/Clarendon.

Wiggins, D. 1967. *Identity and Spatio-Temporal Continuity*. Oxford: Basil Blackwell.

Wilkerson, T. 1980. Kant on self-consciousness. *Philosophical Quarterly* 30, 47-60.

Wittgenstein, L. 1958. *Philosophical Investigations*, trans. by G.E.M. Anscombe. New York: Macmillan.

Woodfield, A. (ed). 1982. *Thought and Object*. Oxford: Clarendon.

Index of Topics

Index of Names

In the series ADVANCES IN CONSCIOUSNESS RESEARCH (AiCR) the following titles have been published thus far or are scheduled to appear in the course of 1996:

1. GLOBUS, Gordon G.: *The Postmodern Brain.* 1995.
2. ELLIS, Ralph D.: *Questioning Consciousness. The interplay of imagery, cognition, and emotion in the human brain.* 1995.
3. JIBU, Mari and Kunio YASUE: *Quantum Brain Dynamics and Consciousness. An introduction.* 1995.
4. HARDCASTLE, Valerie Gray: *Locating Consciousness.* 1995.
5. STUBENBERG, Leopold: *Consciousness and Qualia.* n.y.p.
6. GENNARO, Rocco J.: *Consciousness and Self-Consciousness. A defense of the higher-order thought theory of consciousness.* 1996.
7. MAC CORMAC, Earl and Maxim I. STAMENOV (eds): *Fractals of Brain, Fractals of Mind. In search of a symmetry bond.* n.y.p.
8. GROSSENBACHER, Peter G. (ed.): *Finding Consciousness in the Brain. A neurocognitive approach.* n.y.p.
9. Ó'NUALLÁIN, Seán, Paul MC KEVITT and Eoghan MAC AOGÁIN (eds): *Two Sciences of Mind. Readings in cognitive science and consciousness.* n.y.p.
10. NEWTON, Natika: Foundations of Understanding. n.y.p.